THE ECONOMICS
OF PUBLIC ISSUES

THE ECONOMICS OF PUBLIC ISSUES

SIXTEENTH EDITION

Roger LeRoy Miller
Institute for University Studies
Arlington, Texas

Daniel K. Benjamin
Clemson University, South Carolina
and PERC, Bozeman, Montana

Douglass C. North
Washington University
St. Louis, Missouri

Addison-Wesley

New York Boston San Francisco
London Toronto Sydney Tokyo Singapore Madrid
Mexico City Munich Paris Cape Town Hong Kong Montreal

Editor in Chief: Donna Battista
Acquisitions Editor: Noel Kamm Seibert
Editorial Assistant: Carolyn Terbush
Managing Editor: Nancy H. Fenton
Senior Production Supervisor: Kathryn Dinovo
Executive Marketing Manager: Lori DeShazo
Marketing Assistant: Justin Jacob
Permissions Project Manager: Shannon Barbe
Senior Manufacturing Buyer: Carol Melville
Senior Design Supervisor: Andrea Nix
Cover Designer: Christina Gleason
Text Designer: Joseph Sherman, Dutton & Sherman
Production Coordination: Orr Book Services
Composition: Nesbitt Graphics

Cover image: © Pete Saloutos/CORBIS

Library of Congress Cataloging-in-Publication Data

Miller, Roger LeRoy.
  The economics of public issues / Roger LeRoy Miller, Daniel K. Benjamin,
Douglass C. North. -- 16th ed.
     p. cm.
  Includes bibliographical references and index.
  ISBN 978-0-321-59455-6
  1. Economics. 2. Industrial policy. 3. Economic policy. I. Benjamin, Daniel
K. II. North, Douglass Cecil. III. Title.
  HB171.M544 2010
  330.973--dc22

                                                            2009018248

1 2 3 4 5 6 7 8 9 10—CRW—13 12 11 10 09

Addison-Wesley
is an imprint of

www.pearsonhighered.com

ISBN-10: 0-321-59455-X
ISBN-13: 978-0-321-59455-6

To Annette,
You've always weathered the ups and downs of life because
of your great inner strength.

—R.L.M.

To Ryan Moore Benjamin,
Look up,
And bear a valiant heart.

—D.K.B.

CONTENTS

PART FIVE
Political Economy 117

PART SIX
Property Rights and the Environment 153

PART SEVEN
Globalization and Economic Prosperity 181

PREFACE

This book is about some issues of our times. Several of these issues are usually thought of as being inherently noneconomic. Others provide classic illustrations of the core of economic science. Many are controversial and thus are likely to evoke noneconomic reactions to what we have to say. In our view, however, the one feature that ties all of the issues together is that they illustrate the power of economics in explaining the world around us. And, we might add, we hope all of them illustrate that economics can be entertaining as well as informative.

New Chapters

Over the years, we have sought to select issues for this book that, in addition to the attributes just noted, possess a sense of immediacy. We hope you will find that the issues we have added for this edition meet this criterion. The new issues include the following:

- Kidneys for Sale (*does a market for human organs make sense?*)
- When High Prices Are Low Prices (*why "record high prices" are often much lower than they seem*)
- Are We Running Out of Water? (*on a planet that's two-thirds water, how can we be running out of the stuff?*)
- The (Dis)incentives of High Taxes (*how high taxes illustrate the old adage that "there is no free lunch"*)
- Mortgage Meltdown (*how Congress got us into the mortgage market mess*)
- The Political Economy of Collapsing Bridges (*when shortsighted political decisions lead to long-term troubles*)
- Is Your Bank Manager Headed to Vegas with Your Money? (*how deposit insurance encourages risky behavior by commercial banks*)

Market Meltdown of 2007–2009

As a glance at this list should reveal, one key element of this new edition is a clear focus on the causes and consequences of the housing market meltdown of 2007–2009 and the credit crisis and economic recession that ensued. Because this episode will so profoundly affect public policy for years to come, we believe it is crucial for students to understand what got us into this mess and what we might—or might not—do to get out of it. Here and elsewhere in the book, we continue our emphasis on the interplay between economics and the process of making the policies that address (or create) the public issues we analyze. In numerous chapters, for example, we show that the rational ignorance that results from the diffuse costs of many government policies helps explain why those programs are able to concentrate so many benefits in the hands of so few.

Complete Overhaul of Supply and Demand

Longtime users of this book will also note that we have completely overhauled Part Two, "Supply and Demand." In so doing, we apply economic analysis in some unconventional settings. But we also explode a host of common public policy myths that have routinely made the application of economic principles more difficult than necessary. We think that students will be both surprised and stimulated by these new illustrations of the power of economic analysis.

Glossary and Selected Readings and Web Links

This edition also continues two features that seem universally appreciated by students and faculty: A glossary and a list of selected readings, both at the back of the book. The glossary terms are set in boldface the first time they are used, and the terms are arranged alphabetically in the glossary, with a succinct definition for each. The selected readings only scratch the surface of the rich literature we have drawn upon in preparing this book, but the interested reader will be able to use them as a springboard for as much research as she or he wishes to undertake.

A Complete Revision in Seven Parts

All of the other chapters in this edition have been partly or completely rewritten, and every chapter is as up-to-date as we can make it. What you will consistently find is a straightforward application of economic principles as they are taught in virtually all courses in economics, public policy, and the social sciences. This book can be understood by anyone who has taken a course in economics, is taking a course in economics, or has never taken a course in economics. We have made it self-contained, as well as accessible to a wide range of students.

The chapters are organized into seven parts. Part One examines the foundations of all economic analysis, including the concepts of scarcity, trade-offs, opportunity cost, and marginal analysis. In a sense, the four chapters in this introductory part set the stage for the remaining twenty-eight chapters. Parts Two through Six cover the topics—demand and supply, labor markets, imperfect competition, environmental issues, and the impact of government policies—that are integral to virtually every course in which economics plays a role. Finally, Part Seven examines global affairs because these matters are an essential part of the public issues of today.

Every part has an introduction that prepares the reader for the material in the following chapters. These part openers summarize and tie together the relevant issues, thus serving as launch pads for the analyses that follow. Students would be well advised to read these part openers before they launch into any of the chapters they precede.

Instructor's Manual

Every instructor will want to access the *Instructor's Manual* that accompanies *The Economics of Public Issues*. It is available online to all adopters of the book. In writing this manual, we have tried to incorporate the very best of the teaching aids that we use when we teach from *The Economics of Public Issues*. For each chapter, the manual provides the following:

- A synopsis that cuts to the core of the economic issues involved in the chapter.
- A concise exposition of the "behind the scenes" economic analysis on which the discussion in the text is based. In almost all cases, this exposition is supplemented with one or more diagrams that we have found to be particularly useful as teaching tools.
- Answers to the Discussion Questions posed at the end of the chapter—answers that further develop the basic economic analysis of the chapter and almost always suggest new avenues of discussion.

The Future

The world of public issues continues to evolve. By the time you read these words, we will be working on the next edition. If you have any particular subjects you would like included in the future, let us know by writing us in care of Pearson Higher Education.

Special Thanks and Acknowledgments

Several chapters in this edition draw on the "Tangents" column that Benjamin writes for *PERC Reports*. We are grateful to the Property and Environment Research Center (PERC) for permission to use that material. In addition, literally dozens of kind users of the last edition of this book, as well as several extremely diligent and thoughtful reviewers, offered suggestions for the current edition:

> Kenny Christianson, Binghamton University and Ithaca College
> Christopher Coyne, West Virginia University
> Jill Hendrickson, University of St. Thomas
> Mehrdad Madresehee, Lycoming College
> Michael Marsh, United States Air Force Academy
> John McArthur, Wofford College
> Cyril Morong, San Antonio College
> Valerie Ramey, University of California, San Diego
> Randall Russell, Yavapai College
> Dennis Shannon, Southwestern Illinois College
> Russell Sobel, West Virginia University
> Jeff Summers, Linfield College

Scarcity precluded us from adopting all of their recommendations, but we believe they will be able to identify the impact they each had on this edition. To them and to readers who wrote to us, we offer our sincere thanks and hope that the end result was worthy of their time and concern. We also thank Noel Seibert, Courtney Schinke, and Carolyn Terbush for shepherding the project, Sue Jasin for her expert manuscript preparation, and Robbie Benjamin, whose editorial skills once again have improved the final product. All errors remain, of course, solely our own.

R.L.M.
D.K.B.
D.C.N.

SUGGESTIONS FOR USE

At the request of our readers, we include the following table to help you incorporate the chapters of this book into your syllabus. Depending on the breadth of your course, you may also want to consult the companion paperback, *The Economics of Macro Issues,* 4th edition, which features macroeconomic topics and a similar table in its preface.

Economics Topics	Recommended Chapters in The Economics of Public Issues, *16th Edition*
Introduction to Economics	1, 3, 4, 24
Opportunity Costs and Scarcity	1, 2, 10, 13, 26, 29
Demand and Supply	5, 6, 7
Demand and Supply Applications	5, 6, 7, 8, 9, 10, 11, 12, 15, 23, 28
The Public Sector and Public Choice	1, 18, 19, 20, 21, 23, 24, 25, 27, 28
Taxes, Transfers, and Public Spending	9, 14, 16, 21, 24, 25
Consumer Behavior	1, 3, 5, 6, 7, 8, 9, 10
Elasticity of Demand and Supply	2, 3, 5, 6, 8, 11, 16, 17, 24
Rents, Profits, and the Financial Environment of Business	10, 13, 15, 19, 20, 22
Firm Production and Cost	1, 3, 10, 15
Perfect Competition	23
Monopoly	15, 16, 19
Monopolistic Competition	16, 17, 18
Oligopoly	15, 22
Regulation and Antitrust	3, 6, 10, 16, 19, 20
Unions and the Labor Market	12, 13, 14, 16
Income, Poverty, and Health Care	4, 13, 14, 25
Environmental Economics	1, 2, 8, 26, 27, 28, 29
International Trade	14, 30, 31, 32
International Finance	32

PART ONE

The Foundations of Economic Analysis

Introduction

Our world is one of **scarcity;** we want more than we have. The reason is simple. Although we live in a world of limited **resources,** we have unlimited wants. This does not mean we all live and breathe solely to drive the fastest cars or wear the latest clothes. It means that we all want the right to make decisions about how resources are used—even if what we want to do with those resources is to feed starving children in developing nations.

Given the existence of scarcity, we must make choices; we cannot have more of everything, so to get more of some things, we must give up other things. Economists express this simple idea by saying that we face **trade-offs.** For example, a student who wants higher grades generally must devote more time to studying and less time to, say, going to the movies; the trade-off in this instance is between grades and entertainment.

The concept of a trade-off is one of the (surprisingly few) basic principles you must grasp to understand the economics of public issues. We illustrate the simplicity of these principles with Chapter 1, "Death by Bureaucrat," which examines a behind-the-scenes trade-off made every day on our behalf by the U.S. Food and Drug Administration (FDA). This federal government agency is charged with ensuring that new prescription medicines are both safe and effective. In carrying out its duties, the FDA requires pharmaceutical companies to subject proposed new drugs to extensive testing. Additional testing improves the chances that a drug will be both safe and effective, but it also slows the approval of new drugs, thus depriving some individuals of the ability to use the drugs to treat their illnesses.

The drug-approval process undoubtedly reduces pain and suffering for some people and even saves the lives of others because it lowers the chances that an unsafe or ineffective drug will reach the market. Yet because the process also slows the rate at which drugs reach the market (and may even prevent some safe and effective drugs from ever being introduced), the pain and suffering of other individuals are increased. Indeed, some people die as a result. This, then, is the terrible trade-off we face in Chapter 1: Who shall live and who shall die?

As Chapter 1 suggests, there are times when government bureaucrats don't always make the choices we would expect and may not even make the choices we would prefer. We explore the reasons behind such decisions in Chapter 2, "Ethanol Madness," where we answer this simple query: If the **biofuel** ethanol doesn't protect the environment or conserve resources, why do we mandate its use as a gasoline additive and subsidize its production? The answer lies at the heart of **political economy,** the use of economics to study the causes and consequences of political decision making. It is true (as we emphasize in Chapter 4) that a critical function of government is to provide the institutional structure necessary for the creation and retention of our total wealth, broadly construed. Nevertheless, the essence of much government policymaking has nothing to do with making the economic pie larger. Instead, many government policies are directed at dividing up the pie in new ways, so that one group gets more resources at the expense of some other group. To do this successfully, politicians must be adept at exploiting the **rational ignorance** of voters, concentrating the benefits of policies among a few favored recipients while dispersing the costs of those policies across a large number of disfavored individuals. In the case of ethanol, we see that members of Congress do this in ways that enrich farmers and large ethanol producers at the expense of motorists and taxpayers.

All public issues compel us to face the question of how to make the best choices. Economists argue that doing so requires the use of what we call **marginal analysis.** The term *marginal* in this context means "incremental" or "additional." All choices involve costs and benefits—we give up something for anything that we get. As we engage in more of any activity (eating, studying, or sleeping, for example), the **marginal benefits** of that activity eventually decline: The *additional* benefits associated with an *additional* unit of the activity get lower. In contrast, the **marginal costs** of an activity eventually rise as we engage in more and more of it. The best choices are made when we equate the marginal benefits and marginal costs of activity; that is, we try to determine whether engaging in any more of a given activity would produce additional costs that exceed the additional benefits.

In Chapter 3, "Flying the Friendly Skies?" we apply the principles of marginal analysis to the issue of airline safety. How safe is it to travel at 600 miles per hour 7 miles above the ground? How safe *should* it be? The answers to these and other questions can be explored using marginal analysis. One of the conclusions we reach is that *perfect* safety is simply not in the cards. Every time you step into an airplane (or even the street), there is some risk that your journey will end unhappily. As disconcerting as this might sound at first, we think you will find after reading this chapter that once the costs and benefits are taken into account, you would have it no other way.

Every choice we make entails a **cost:** In a world of scarcity, something must be given up to obtain anything of value. Costs, combined with the benefits of our choices, comprise the **incentives** that ultimately inform and guide our decisions. That these decisions—and thus the incentives—have real and lasting consequences is nowhere more evident than in Chapter 4, "The Mystery of Wealth." Here we seek to answer a simple but profound question: Why are the citizens of some nations rich while the inhabitants of others are poor? Your initial answer might be "because of differences in the **natural-resource endowments** of the nations." It is true that ample endowments of energy, timber, and fertile land all help raise wealth. But it turns out that natural resources are only a very small part of the answer.

Far more important in determining the wealth of the citizenry are the fundamental political and legal **institutions** of a nation. Institutions such as political stability, secure private property rights, and legal systems based on the **rule of law** create the incentives that encourage people to make long-term investments in improving land and in all forms of **physical** and **human capital.** These investments raise the **capital stock,** which in turn provides for more growth long into the future. And the cumulative effects of this growth over time eventually yield much higher standards of living: They make us rich. Thus incentives, comprising both costs and benefits, turn out to be an integral component of the foundations of economic analysis, as well as the foundations of society.

Chapter 1

DEATH BY BUREAUCRAT

How would you rather die? From a lethal reaction to a drug prescribed by your doctor? Or because your doctor failed to prescribe a drug that would have saved your life? If this choice sounds like one you would rather not make, consider this: Employees of the Food and Drug Administration (FDA) make that decision on behalf of millions of Americans many times each year. More precisely, FDA bureaucrats decide whether or not new medicines (prescription drugs) should be allowed to go on sale in the United States. If the FDA rules against a drug, physicians in America may not legally prescribe it, even if thousands of lives are being saved by the drug each year in other countries.

The FDA's authority to make such decisions dates back to the passage of the Food and Drug Safety Act of 1906. That law required that medicines be correctly labeled as to their contents and that they not contain any substances harmful to the health of consumers. Due to this legislation, Dr. Hostatter's Stomach Bitters and Kickapoo Indian Sagwa, along with numerous rum-laden concoctions, cocaine-based potions, and supposed anticancer remedies, disappeared from druggists' shelves. The law was expanded in 1938 with the passage of the Food, Drug, and Cosmetic Act, which forced manufacturers to demonstrate the safety of new drugs before being allowed to offer them for sale. (This law was prompted by the deaths of 107 people who had taken Elixir Sulfanilamide, an antibiotic that contained poisonous diethylene glycol, a chemical cousin of antifreeze.)

The next step in U.S. drug regulation came after a rash of severe birth defects among infants whose mothers during pregnancy had taken a sleep aid known as thalidomide. When these birth defects first became apparent, the drug was already widely used in Europe and Canada, and the FDA was nearing approval for its use in America. In fact, about 2.5 million thalidomide tablets were already in the hands of U.S. physicians as samples. The FDA ordered all of the samples destroyed and prohibited the sale of the drug here. This incident led to the 1962 Kefauver-Harris Amendments to the 1938 Food, Drug, and Cosmetic Act, radically altering the drug-approval process in the United States.

Prior to the 1962 amendments, the FDA was expected to approve a new drug application within 180 days unless the application failed to show that the drug was safe. The 1962 amendments added a "proof of efficacy" requirement and also removed the time constraint on the FDA. The FDA has free rein to determine how much and what type of evidence it will demand before approving a drug for sale and thus may take as long as it pleases before either granting or refusing approval.

The 1962 amendments drastically increased the costs of introducing a new drug and markedly slowed the approval process. Prior to 1962, for example, the average time between filing and approval of a new drug application was seven months; by 1967, it was thirty months; and by the late 1970s, it had risen to eight to ten *years*. The protracted approval process involves costly testing by the drug companies—$800 million or more for each new drug—and delays the receipt of any potential revenue from new drugs. Because this reduced the expected profitability of new drugs, fewer of them have been brought onto the market.

Debate continues over how much FDA regulation is needed to ensure that drugs are both safe and efficacious, but there is little doubt that the 1962 amendments have resulted in a U.S. "drug lag." On average, drugs take far longer to reach the market in the United States than they do in Europe. Admittedly, it takes time to ensure that patients benefit from, rather than are harmed by, new drugs, but regulation-induced drug lag can itself be life-threatening. Dr. George Hitchings, a winner of the Nobel Prize in Medicine, has estimated that the five-year lag in introducing Septra (an antibiotic) to the United States killed 80,000 people in this country. Similarly, the introduction of a class of drugs called beta blockers (used to treat heart attack victims and people with high blood pressure) was delayed nearly a decade in America relative to Europe. According to several researchers, the lag in the FDA approval of these drugs cost the lives of at least 250,000 Americans.

In effect, the law requires FDA bureaucrats to make what is truly a terrible trade-off. Lives are saved because unsafe or ineffective drugs are kept off the market, but the regulatory process delays (or even prevents) the introduction of some safe and efficacious drugs, thereby costing lives. Let us now take a more systematic look at this trade-off.

Every time a new drug is introduced, there is a chance that it should not have been—either because it has adverse side effects that outweigh the therapeutic benefits (it is not safe) or because it really does little to help the individuals who take it (it is not effective). When such a drug is introduced, we say that a **Type I error** has been committed. Since 1962, the incidence of Type I error—the thalidomide possibility—has been reduced by the added testing required by the FDA. But other people have been the victims of what is called **Type II error.** Their cost is the pain, suffering, and death that occur because the 1962 amendments have prevented or delayed the introduction of safe, efficacious drugs. Type II error—as with Septra or beta blockers—occurs when a drug *should* be introduced but is held back by FDA regulation.

Over the past twenty or thirty years, outcries over the harm caused by the drug lag have in some cases induced the agency to shorten the testing period when the costs of Type I error are small relative to the damages due to Type II error—as in the case of terminally ill patients. One famous example involved azidothymidine (AZT), which emerged as a possible treatment for AIDS. Gay men, among whom AIDS was most prevalent at the time, took the lead in pressuring the FDA to approve the drug quickly, and the FDA responded accordingly, giving it the OK after only eighteen months of testing. Similarly, Taxol, an important new drug used to treat breast cancer, received expedited review by the FDA, in this case because of pressure applied by women in whose families there was a history of breast cancer. The FDA now has a formal program in which it seeks to expedite testing for drugs that seem to offer great promise for alleviating death or suffering. Nevertheless, although the average approval time for new drugs has shortened considerably, it still takes more than ten times as long for a new drug to be approved as it did before the 1962 amendments.

What can we learn from the FDA regulation of new drugs that will guide us in thinking about other public issues of our time? There are several key principles:

1. *There is no free lunch.* Every choice, and thus every policy, entails a **cost**—something must be given up. In a world of **scarcity,** we cannot have more of everything, so to get more of some things, we must give up other things. Although FDA review of drugs saves lives by preventing the introduction of unsafe or ineffective drugs, the cost is billions of dollars of added expenses, plus delayed availability of safe and efficacious drugs, resulting in the deaths of hundreds of thousands of people.

2. *The cost of an action is the alternative that is sacrificed.* Economists often express costs (and benefits) in terms of dollars because this is a simple means of accounting for and measuring them. But that doesn't

mean that costs have to be monetary, nor does it mean that economics is incapable of analyzing costs and benefits that are quite human. The costs that led to the 1938 and 1962 amendments were the very visible deaths caused by sulfanilamide and the terrible birth defects due to thalidomide. Subsequent revisions to the FDA process for reviewing drugs, as with AZT and Taxol, have been in response to the adverse effects caused by the regulation-induced drug lag.

3. *The relevant costs and benefits are the marginal (incremental) ones.* The relevant question is not whether safety is good or bad; it is instead how much safety we want—which can only be answered by looking at the added (marginal) benefits of more safety compared to the added (marginal) costs. One possible response to the sulfanilamide poisonings or thalidomide was to have outlawed new drugs altogether. That would guarantee that no more people would be harmed by new drugs. But surely this "solution" would not be sensible, because the marginal cost (due to higher Type II errors) would exceed the marginal benefit (caused by reduced Type I errors).

4. *People respond to incentives.* And this is true whether we are talking about consumers, suppliers, or government bureaucrats. Here the incentive to amend the law in 1938 and 1962 was the very visible death and disfigurement of individuals. The eventual FDA decision to speed up the review process was prompted by intense lobbying by individuals who believed (correctly, as it turned out) that they might be benefited by drugs not yet approved.

5. *Things aren't always as they seem.* Many analyses of the effects of government policies take an approach that doesn't fully recognize the actions that people would otherwise have taken. Thus official pronouncements about the effects of policies routinely misrepresent their impact—not because there is necessarily any attempt to deceive but because it is often difficult to know what would have happened otherwise. Pharmaceutical manufacturers, for example, have strong incentives to avoid introducing drugs that are unsafe or ineffective because the companies are subject to loss of reputation and to lawsuits. For similar reasons, physicians have strong incentives to avoid prescribing such drugs for their patients. Even without FDA regulation, there would thus be extensive testing of new drugs before their introduction. Hence it is incorrect to ascribe the generally safe and effective nature of modern drugs entirely to FDA protection. The flip side, however, is that the drug development process is inherently long, complicated, and costly. Even without FDA oversight, some people would die waiting for new drugs because self-interested

manufacturers would insist on some testing and cautious physicians would proceed slowly in prescribing new drugs.

The people who work at the FDA (and members of Congress) are publicly castigated when they "allow" a Type I error to occur—especially when it is a drug that kills people. Thus FDA bureaucrats have a strong incentive to avoid such errors. But when testing delays cause a Type II error, as with Septra, it is almost impossible to point to specific people who died because the drug was delayed. As a result, officials at the FDA are rarely attacked directly for such delays. Because the costs of Type II errors are much more difficult to discern than the costs of Type I errors, many observers believe that there is an inherent bias at the FDA in favor of being "safe rather than sorry"—in other words, excessive testing.

6. *Policies always have unintended consequences, and as a result, their net benefits are almost always less than anticipated.* In the case of government regulations, balancing incremental costs and benefits (see principle 3) fails to make good headlines. Instead, what gets politicians reelected and regulators promoted are *absolute* notions such as safety (and motherhood and apple pie). Thus if a little safety is good, more must be better, so why not simply mandate that drug testing "guarantee" that everyone is free of risk from dangerous drugs? Eventually, the reality of principle 3 sinks in, but in this case not before the drug lag had killed many people.

As is often true with important public issues, our story has one more interesting twist. Thalidomide is back on the market. In 1998, it was approved by the FDA for use in treating Hansen's disease (leprosy), and in 2006, the FDA gave physicians the OK to use it in treating bone marrow cancer. In each instance, there are strong protections to prevent pregnant women from taking the drug. And so perhaps the very drug that brought us the deadly drug lag will turn out to be a lifesaver for a new generation of patients.

DISCUSSION QUESTIONS

1. Does the structure of the drug industry have any bearing on the types of errors that drug firms are likely to make? That is, would a drug industry made up of numerous highly competitive firms be more or less likely to introduce unsafe drugs than an industry consisting of a few large firms?

2. How could the incentives facing the people at the FDA be changed to reduce the incidence of Type II errors? (*Hint:* Is it possible to compare the FDA approval process with the drug-approval process in other nations?)

3. What would be the advantages and disadvantages of a regulatory system in which, rather than having the FDA permit or prohibit new drugs, the FDA merely published its opinions about the safety and efficacy of drugs and then allowed physicians to make their own decisions about whether or not to prescribe the drugs for their patients?

4. Suppose, for simplicity, that Type I and Type II errors resulted in deaths only. Keeping in mind that too little caution produces Type I errors and too much caution produces Type II errors, what would be the best mix of Type I and Type II errors?

Chapter 2

ETHANOL MADNESS

Henry Ford built his first automobile in 1896 to run on pure ethanol. If Congress has its way, the cars of the future will be built the same way. But what made good economic sense in the late nineteenth century doesn't necessarily make economic sense in the early twenty-first century—although it does make for good politics. Indeed, the ethanol story is a classic illustration of how good politics routinely trumps good economics to yield bad policies.

Ethanol is made in the Midwest just like moonshine whiskey is made in Appalachia: Corn and water are mixed into a mash, enzymes turn starch to sugar, yeast is added, and heat ferments the brew. Once this is distilled, the liquid portion is ethanol and the solids are used as a high-protein animal food. The high-proof ethanol is combustible but yields far less energy per gallon than gasoline does. Despite this inefficiency, federal law requires that ethanol be added to gasoline, in increasing amounts through 2022. This requirement is supposed to conserve resources and improve the environment. It does neither. Instead, it lines the pockets of American corn farmers and ethanol makers and incidentally enriches some Brazilian sugarcane farmers along the way.

Federal law has both encouraged and subsidized ethanol as a so-called alternative fuel for more than thirty years. But it was not until 2005 that ethanol really achieved national prominence. The use mandates of the Energy Policy Act, combined with surging gas prices and an existing 51-cent-per-gallon federal ethanol subsidy, created a boom in ethanol production. Soon ethanol refineries were springing up all over the Midwest, and imports of ethanol from Brazil reached record-high levels.

Three factors are typically used to justify federal use mandates and subsidies for ethanol. First, it is claimed that adding ethanol to gasoline reduces air pollution and so yields environmental benefits. That may have been true fifteen or twenty years ago, but even the Environmental

Protection Agency acknowledges that ethanol offers no environmental advantages over other modern methods of making reformulated gasoline. Hence neither the congressional mandate to add ethanol nor the 51-cent-per-gallon subsidy for its use as a fuel additive can be justified on environmental grounds.

A second argument advanced on behalf of ethanol is that it is "renewable," in that fields on which corn is grown to produce ethanol this year can be replanted with more corn next year. This is true enough, but we are in little danger of running out of "nonrenewable" crude oil any time in the next century. Indeed, proven reserves of oil are at record-high levels. Perhaps more to the point, the production of ethanol uses so much fossil fuel and other resources that under most circumstances, its production actually *wastes* resources overall compared to gasoline. In part, this is because ethanol is about 25 percent less efficient than gasoline as a source of energy. But it is also because the corn used to make ethanol in the United States has a high **opportunity cost:** If it were not being used to make fuel, it would be used to feed humans and livestock. Moreover, because ethanol production is most efficiently conducted on a relatively small scale, it must be transported by truck or rail, which is far more costly than the pipelines used for gasoline.

The third supposed advantage of ethanol is that its use reduces our dependence on imports of oil. In principle, this argument is correct, but its impact is tiny, and the likely consequences are not what you might expect. Total consumption of all **biofuels** in the United States amounts to less than 3 percent of gasoline usage. To replace the oil we import from the Persian Gulf with corn-based ethanol, at least *50 percent* of the nation's total farmland would have to be devoted to corn for fuel. Moreover, any cuts in oil imports will likely *not* come from Persian Gulf sources. Canada and Mexico are two of the three biggest suppliers of crude oil to the United States, and both countries send almost 100 percent of their exports to the U.S. market.

All of this raises an interesting question: If ethanol doesn't protect the environment, conserve resources, or have any compelling foreign policy advantages, why do we mandate its use and subsidize its production? The answer lies at the heart of **political economy,** the use of economics to study the causes and consequences of political decision making. It is true that a critical component of what the government does (such as providing for national defense and law enforcement) provides an institutional structure necessary for the creation and retention of our total wealth. Nevertheless, the essence of much government policymaking has nothing to do with making the size of the economic pie larger than it otherwise would be. Instead, many government policies are directed at dividing up the pie in new ways so that one group gets more resources at the expense of some other group. To do this successfully, politicians must be adept at concentrating the benefits of policies among a few favored recipients while dispersing the costs of those policies across a large number of disfavored individuals.

At first blush, such an approach sounds completely at odds with the essence of democracy. After all, under the principle of "one person, one vote," it seems that benefits should be widely spread (to gain votes from many grateful beneficiaries) and costs should be concentrated (so that only the votes of a few disfavored constituents are lost). The concept of **rational ignorance** explains what is really going on. It is costly for individuals to keep track of exactly how the decisions of their elected representatives affect them. When the consequences of political decisions are large enough to outweigh the **monitoring costs,** voters swiftly and surely express their pleasure or displeasure, both in the voting booth and in their campaign contributions. But when the consequences to each of them individually are small relative to the monitoring costs, people don't bother to keep track of them—they remain "rationally ignorant."

In the case of ethanol, about one-fifth of all ethanol for fuel is made by one company, Archer Daniels Midland (ADM). Clearly, even small changes in the price of ethanol are important to ADM. Because federal use mandates and the federal ethanol subsidy both increase the profitability of making ethanol, ADM has strong incentives to ensure that members of Congress are aware of the benefits (to ADM) of such policies. Similarly, corn farmers derive most of their income from sales of corn. Federal ethanol policies increase the demand for corn and thus increase its price; again, because the resulting benefits are highly concentrated on corn farmers, each has a strong incentive to ensure that his or her members of Congress understand the benefits (to the farmer) of such policies.

Contrast this with the typical taxpayer or consumer of gasoline. It is true that the $3 billion or so spent on ethanol subsidies each year must come out of taxpayers' pockets. Nevertheless, this amount is spread thinly across tens of millions of federal taxpayers. Similarly, although the mandated use of ethanol in gasoline is estimated to raise the cost of gas by about 8 cents per gallon, this amounts to no more than $50 per year for the typical driver. Neither taxpayer nor motorist is likely to spend much time complaining to his or her senator.

Thus it is that farmers and ethanol producers are willing to lobby hard for use mandates and subsidies at the same time that taxpayers and drivers put up little effective resistance to having their pockets picked. It may make for bad economics, but it is classic politics.

DISCUSSION QUESTIONS

1. Brazilian ethanol producers (who make ethanol from sugarcane) have lower production costs than U.S. producers. Indeed, even though it costs 16 cents per gallon to transport ethanol from Brazil to the United States, which also imposes an **import tariff** of nearly 60 cents per gallon on Brazilian ethanol, the United States still imports millions of gallons of ethanol per year from Brazil. If Congress really cares about protecting the environment and reducing our reliance on foreign crude oil, why do you suppose we have a large import tariff on ethanol?

2. If imports of Brazilian ethanol begin to rise sharply in the future, what do you predict will happen to the size of the import tariff levied on this good?

3. Why do you suppose the federal government gives special treatment to owners of fertile farmland rather than, say, automobile mechanics?

4. Use the theory of rational ignorance to explain why the ethanol subsidy is only 51 cents per gallon rather than, say, $5 per gallon.

Chapter 3

FLYING THE FRIENDLY SKIES?

Most of us hop into our car with little thought for our personal safety, beyond perhaps the act of putting on seat belts. Yet even though travel on scheduled, commercial airlines is safer than driving to work or to the grocery store, many people approach air travel with a sense of foreboding, if not downright fear.

If we were to think carefully about the wisdom of traveling 600 miles per hour in an aluminum tube 7 miles above the earth, several questions might come to mind: How safe is this? How safe should it be? Because the people who operate airlines are not in it for fun, does their interest in making a buck ignore our interest in making it home in one piece? Is some form of government regulation the only way to ensure safety in the skies?

The science of economics begins with one simple principle: We live in a world of **scarcity,** which implies that to get more of any good, we must sacrifice some of other goods. This is just as true of safety as it is of pizzas or haircuts or works of art. Safety confers benefits (we live longer and more enjoyably), but achieving it also entails **costs** (we must give up something to obtain that safety).

As the degree of safety rises, the total benefits of safety rise, but the marginal (or incremental) benefits of additional safety decline. Consider a simple example: Adding exit doors to an airplane increases the number of people who can escape in the event of an emergency evacuation. Nevertheless, each *additional* door adds less in safety benefits than the previous one; if the fourth door enables, say, an extra ten people to escape, the fifth may enable only an extra six to escape. (If this sounds implausible, imagine having a door for each person; the last door added will enable at most one more person to escape.) So we say that the marginal (or incremental) benefit of safety declines as the amount of safety increases.

Let's look now at the other side of the equation: As the amount of safety increases, both the total and the marginal (incremental) costs of providing safety rise. Having a fuel gauge on the plane's instrument panel clearly enhances safety, because it reduces the chance that the plane will run out of fuel while in flight.[1] It is always possible that a fuel gauge will malfunction, so having a backup fuel gauge also adds to safety. Because having two gauges is more costly than having just one, the total costs of safety rise as safety increases. It is also clear, however, that while the cost of the second gauge is (at least) as great as the cost of the first, the second gauge has a smaller positive impact on safety. Thus the cost per unit of additional (incremental) safety is higher for the second fuel gauge than for the first.

How much safety should we have? For an economist, the answer to such a question is generally expressed in terms of **marginal benefits** and **marginal costs.** The economically *efficient* level of safety occurs when the marginal cost of increasing safety just equals the marginal benefit of that increased safety. Put somewhat differently, if the marginal benefits of adding (or keeping) a safety feature exceed the marginal costs of doing so, the feature is worthwhile. But if the added benefits of a safety device do *not* exceed the added costs, we should refrain from installing the device. Note there are two related issues here: How safe should we *be,* and how should we *achieve* that level of safety?

Both of these issues took on added urgency on the morning of September 11, 2001, when terrorists hijacked and crashed four U.S. commercial jetliners. This episode revealed that air travel was far less safe than previously believed. Immediately, it was clear that we should devote additional resources to airline safety; what was not clear was how *much* additional resources should be thus devoted and precisely *what* changes should be made. For example, almost everyone agreed that more careful screening of passengers and baggage at airports would produce important safety benefits. But how should we achieve this? Should carry-on bags be prohibited or just examined more carefully? How thoroughly should checked luggage be screened for bombs? Even now, our answers to these questions are evolving as we learn more about the extent of the threat and the costs of alternative responses to it. Nevertheless, throughout the process, economic principles can help us make the most sensible decisions.

---

1. Notice that we say "reduces" rather than "eliminates." In 1978, a United Air Lines pilot preoccupied with a malfunctioning landing gear evidently failed to pay sufficient attention to his cockpit gauges. When the plane was forced to crash-land after running out of fuel, eight people died.

In general, the efficient level of safety will not be perfect safety, because perfection is simply too costly to achieve. For example, to be absolutely certain that no one is ever killed or injured in an airplane crash, we would have to prevent all travel in airplanes—an unrealistic and impracticable prospect. This means that if we wish to enjoy the advantages of flying, we must be willing to accept *some* risk—a conclusion that each of us implicitly accepts every time we step aboard an airplane.

Changes in circumstances can alter the efficient level of safety. For example, if a technological change reduces the costs of bomb-scanning equipment, the marginal costs of preventing terrorist bomb attacks will be lower. It will be efficient to have more airports install the machines and to have extra machines at large airports to speed the screening process. Air travel will become safer because of the technological change. Similarly, if the marginal benefits of safety rise for some reason—perhaps because the president of the United States is on board—it could be efficient to take more precautions, resulting in safer air travel. Given the factors that determine the benefits and costs of safety, the result of a change in circumstances will be some determinate level of safety that generally will be associated with some risk of death or injury.

Airplanes are complex systems, and an amazing number of components can fail. Over the century that humans have been flying, airplane manufacturers and airlines have studied every one of the malfunctions thus far and have put into place design changes and operating procedures aimed at preventing recurring error. Of course, consumers have the greatest incentive to ensure that air travel is safe, and if information were free, we could assert with some confidence that the actual level of safety supplied by firms was the efficient level of safety. Consumers would simply observe the safety offered by different airlines, the prices they charge, and select the degrees of safety that best suited their preferences and budgets, just as with other goods. But information is not free; it is a **scarce good,** costly to obtain. As a result, passengers may be unaware of the safety record of various airlines or the competence of the pilots and the maintenance procedures of an airline's mechanics. Indeed, even the airlines themselves may be uncertain about the efficient level of safety, perhaps because they have no way of estimating the true threat of terrorist attacks, for example. Such possibilities have been used to argue that the federal government should mandate certain minimum levels of safety, as it does today through the operation of the Federal Aviation Administration (FAA). Let's look at this issue in some detail.

One argument in favor of government safety standards rests on the presumption that, left to their own devices, airlines would provide less safety than passengers want. This might happen, for example, if customers could not tell (at a reasonable cost) whether the equipment, training, and procedures employed by an airline are safe. If passengers cannot cheaply gauge the level of safety, they will not be willing to reward airlines for being safe or punish them for being unsafe. If safety is costly to provide and consumers are unwilling to pay for it because they cannot accurately measure it, airlines will provide too little of it. The conclusion is that government experts, such as the FAA, should set safety standards for the industry.

This conclusion seems plausible, but it ignores two simple points. First, how is the government to know the efficient level of safety? Even if the FAA knows the costs of all possible safety measures, it still does not have enough information to set efficient safety standards because it does not know the value that people place on safety. Without such information, the FAA has no way to assess the benefits of additional safety and hence no means of knowing whether those benefits are greater or less than the added costs.

The second point is that people want to reach their destinations safely. Even if they cannot observe whether an airline hires good pilots or bad pilots, they can see whether that airline's planes land safely or crash. If it is *safety* that is important to consumers—and not the obscure, costly-to-measure *reasons* for that safety—the fact that consumers cannot easily measure metal fatigue in jet engines may be totally irrelevant to the process of achieving the efficient level of safety.

Interestingly, evidence shows that consumers are indeed cognizant of the safety performance of airlines and that they "punish" airlines that perform in an unsafe manner. Researchers have found that when an airline is at fault in a fatal plane crash, consumers appear to downgrade their safety rating of the airline (that is, they revise upward their estimates of the likelihood of future fatal crashes). As a result, the offending airline suffers substantial adverse financial consequences over and above the costs of losing the plane and being sued on behalf of the victims. These findings suggest a striking degree of safety awareness on the part of supposedly ignorant consumers.

Of course, this discussion leaves open the issue of how to handle safety threats posed by terrorists and other miscreants. For example, much of the information that goes into assessing terrorist threats is classified as secret, and its revelation to airlines or consumers might compromise key sources of the data. Hence there could be an advantage to having the government try to approximate the efficient safety outcome by mandating certain screening provisions without revealing exactly why they are being chosen. Similarly, because airlines are connected in networks (so that people and baggage move from one airline to another in the course of a trip), achieving the efficient level of safety might require a common set of screening rules for all airlines. Even so, this does not inform us whether the government should impose those rules or the airlines should come to a voluntary joint agreement on them.

We began this chapter with the commonplace observation that airlines are safer than cars. Yet many people still worry for their safety every time they get on an airplane. Are they being irrational? Well, the answer, it seems, is in the eye of the beholder. Measured in terms of fatalities per mile traveled, airplanes are some 15 times safer than cars (and 176 times safer than walking, we might add). But this number masks the fact that 68 percent of aircraft accidents happen on takeoff and landing, and these operations occupy only 6 percent of flight time. It is presumably this fact that quite sensibly makes people nervous whenever they find themselves approaching an airport.

DISCUSSION QUESTIONS

1. Is it possible to be too safe? Explain what you mean by "too safe."

2. Many automobile manufacturers routinely advertise the safety of their cars, yet airlines generally do not mention safety in their advertising. Can you suggest an explanation for this difference?

3. Many economists would argue that private companies are likely to be more efficient than the government at operating airlines. Yet many economists would also argue that there is a valid reason for government to regulate the safety of those same airlines. Can you explain why the government might be good at ensuring safety, even though it might not be good at operating the airlines?

4. Professional football teams sometimes charter airplanes to take them to their away games. Would you feel safer on a United Air Lines plane that had been chartered by the Washington Redskins than on a regularly scheduled United Air Lines flight?

Chapter 4

THE MYSTERY OF WEALTH

Why are the citizens of some nations rich while the inhabitants of others are poor? Your initial answer might be "because of differences in the **natural-resource endowments** of the nations." It is true that ample endowments of energy, timber, and fertile land all help raise wealth. But natural resources can be only a very small part of the answer, as witnessed by many counterexamples. Switzerland and Luxembourg, for example, are nearly devoid of key natural resources, yet the real incomes of citizens of those lands are among the world's highest. Similarly, Hong Kong, which consists of a few square miles of rock and hillside, is one of the economic miracles of modern times, while in Russia, a land amply endowed with vast quantities of virtually every important resource, most people remain mired in economic misery.

A number of studies have begun to unravel the mystery of **economic growth.** Repeatedly, they have found that it is the fundamental political and legal **institutions** of society that are conducive to growth. Of these, political stability, secure private property rights, and legal systems based on the **rule of law** are among the most important. Such institutions encourage people to make long-term investments in improving land and in all forms of **physical capital** and **human capital.** These investments raise the **capital stock,** which in turn provides for more growth long into the future. And the cumulative effects of this growth over time eventually yield much higher standards of living.

Consider first the contrasting effects of different legal systems on economic growth. Many legal systems around the world today are based on one of two models: the English **common law system** and the French **civil law system.** Common law systems reflect a conscious decision in favor of a limited role for government and emphasize the importance of the judiciary in constraining the power of the executive and legislative branches of government. In contrast, civil law systems favor the creation

TABLE 4–1 Differing Legal Systems

Common Law Nations	Civil Law Nations
Australia	Brazil
Canada	Egypt
India	France
Israel	Greece
New Zealand	Italy
United Kingdom	Mexico
United States	Sweden

of a strong centralized government in which the legislature and the executive branches have the power to grant preferential treatment to special interests. Table 4–1 shows a sampling of common law and civil law countries.

Research reveals that the security of **property rights** is much stronger in common law systems, such as observed in Britain and its former colonies, including the United States. In nations such as France and its former colonies, the civil law systems are much more likely to yield unpredictable changes in the rules of the game—the structure of **property and contract rights.** This unpredictability makes people reluctant to make long-term fixed investments, a fact that ultimately slows the economic growth of these nations and lowers the standard of living for their citizens.

The reasoning here is simple. If you know that the police will not help you protect your rights to a home or a car, you are less likely to acquire those assets. Similarly, if you cannot easily enforce business or employment contracts that you make, you are less likely to make those contracts—and hence less likely to produce as many goods or services. And if you cannot plan for the future because you don't know what the rules of the game will be in ten years or perhaps even one year from now, you are less likely to make the kinds of productive long-term investments that take years to pay off. Common law systems seem to do a better job at enforcing contracts and securing property rights and so would be expected to promote economic activity now and economic growth over time.

Research into the economic performance of nations around the world from 1960 until the 1990s found that economic growth was one-third higher in the common law nations, with their strong property rights, than in civil law nations. Over the more than three decades covered, the standard of living—measured by real **per capita income**—increased more than 20 percent in common law nations compared to civil law nations. If such a pattern persisted over the span of a century, it would produce a staggering 80 percent real per capita income differential in favor of nations with secure property rights.

Other research has taken a much broader view, both across time and across institutions, in assessing economic growth. Institutions such as political stability, protection against violence or theft, security of contracts, and freedom from regulatory burdens all contribute to sustained economic growth. Indeed, it is key institutions such as these, rather than natural-resource endowments, that explain long-term differences in economic growth and thus present-day differences in levels of real income. To illustrate the powerful effect of institutions, consider the contrast between Mexico, with per capita real income of about $12,000 today, and the United States, with per capita real income of about $48,000. Had Mexico developed with the same political and legal institutions that the United States has enjoyed, per capita income in Mexico would today be equal to that in the United States.

Given the great importance of such institutions in determining long-term growth, one might ask another important question: How have countries gotten the political and legal institutions they have today? The answer has to do with disease, of all things. An examination of more than seventy former European colonies reveals that a variety of strategies were pursued. In Australia, New Zealand, and North America, the colonists found geography and climates that were conducive to good health. Permanent settlement was attractive, so colonists created institutions to protect private property and curb the power of the state. But when Europeans arrived in Africa and South America, they encountered tropical diseases, such as malaria and yellow fever, that produced high mortality rates. This discouraged permanent settlement and encouraged a mentality focused on extracting metals, cash crops, and other resources. As a result, there were few **incentives** to promote democratic institutions or stable long-term property rights systems. The differing initial institutions helped shape economic growth over the years and, because of the broad persistence of those institutions, continue to shape the political and legal character and the standard of living in these nations today.

Recent events also illustrate that the effects of political and legal institutions can be drastically accelerated—in either direction. Consider China, which in 1979 began to change its institutions in two key ways. First, as we discuss more fully in Chapter 32, China began to experiment with private property rights for a few of its citizens, under narrow circumstances. Second, the Chinese government began to clear away obstacles to foreign investment, making China a more secure place for

Western companies to do business. Although the institutional changes have been modest, their combined effects have been substantial. Over the years since, economic growth in China has accelerated, averaging almost 7 percent per year. And if that doesn't sound like much, keep in mind that it has been enough over that period to raise real per capita income in China by a factor of 6.

For an example of the potential *destructive* impact of institutional change, we need look no further than Zimbabwe. When that country won its independence from Britain in 1980, it was one of the most prosperous nations in Africa. Soon after taking power as Zimbabwe's first (and so far only) president, Robert Mugabe began disassembling that nation's rule of law, tearing apart the institutions that had helped it grow rich. He reduced the security of property rights in land and eventually confiscated those rights altogether. Mugabe has also gradually taken control of the prices of most goods and services in his nation and even controls the price of its national currency, at least the price at which Zimbabweans are allowed to trade it. Moreover, the Mugabe government has confiscated large stocks of food and much of anything of value that might be exported out of or imported into Zimbabwe. In short, anything that is produced or saved has become subject to confiscation, so the incentives to do either are—to put it mildly—reduced.

As a result, between 1980 and 1996, real per capita income in Zimbabwe fell by one-third, and since 1996, it has fallen by an additional third. Eighty percent of the workforce is unemployed, investment is nonexistent, and the annual inflation rate reached an astonishing 231 million percent in recent years. (At that rate, the price level *doubles* every thirteen days.) The fruit of decades of labor and capital investment has been destroyed because the institutions that made that progress possible have been eliminated. It is a lesson we ignore at our peril.

DISCUSSION QUESTIONS

1. Consider two countries, A and B, that have identical *physical* endowments of a key natural resource. In country A, any profits that are made from extracting that resource are subject to confiscation by the government, while in country B, there is no such risk. How does the risk of expropriation affect the *economic* endowment of the two nations? In which nation are people richer?

2. In light of your answer to question 1, how do you explain the fact that in some countries there is widespread political support for government

policies that expropriate resources from some groups for the purpose of handing them out to other groups?

3. If the crucial factor determining a country's low standard of living is the adverse set of legal and cultural institutions it possesses, can you offer suggestions for how the other nations of the world might help in permanently raising that country's standard of living?

PART TWO

Supply and Demand

Introduction

The tools of **demand** and **supply** are the most basic and useful elements of the economist's kit. Indeed, many economists would argue that the **law of demand**—the lower the price of a good, the greater the quantity of that good demanded by purchasers—is the single most powerful proposition in all of economics. Simply stated, the law of demand has the capacity, unmatched by any other proposition in economics, to explain an incredibly diverse range of human behaviors. For example, the law of demand explains why buildings are taller in downtown areas than in outlying suburbs and also why people are willing to sit in the upper deck of football stadiums even though lower-deck seats are clearly superior. The great explanatory power of the law of demand is almost matched by that of the **law of supply,** which states that the higher the price of a good, the greater will be the quantity of that good supplied by producers. The law of supply helps us understand why people receive a premium wage when they work overtime, as well as why parking places at the beach are so much more expensive during the summer months than during the winter.

When the laws of demand and supply are combined, they illuminate the enormous **gains from trade** that arise from voluntary exchange. In Chapter 5, "Sex, Booze, and Drugs," we examine what happens when the government attempts to prohibit the exchanges that give rise to these gains. The consequences are often surprising, always costly, and—sadly—sometimes tragic. We find, for example, that when the federal government made alcoholic beverages illegal during the era known as Prohibition, Americans responded by switching from beer to hard liquor and by getting drunk more often when they drank. We also show that the government's ongoing efforts to prevent individuals from using drugs such as marijuana and cocaine cause the drive-by shootings that occur in many major cities and also encourage drug overdoses among users. Finally, we explain why laws against prostitution help foster the spread of AIDS.

Sometimes markets can create gains for humanity in the most unexpected places. One instance involves the transplantation of human organs. Many thousands of people die each year waiting in vain for the donation of a lifesaving organ. As we see in Chapter 6, "Kidneys for Sale," one key impediment to saving their lives lies in the fact that although we allow voluntary organ donations at a zero price, we prohibit individuals from being paid for a human organ for transplant. It is legal to pay the surgeons who perform the transplants and lawful for hospitals to make a profit on organ transplants performed in their operating rooms. But it is against the law for you to sell a cornea or a kidney or a lobe of your liver; it is even unlawful for your loved ones to benefit from the harvesting of any of your organs after your death. This reduces the number of human organs available for transplant and so results in the deaths of many thousands of people. We know from the experience of other nations that paying for organs induces many more donations. Safeguards against abuse (such as involuntary "donations") are also relatively easy to implement. Moreover, paying for transplant organs would add relatively little to the costs of the insurance programs that already pay for virtually all transplants. On balance, it thus appears that allowing payment for transplant organs would benefit the donors and, even more important, save the lives of many thousands of recipients—which is surely a classic illustration of the gains from trade.

Our focus in Chapter 7, "When High Prices Are Low Prices," is that when using the tools of supply and demand to assess the world around us, it is essential that we measure prices correctly. This sounds easy enough; after all, we encounter prices every day in our market transactions. But what we directly observe are **nominal prices,** which are expressed in terms of dollars (or euros or yen) per unit of the good in question. What is critical for analysis (and for our own decision making in the market) are **relative prices,** that is, prices that have been adjusted for inflation and so account for the true cost of items. We must also ensure that we adjust for the quality of items when comparing the relative prices across goods or across time. Humans seem to have the ability to make these adjustments automatically in the case of their day-to-day purchase and sale decisions. But when it comes to journalists writing about economic affairs or politicians making economic policy, the common sense of everyday choices seems to be forgotten, sometimes resulting in foolish news stories at best and damaging political decisions at worst.

Despite abundant everyday evidence of the power of prices to stimulate production, ration consumption, and ensure the efficient allocation of scarce goods, sometimes people forget that prices can perform their wonders even for goods like water, so essential to human life. This forgetfulness appears to be based on a variety of myths that surround water—notions that the planet is somehow drying up or that water cannot (because it is essential to life) be allocated through markets or that salty ocean water cannot readily be converted into freshwater. As we see in Chapter 8, "Are We Running Out of Water?" such ideas simply can't stand up to careful scrutiny. The earth is a closed system: Water can be dirtied, cleaned up, or moved around, but when we use it, we don't destroy it. Moreover, because it *is* so precious to us, water is an *ideal* candidate for the unfettered operation of competitive markets. Any attempts to interfere with open markets for water will reduce our total wealth and will place a disproportionate share of the burden on the people least able to bear it—those at the bottom of the income distribution.

One important conclusion of this chapter is that the water shortages and water crises that periodically afflict various parts of the world are rarely the result of droughts. They are far more often caused by government officials who are unwilling or unable to accept the reality of the laws of demand and supply.

As we see in Chapter 9, "The (Dis)Incentives of Higher Taxes," the effective prices faced by demanders and suppliers are importantly influenced by the taxes we impose on activities or goods. The consequences can be large-scale and sometimes confounding or counterproductive. When we tax income more heavily, people work less. When we tax goods more heavily, people consume less of those goods. Even so, at low levels of taxes, such responses are often modest, so that a higher **tax rate** can yield more **tax revenue.** But at some point, the disincentive effects of higher taxes can so discourage demanders or suppliers that revenues collected from the tax actually *fall*. When combined with the fact that the disincentive effects of taxes cause a reduction in the overall output produced in society, the result is surely a "lose-lose" outcome by any definition.

Our final application of demand and supply analysis comes in Chapter 10, "Bankrupt Landlords, from Sea to Shining Sea." This chapter brings us back to the issue discussed in Chapter 5, the effects of government interference with free markets, in this case in the form of **rent controls**—legal ceilings on the rent that landlords may charge for apartments. Although the effects of rent controls are perhaps less tragic than some of the effects observed in Chapter 5 or 6, they are just as surprising and often as costly. We find, for example, that legal ceilings on rents have increased the extent of homelessness in the United States, have led to a rise in racial discrimination, and have caused the wholesale destruction of hundreds of thousands of dwelling units in our nation's major cities. We cannot escape one simple fact: Politicians may pass legislation, and bureaucrats may do their best to enforce it, but the laws of demand and supply ultimately rule the economy.

Chapter 5

SEX, BOOZE, AND DRUGS

Before 1914, cocaine was legal in this country; today it is not. Alcoholic beverages are legal in the United States today; from 1920 to 1933, they were not. Prostitution is legal in Nevada today; in the other forty-nine states, it is not.[1] All these goods—sex, booze, and drugs—have at least one thing in common: The consumption of each brings together a willing seller with a willing buyer, creating an act of mutually beneficial exchange (at least in the opinion of the parties involved). Partly because of this property, attempts to proscribe the consumption of these goods have met with less than spectacular success and have yielded some peculiar patterns of production, distribution, and usage. Let's see why.

When the government seeks to prevent voluntary exchange, it must generally decide whether to go after the seller or the buyer. In most cases—and certainly where sex, booze, and drugs are concerned—the government targets sellers because this is where the authorities get the most benefit from their enforcement dollars. A cocaine dealer, even a small retail pusher, often supplies dozens or even hundreds of users each day, as did speakeasies (illegal saloons) during Prohibition; a hooker typically services three to ten "tricks" per day. By incarcerating the supplier, the police can prevent several, or even several hundred, transactions from taking place, which is usually much more cost-effective than going after the buyers one by one. It is not that the police ignore the consumers of illegal goods; indeed, sting operations, in which the police pose as illicit sellers, often make the headlines. Nevertheless, most enforcement efforts focus on the supply side, and so shall we.

---

1. These statements are not entirely correct. Even today, cocaine may be obtained legally by prescription from a physician. Prostitution in Nevada is legal only in counties that have chosen to permit it. Finally, some counties in the United States remain "dry," prohibiting the sale of beer, wine, and distilled spirits.

Law enforcement activities directed against the suppliers of illegal goods increase the suppliers' operating costs. The risks of fines, jail sentences, and possibly even violence become part of the costs of doing business and must be taken into account by existing and potential suppliers. Some entrepreneurs will leave the business, turning their talents to other activities; others will resort to clandestine (and costly) means to hide their operations from the police; still others will restrict the circle of buyers with whom they are willing to deal to minimize the chances that a customer is a cop. Across the board, the costs of operation are higher, and at any given price, less of the product will be available. There is a reduction in supply, and the result is a higher price for the good.

This increase in price is, in a sense, exactly what the enforcement officials are after, for the consumers of sex, booze, and drugs behave according to the **law of demand:** The higher the price of a good, the lower the amount consumed. So the immediate impact of the enforcement efforts against sellers is to reduce the consumption of the illegal good by buyers. There are, however, some other effects.

First, because the good in question is illegal, people who have a **comparative advantage** in conducting illegal activities will be attracted to the business of supplying (and perhaps demanding) the good. Some may have an existing criminal record and are relatively unconcerned about adding to it. Others may have developed skills in evading detection and prosecution while engaged in other criminal activities. Some may simply look at the illegal activity as another means of thumbing their noses at society. The general point is that when an activity is made illegal, people who are good at being criminals are attracted to that activity.

Illegal contracts are usually not enforceable through legal channels (and even if they were, few suppliers of illegal goods would be foolish enough to complain to the police about not being paid for their products). So buyers and sellers of illegal goods must frequently resort to private methods of contract enforcement, which often entails violence.[2] Hence people who are relatively good at violence are attracted to illegal activities and have greater **incentives** to employ their talents. This is one reason why the murder rate in America rose to record levels during Prohibition and then dropped sharply when liquor was again made legal. It also helps explain why the number of drug-related murders soared during the 1980s and why drive-by shootings became commonplace in many drug-infested cities. The Thompson submachine gun of the 1930s and

---

2. Fundamentally, violence—such as involuntary incarceration—also plays a key role in the government's enforcement of legal contracts. We often do not think of it as violence, of course, because it is usually cushioned by constitutional safeguards and procedural rules.

the MAC-10 machine gun of the 1980s were just low-cost means of contract enforcement.

The attempts of law enforcement officials to drive sellers of illegal goods out of business have another effect. Based on recent wholesale prices, $50,000 worth of pure heroin weighs about one pound; $50,000 worth of marijuana weighs about 100 pounds. As any drug smuggler can tell you, hiding a pound of contraband is a lot easier than hiding 100 pounds. Thus to avoid detection and prosecution, suppliers of the illegal good have an incentive to deal in the more valuable versions of their product, which for drugs and booze mean the more potent versions. Bootleggers during Prohibition concentrated on hard liquor rather than beer and wine; even today, moonshine typically has roughly twice the alcohol content of legal hard liquor such as bourbon, scotch, or vodka. After narcotics became illegal in this country in 1914, importers switched from the milder opium to its more valuable, more potent, and more addictive derivative, heroin.

The move to the more potent versions of illegal commodities is enhanced by enforcement activities directed against users. Not only do users, like suppliers, find it easier (cheaper) to hide the more potent versions, but there is also a change in relative prices due to user penalties. Typically, the law has lower penalties for using an illegal substance than for distributing it. Within each category (use or sale), however, there is commonly the same penalty regardless of value per unit. For example, during Prohibition, a bottle of wine and a bottle of more expensive, more potent hard liquor were equally illegal. Today, the possession of one gram of 90 percent pure cocaine brings the same penalty as the possession of one gram of 10 percent pure cocaine. Given the physical quantities, there is a fixed cost (the legal penalty) associated with being caught, regardless of value per unit (and thus potency) of the substance. Hence the structure of legal penalties raises the relative price of less potent versions, encouraging users to substitute more potent versions—heroin instead of opium, hashish instead of marijuana, hard liquor instead of beer.

Penalties against users also encourage a change in the nature of usage. Prior to 1914, cocaine was legal in this country and was used openly as a mild stimulant, much as people today use caffeine. (Cocaine was even an ingredient in the original formulation of Coca-Cola.) This type of usage—small, regular doses over long time intervals—becomes relatively more expensive when the substance is made illegal. Extensive usage (small doses spread over time) is more likely to be detected by the authorities than intensive usage (a large dose consumed at once), simply because possession time is longer and the drug must be accessed more frequently. Thus when a substance is made illegal, there is an incentive for consumers to switch toward usage that is more intensive. Rather than ingesting cocaine orally in the form of a highly diluted liquid solution, as was commonly done before 1914, people switched to snorting or injecting it. During Prohibition, people dispensed with cocktails before dinner each night; instead, on the less frequent occasions when they drank, they more often drank to get drunk. The same phenomenon is observed today. People under the age of twenty-one consume alcoholic beverages less frequently than people over the age of twenty-one. But when they do drink, they are more likely to drink to get drunk.

Not surprisingly, the suppliers of illegal commodities are reluctant to advertise their wares openly; the police are as capable of reading billboards and watching TV as potential customers are. Suppliers are also reluctant to establish easily recognized identities and regular places and hours of business because to do so raises the chance of being caught by the police. Information about the price and quality of products being sold goes underground, often with unfortunate effects for consumers.

With legal goods, consumers have several means of obtaining information. They can learn from friends, advertisements, and personal experience. When goods are legal, they can be trademarked for identification. The trademark cannot legally be copied, and the courts protect it. Given such easily identified brands, consumers can be made aware of the quality and price of each. If their experience does not meet expectations, they can assure themselves of no further contact with the unsatisfactory product by never buying that brand again.

When a general class of products becomes illegal, there are fewer ways to obtain information. Brand names are no longer protected by law, so falsification of well-known brands ensues. When products do not meet expectations, it is more difficult (costly) for consumers to punish suppliers. Frequently, the result is degradation of and uncertainty about product quality. The consequences for consumers of the illegal goods are often unpleasant and sometimes fatal.

Consider prostitution. In Nevada counties where prostitution is legal, the prostitutes are required to register with the local authorities, and they generally conduct their business in well-established bordellos. These establishments advertise openly and rely heavily on repeat business. Health officials test the prostitutes weekly for venereal disease and monthly for AIDS. Contrast this with other areas of the country, where prostitution is illegal. Suppliers are generally streetwalkers because a fixed, physical location is too easy for the police to detect and raid. Suppliers change locations frequently to reduce harassment by police. Repeat business is reported to be minimal; frequently, customers have never seen the prostitute before and never will again.

The difference in outcomes is striking. In Nevada, the spread of venereal disease by legal prostitutes is estimated to be almost nonexistent; to date, none of the registered prostitutes in Nevada has tested positive for AIDS. By contrast, in some major cities outside Nevada, the incidence of venereal disease among prostitutes is estimated to be near 100 percent. In Miami, one study found that 19 percent of all incarcerated prostitutes tested positive for AIDS; in Newark, New Jersey, 52 percent of the prostitutes tested were infected with the AIDS virus, and about half of the prostitutes in Washington, D.C., and New York City are also believed to be carrying the AIDS virus. Because of the lack of reliable information in markets for illegal goods, customers frequently do not know exactly what they are getting; as a result, they sometimes get more than they bargained for.

Consider alcohol and drugs. Today, alcoholic beverages are heavily advertised to establish their brand names and are carried by reputable dealers. Customers can readily punish suppliers for any deviation from the expected potency or quality by withdrawing their business, telling their friends, or even bringing a lawsuit. Similar circumstances prevailed before 1914 in this country for the hundreds of products containing opium or cocaine.

During Prohibition, consumers of alcohol often did not know exactly what they were buying or where to find the supplier the next day if they were dissatisfied. Fly-by-night operators sometimes adulterated liquor with far more lethal methyl alcohol. In tiny concentrations, this made watered-down booze taste like it had more kick, but in only slightly higher concentrations, the methyl alcohol blinded or even killed the unsuspecting consumer. Even in "reputable" speakeasies (those likely to be in business at the same location the next day), bottles bearing the labels of high-priced foreign whiskeys were refilled repeatedly with locally (and illegally) produced rotgut until their labels wore off.

In the 1970s, more than one purchaser of what was reputed to be high-potency Panama Red or Acapulco Gold marijuana ended up with low-potency pot heavily loaded with stems, seeds, and maybe even oregano. Buyers of cocaine must worry about not only how much the product has been cut along the distribution chain but also what has been used to cut it. In recent years, the purity of cocaine at the retail level has ranged between 10 percent and 95 percent; for heroin, the degree of purity has ranged from 5 percent to 50 percent. Cutting agents can turn out to be any of various sugars, local anesthetics, or amphetamines; on occasion, rat poison has been used.

We noted earlier that the legal penalties for the users of illegal goods encourage them to use more potent forms and to use them more intensively. These facts and the uncertain quality and potency of the illegal products yield a deadly combination. During Prohibition, the death rate from acute alcohol poisoning (due to overdose) was more than thirty times higher than today. In 1927 alone, twelve thousand people died from acute alcohol poisoning, and many thousands more were blinded or killed by contaminated booze. Today, about four thousand people a year die as a direct result of consuming either cocaine or heroin. Of that total, it is estimated, roughly 80 percent die from either an overdose caused by an unexpectedly potent product or an adverse reaction to the material used to cut the drug. Clearly, *caveat emptor* ("let the buyer beware") is a warning to be taken seriously if one is consuming an illegal product.

We noted at the beginning of this chapter that one of the effects of making a good illegal is to raise its price. One might well ask, by how much? During the early 1990s, the federal government was spending about $2 billion a year in its efforts to stop the importation of cocaine from Colombia. One study concluded that these efforts had hiked the price of cocaine by 4 percent relative to what it would have been had the federal government done nothing to interdict cocaine imports. The study estimated that the cost of raising the price of cocaine an additional 2 percent would be $1 billion per year. More recently, Nobel Laureate Gary Becker and his colleagues have estimated that America's war on drugs costs at least $100 billion per year. And the results? The prices of heroin and cocaine are at record-low levels.

The government's efforts to halt imports of marijuana have had some success, presumably because that product is easier to detect than cocaine. Nevertheless, suppliers have responded by cultivating marijuana domestically instead of importing it or by bringing it in across the relatively open U.S.-Canadian border rather than from elsewhere. The net effect has been an estimated tenfold increase in potency due to the superior farming techniques available in this country and Canada, as well as the use of genetic bioengineering to improve strains.

A few years ago, most states and the federal government began restricting sales of cold medicines containing pseudoephedrine because that ingredient was widely used for making the illegal stimulant methamphetamine in home laboratories. The restrictions succeeded in sharply curtailing home production of "meth." They also led to a huge increase in imports of a far more potent version of meth from Mexico. Overall, it is estimated that neither consumption of nor addiction to methamphetamine was reduced by the restrictions. But overdoses from the drug rose sharply because of the greater purity of the imports.

Consider also the government's efforts to eliminate the consumption of alcohol during the 1920s and 1930s. They failed so badly that the Eighteenth Amendment, which put Prohibition in place, was the first (and so far the only) constitutional amendment ever to be repealed. As for prostitution, it is reputed to be "the oldest profession" and by all accounts continues to flourish today, even in Newark and Miami.

The government's inability to halt the consumption of sex, booze, or drugs does not mean that those efforts have failed. Indeed, the impact of these efforts is manifested in their consequences, ranging from tainted drugs and alcohol to disease-ridden prostitutes. The message instead is that when the government attempts to prevent mutually beneficial exchange, even its best efforts are unlikely to meet with spectacular success.

DISCUSSION QUESTIONS

1. The federal government currently taxes alcohol on the basis of the 100-proof gallon. (Alcohol that is 100 proof is 50 percent pure ethyl alcohol; most hard liquor sold is 80 proof, or 40 percent ethyl alcohol, whereas wine is usually about 24 proof, and most beer is 6 to 10 proof.) How would alcohol consumption patterns change if the government taxed alcohol strictly on the basis of volume rather than also taking its potency into account?

2. During Prohibition, some speakeasy operators paid bribes to ensure that the police did not raid them. Would you expect the quality of the liquor served in such speakeasies to be higher or lower than in those that did not pay bribes? Would you expect to find differences (for example, with regard to income levels) among the customers patronizing the two types of speakeasies?

3. The markets for prostitution in Nevada and New Jersey have two important differences: (1) Prostitutes in New Jersey face higher costs because of government efforts to prosecute them, and (2) customers in New Jersey face higher risks of contracting diseases from prostitutes because the illegal nature of the business makes reliable information about product quality much more costly to obtain. Given these facts, in which state would you expect the price of prostitution services to be higher? Which state would have the higher amount of services consumed (adjusted for population differences)? Explain your answer.

4. According to the surgeon general of the United States, nicotine is the most addictive drug known to humanity, and cigarette smoking kills perhaps 300,000 to 400,000 people a year in the United States. Why isn't tobacco illegal in America?

Chapter 6

KIDNEYS FOR SALE

This year, more than seven thousand Americans will die waiting for an organ transplant. They will not die because physicians are unable to transplant organs or because their health insurance does not cover the cost of the transplant. They will die because since 1984, it has been against federal law to pay for human organs.[1] It is lawful to pay a man for his sperm, a woman for her eggs, and members of either gender for their blood. It is even lawful to donate an organ or to receive one as a gift. And it is certainly legal to pay the surgeons who perform the transplants. It is even lawful for hospitals to make a profit on organ transplants performed in their operating rooms. But it is against the law for you to sell a cornea or a kidney or a lobe of your liver; it is even unlawful for your loved ones to benefit from the harvesting of any of your organs after your death. And so seven thousand people die every year, waiting in vain for someone to donate an organ to them.

The transplantation of human body parts is not new. The first cornea was successfully transplanted in Austria in 1905. The first successful kidney transplant (between identical twins) was conducted in Boston in 1954. Since then, successful transplants of the pancreas, liver, heart, lung, hand, and even face have been performed. Indeed, there are now thirty-seven different organs and types of human tissues that can be transplanted. None of this is cheap. In the United States, a kidney transplant costs about $250,000 on average, a liver transplant runs $520,000, and a heart transplant costs an average of $650,000. But there are services that arrange for international transplants (performed, for example, in India or China) of any of these organs at less than half the price. None of these

---

1. This legislation was originally introduced by Rep. Al Gore (D., Tenn.), who went on to become vice president of the United States (1993–2001).

figures include payment for the organ itself because such payments are illegal in the United States and in most other countries.

These astronomical sums are obviously out of the reach of most people. In fact, however, transplants done in the United States are generally not paid for directly by the recipients. For a person under the age of sixty-five with health insurance, private insurance pays for the transplant. For anyone sixty-five or older, the federal Medicare system pays for the transplant. And for people under sixty-five with neither private insurance nor the wealth to pay by themselves, transplants are paid for by the Medicaid system, which is financed jointly by the federal government and the states. (Neither private insurance plans nor Medicare or Medicaid will pay for international transplants, which are generally chosen only by relatively affluent people who are unwilling to wait—or to die waiting.)

Now, to begin our inquiry into the economics of organ transplants, let's consider the case of kidneys. We start here because the technical features of the transplant process have become relatively routine and because we each are born with two kidneys but can get by quite well with only one. In fact, thanks to the technique known as dialysis, humans can actually survive for years without functioning kidneys. In 2009, about eighty thousand people were awaiting kidney transplants in the United States. That same year, ten thousand Americans received transplants from deceased strangers. Another six thousand received a transplant from a living donor (recall that "extra" kidney we each have), usually a close friend or relative. Tragically, five thousand of the people waiting for a kidney either died or were dropped from the list because they had become too sick to qualify for a transplant. Another two thousand died that year waiting for a liver, heart, lung, or other critical organ. Could they be saved, if it were as lawful to pay for kidneys as it is to pay for the surgeons who transplant them? Or would a market for kidneys ultimately become a black market, relying on "donated" organs removed from unwilling victims by unscrupulous brokers motivated by cash rather than kindness? That is precisely the nexus of the debate over whether we should permit people (or the relatives of just-deceased donors) to be remunerated for lifesaving organ donations.

First things first: Surely we cannot object to a market for organs because the act of donating a kidney or the lobe of a liver is potentially hazardous to the donor. After all, we currently permit people to undergo such risks under the current system with *no* monetary compensation. If it is safe enough to allow friends or family to donate without payment, why is it too risky for someone to give up a kidney or part of his or her liver in return for money?

There are, of course, many other contentious issues. To start exploring them, let's look first at a nation where it *is* legal to pay people for human organs: Iran, which just happens to have the highest living-donor rate in the world, at twenty-three donations per million people. Monetary compensation for organs in Iran has been lawful there since 1988, and in the ensuing decade, Iran eliminated the *entire* backlog of kidney transplant patients, something no other nation has achieved.

Under the Iranian system, a person awaiting a kidney must first seek a suitable, willing donor in his or her family. If none is forthcoming, the person must wait up to six months for a suitable deceased donor. At that point, the potential recipient can apply to the national transplant association for a kidney from a willing donor who is paid for the kidney. The donor receives from the government $1,200 plus a year of fully paid health insurance and a payment of $2,300 to $4,500 from the recipient (or a charity, if the recipient is poor). Donor and recipient are also free to agree to an additional cash payment, although in most cases, the sums already mentioned are sufficient to get the job done. There are still purely altruistic donors in Iran, as well as cadaveric donations from the recently deceased. But it is the payment for organs that has permitted essentially all who seek kidney donations in Iran to get them, and the Iranian system has done so *without* leading to "back alley" donations or to people who are unable to afford a transplant because of the high cost of the organs themselves. Meanwhile, the system has saved the lives of thousands of Iranians.

Many people worry about a system of payment for human transplant because of the possibility that it would yield *involuntary* donors. That is, if there is a market for organs, some unscrupulous brokers might be tempted by profits to knock people over the head and harvest their organs for sale at the highest price. Yet it is generally agreed that the Iranian system has worked for more than twenty years without a hint of any such activities. Perhaps this should not be too surprising, given the medical techniques that have been developed to ensure that the tissue match between organ and recipient is close enough to make transplant feasible. These and other DNA tests can now quickly ascertain with substantial certainty that "organ A" came from voluntary "donor A" rather than from involuntary "donor B."

Indeed, apart from gruesome works of fiction, most of the horror stories about the hazards of allowing markets for human organs are stories about behavior caused by the *lack* of a market for organs. In China, for example, many "transplant tourists" in the past received organs taken from the bodies of the thousands of prisoners who are executed there every year. China insisted that the prisoners' organs were used only with their "consent," a claim that many human rights groups have disputed. But on one point all agree: There were no payments to the prisoners or their surviving relatives. The organs were simply taken (a practice now supposedly halted).

In both the United States and Britain, there have been highly publicized cases of what amount to "body snatching"—removal of organs and other body parts from the recently deceased. Some of these cases involved body parts used in research, while other body parts were intended for sale at a profit. In each of these cases, removal was done without the prior consent of the deceased or the postmortem consent of relatives. But this amounts to theft; it is singularly horrifying, but we must remember that it is theft. Consider another form of stealing: Every year many thousands of senior citizens are defrauded of their hard-earned retirement funds by unscrupulous individuals who masquerade as "financial advisers." Should we make it illegal for anyone to pay for investment advice— or should we devote our efforts to prosecuting and incarcerating the perpetrators of such crimes?

In Pakistan and the Philippines, there were small-scale markets for transplant organs until recently, although Pakistan has now banned the trade in human organs and transplants for non-Filipinos have now been outlawed in that nation. In both countries, there were anecdotes of donors who sold kidneys for $2,000 to $3,000 (about a year's worth of per capita income in either nation), but who later came to regret the transaction because of adverse long-term health effects. But this would be a potential issue even with unpaid donors, and in any nation such as the United States, donors in a market for organs would surely receive at least as much medical and psychological counseling as volunteer donors receive now.

Now, what about the added expense of allowing payments for donated organs? Would this break the budgets of Medicare or Medicaid or empty the coffers of the private insurance companies that pay for the bulk of transplants? In the case of kidneys, we have enough information from elsewhere to say the answer is probably not. In Iran, where per capita income is about $12,000 per year, payments to donors smaller than this amount have been sufficient to clear the market for kidneys. In Pakistan and the Philippines, payments equivalent to a year's worth of per capita income were enough to support a substantial transplant tourist market in both countries.

At almost $50,000 a year, average per capita income in the United States is clearly much higher than in any of these nations, suggesting that payments for kidneys would also have to be much larger to induce a substantial increase in the number of donations. But experts have estimated that even if the payment for a kidney were as much as $100,000, private and public insurance systems (which, as we have noted, pay for almost all of the transplants in the United States) could actually *save* money on many transplants because dialysis (at $70,000 per year) and the other treatments associated with chronic kidney disease are so expensive.

It is true that allowing payments for human organs would almost surely increase the number of transplants each year—indeed, this is the very point. Payments would bring forth more organs, and this would in turn reduce deaths among people waiting for transplants. A payment system would have added costs associated with it: There would be more transplant operations (at $250,000 each for kidneys, for example, plus another, say, $100,000 for each of the organs themselves). Suppose that the payments for kidneys enabled an additional five thousand transplants per year (assuming that the U.S. system would be as successful as the Iranian system in eliminating the excess demand for kidneys). That would yield added costs nationwide of about $1.75 billion (five thousand transplants estimated at $350,000 each).

And there is a second cost: Paying for organs would cause a reduction in the number of altruistic donations. How many fewer there would be we cannot know for sure, but let us make two assumptions to be on the safe side. First, we assume that there would be *no* altruistic donations from living donors under a payment system. Second, we assume that the relatives of all deceased donors would insist on payment. Together these assumptions imply there would be an added expense of $100,000 on each of the sixteen thousand kidney transplants performed under the current system. The added cost here would be $1.6 billion a year, which, when added to the $1.75 billion cost of the new transplants, yields a total added annual cost of $3.35 billion for the organ payment system.

In return for this sum, we would surely recoup some savings from the dialysis system, because at least five thousand people a year would no longer be on dialysis at $70,000 per year—they would instead have a kidney to do that work for them. Moreover, the current three- to four-year delay on kidney transplants would be sharply reduced, generating additional savings. But far more important, we would be saving the lives of five thousand people every year, at a cost per life saved of but $600,000—and this number does not count any of the savings from reduced dialysis treatments.

All these calculations seem a callous way to view a human life. But by the standards of medical care of today, allowing payments for human organs is almost surely a safe and remarkably cheap way to alleviate needless suffering and save thousands of lives every year. And once this is clear, aren't the truly callous people those who would deprive human beings of that opportunity?

DISCUSSION QUESTIONS

1. Why might the owners of the private insurance companies that pay for most organ transplants be in favor of a system that prohibits paying for a donated organ? Should the taxpayers of the United States, who ultimately cover the cost of Medicare and Medicaid transplants, similarly be opposed to paying for donated organs?

2. If payment for organs drives up the financial costs of transplants, is it possible that private insurance companies, and even Medicare and Medicaid, might tighten their standards for transplants so as to reduce the number of transplants each year? If they do, who would gain and who would lose compared to the current system?

3. The average waiting time on transplant lists is three to four years for kidneys (although this is expected to rise sharply, due to the rising incidence of diabetes, a major cause of kidney damage). Many of these people waiting must undergo dialysis, at a cost of $70,000 per year, paid for by private insurance, Medicare, or Medicaid. Suppose that if payment for organs were permitted, the transplant waiting time were shortened by three years, and that for the average patient, the result was eighteen months less on dialysis. At what price for a kidney would a system of paying for organs be a "break-even" proposition for insurers? Show all calculations, and explain your reasoning.

4. The United States currently has an "opt-in" system for organ donations from the deceased: People must explicitly choose postmortem donation ahead of time (as when they obtain their driver's licenses). Many other nations have "opt-out" systems: A desire to donate postmortem is presumed to exist unless an individual explicitly chooses ahead of time *not* to permit donation. How—if at all—would a shift to an opt-out system likely change the supply of cadaveric (postmortem) donations?

Chapter 7

WHEN HIGH PRICES ARE LOW PRICES

Every few years, some important commodity, such as gasoline, electricity, or food, experiences a spike in prices. Reporters examine such price spikes and plaster newspapers, magazines, and Web sites with the appropriate headlines—sometimes day after day. Television commentators interview frustrated and worried Americans who proffer the expected negative reaction to the higher prices of essential items in their budgets. The world, it would seem, is coming to an end.

Let's just take one often-in-the-press example: gasoline prices. The authors of the book you are reading are old enough to remember the TV interviews that ensued when the price of gas first hit the unprecedented level of $1 per gallon, back in 1980. The same sorts of interviews occurred when the price of a gallon of gas broke the $2 barrier, early in 2005. Not surprisingly, virtually the same types of interviews occurred when the price of a gallon of gas rose to $3 in 2006 and then to $4 in the summer of 2008. At each point in time, everyone interviewed had the same response, even though years had passed between the price spikes: "I guess I'll just have to stop driving." "I'm going to get a bike." "I'm selling my big car and getting a small one." And of course, each time there was an accompanying story about how record numbers of people were (or soon would be) flocking to their neighborhood motor scooter dealerships.

If we wish to analyze sensibly the effects of higher prices on the quantity demanded and the quantity supplied of any good or service, we can rely neither on what journalists report nor on what Americans say when they are interviewed. After all, what is important is not what people say but what they do. As economists, we best understand consumers by their **revealed preferences.** Similarly, business owners are best understood by their actions, not their words. What people do is reflected in how much they actually buy of any good or service after its price changes—not by their complaints to a TV reporter or what they post on their blog or on Facebook or MySpace or Twitter.

For demand and supply analysis, the relevant price is the price *relative to* all other prices, because people's decisions are based on **relative prices,** not **nominal prices.** The latter simply tell us the number of pieces of paper (dollar bills) we must hand over for a good. Nominal prices tell us nothing about the real sacrifice (measured in terms of goods or our labor services) that we must make to obtain those goods. Relative prices, in contrast, tell us the real sacrifice involved in acquiring a good, because they tell us how much of other goods we must sacrifice.

Said another way, we have to separate the rise in the general price level, called **inflation,** from the rise in the nominal price of a particular good or service. If *all* nominal prices went up 3 percent in a given year, there would be no change in relative prices, but this inflation of 3 percent per year would not change the real sacrifice entailed in acquiring any particular good. In the real world, even during periods of inflation, some prices go up faster than others and some prices even go down— witness the price of computing power, of DVD players, and of MP3 players. Nevertheless, if we want to predict people's behavior, we must know what has happened to the *relative* price of a good, and to determine this, we must adjust for inflation.

Now let's get back to our example of gasoline prices. Your grandparents might be able to talk about buying gas for 30 cents a gallon (its typical nominal price most of the time between 1956 and 1964). Today, what you pay in dollars per gallon is many times that level. People still drive nonetheless; indeed, the use of gasoline for cars and trucks in the United States is roughly *triple* what it was when the nominal price of gas was only 30 cents. Something must have happened. The most important is a general rise in all nominal prices, including gasoline prices.

In the summer of 2008, the price of gasoline edged beyond $4 per gallon. Then-presidential candidate Barack Obama argued that the government should intervene on gas prices to "give families some relief." Two-thirds of American voters at that time said they thought that the price of gas was "an extremely important political issue." (Of course, when gas prices started tumbling in the fall of 2008, there were not many front-page articles or TV interviews with happy consumers. And the politicians simply became silent on this subject.) Consider, though, that at its nominal price at the end of 2008, the *relative* price of gas was lower than it had been in 1980, after correcting for overall inflation. For many people, this is a shocking revelation. But correcting for inflation is absolutely essential if you want to sensibly analyze the price of anything over time.

There is something else that we should mention here, particularly relevant when thinking about the real burden of gasoline. People are becoming more productive over time, because they are getting better educated and because ongoing technological change enables us to produce more with a given input of our time. As a result of this higher productivity, U.S. consumers' **disposable income** generally rises from one year to the next—and rises on average over longer periods of time. As Americans become richer on average, they are financially able to handle even higher relative prices of the items they wish to purchase, gasoline included.

To help us understand this point better, researchers Indur Goklany and Jerry Taylor came up with an "affordability index." They compared family income to the price of gas from 1949 to 2008. They arbitrarily set 1960 at an affordability index of 1; relative to this, a higher affordability index number means that something is more affordable. Even when gas was $4.15 per gallon, the affordability gas index was 1.35. In other words, the ratio of the average person's disposable income to the price of gasoline was higher by about 35 percent in 2008 than it was in 1960; gasoline was *more* affordable than it had been back in 1960, when your grandparents were filling up their tanks at 30 cents a gallon—hard to believe for some of us, but true nonetheless. And once gas prices started going down at the end of 2008, the gas affordability index rose even more, passing 2.0.

The quality of gasoline does not change over time. But the quality of many other products does change over time, usually for the better. Often we forget about this crucial aspect when we start comparing prices of a good or service over time. If you ask senior citizens today how much they paid for their first car, you might get prices in the range of $2,000 to $5,000. The average new car today costs around $24,000. By now, of course, you know that if you want to compare these numbers, you must first account for the inflation that has occurred over the time period you are examining. In this case, adjusting for inflation still means that the relative price of a car appears to be about 30 percent higher than it was, say, fifty years ago.

Does that necessarily mean that a car is really 30 percent more expensive than it was in 1960? Probably not. We must take into account improved quality features of cars today compared to those of half a century ago. Today, the average car has the following:

- Computer-controlled antilock power brakes
- Power steering
- Digital radio with CD or MP3 player
- Air conditioning
- Steel-belted radial tires

- Cruise control
- Power windows and locks
- Air bags
- Forty percent better fuel economy

The list of improved and new features is actually much longer. Today, the average car is safer, breaks down less often, needs fewer tune-ups, has a host of amenities that were not even dreamed of fifty years ago, and almost certainly lasts for at least twice as many miles. If you correct for not only inflation but also for these quality increases, the relative price of cars today has almost certainly *fallen* appreciably in the past fifty years, despite the "sticker shock" that you may experience when you go shopping for a new car. That is, appearances to the contrary, the inflation-corrected **constant-quality price** of automobiles is actually lower today than it was five decades ago.

The necessity of adjusting for inflation and quality changes continues to apply even when we are examining goods whose nominal prices have declined over time. A good example is computing power. The nominal price of the average personal computer has gone down in spite of general inflation over the past several decades. These days, a Windows-based desktop computer has an average price of about $550; for a laptop, the average price is around $700. A decade ago, the average machines in each category would have had nominal prices twice as high. You might be tempted to conclude, then, that the price of personal computing has fallen by 50 percent, but you'd be wrong. The price has actually fallen by more than 50 percent.

Why? There are two reasons. First, over the past ten years, the average dollar prices of all goods increased by 30 percent; that is how much overall inflation there has been. That means that the *relative* price of the average computer has fallen by two-thirds, which of course is greater than 50 percent. But even here we are missing something extremely important: The quality of what you are buying—computing power—has skyrocketed. The processor speed of the average computer today is at least ten times greater than it was ten years ago and is increasing exponentially. Moreover, hard drives are bigger; monitors are flat-screen LCDs instead of bulky old cathode ray tubes; laptops are lighter; RAM is larger—so the list of improvements grows. And despite people's frustrations with both the hardware and software of the personal computer today, longtime users can tell you that both are vastly more reliable than they were a decade ago. Thus if you look only at the inflation-corrected decrease in computer prices, you will be underestimating the true decrease in the *relative* price of computers.

The moral of our story is simple. At some point in your education, you learned that "what goes up must come down." Now you know that when it comes to prices, it is often the case that "what goes up has actually gone down." It is a lesson worth keeping in mind if you really want to understand the behavior of consumers and businesses alike.

DISCUSSION QUESTIONS

1. Try to explain why price increases for crude oil, gas, heating oil, electricity, and food are widely reported by the media, yet when these prices decline, there is almost no discussion in the media.

2. Make a list of goods (or services) whose qualities have improved over time to such an extent that the prices do not accurately reflect their real prices, even after adjusting for inflation. Now see if you can come up with a list of items whose quality has systematically *decreased* over time. Can you suggest why it is easier to find examples of the former than it is of the latter?

3. The demand for small-engine motor scooters jumped when the price of gasoline started moving up in the summer of 2008. Make a prediction about the demand for this form of transportation in, say, two years from today. Explain your answer.

4. Explain why you will make more accurate predictions if you focus on the changing incentives people face rather than listening to what they say they are going to do.

C h a p t e r   8

ARE WE RUNNING
OUT OF WATER?

If you believe the headlines, humans are about to die of thirst. A few samples should be enough to convince you:

"A World of Thirst" (*U.S. News & World Report*)
"Water Shortages May Lead to War" (*Financial Times*)
"Drying Up" (*The Economist*)
"Water Shortages Could Leave World in Dire Straits" (*USA Today*)

The world, it seems, is running out of water.

But how can this be true? After all, about 71 percent of the earth's surface is covered in water. Lake Michigan alone contains more water than the world's population uses in two years. Even more to the point, the earth is a closed system. Using water does not destroy water. Whether we drink it, flush it, irrigate with it, or even let it evaporate, it comes back to us eventually, just as clean and pure as the raindrops of a spring shower. In fact, every three weeks, enough rain falls to satisfy the water uses of the entire world's population for a year. So what, exactly, is the problem?

Water is the ultimate renewable resource: The act of using it begins the process that returns it to us. But—and this is the crux—water is also *scarce*. That is, having the amount of clean water we want, where we want it, when we want it there, is not free. We must sacrifice other resources to accomplish this. And as the level of economic activity grows, the demand for water grows, and so the costs of consuming water grow.

In this sense, water is no different from any other **scarce good.** If we want more of it, we must sacrifice more of other things to achieve that goal. But what makes water seem different is that unlike, say, broccoli, if we do entirely without it, disastrous things happen in a relatively short period of time. If water gets sufficiently scarce, people may start doing some pretty unpleasant things to each other to ensure that they, rather than their neighbors or enemies, are the ones who end up with it. But before we see if this is really something we should worry about, we had better start by learning a little more about water.

Of the enormous amount of water on the earth's surface, about 97.2 percent is ocean water, which is too saline under normal circumstances to drink or use for irrigation. Another 2.15 percent is polar ice, which is certainly not a very convenient source. Of the remaining 0.65 percent, about 0.62 percent is underground in aquifers and similar geological structures; this groundwater takes hundreds of years to recharge and so is not really a sustainable source of freshwater over the relevant time span. That leaves us with rain.

Fortunately, it rains a lot, and despite the headlines, on a *worldwide* basis, the amount of rainfall doesn't vary much from year to year. About two-thirds of the rain falls on the world's oceans, where almost no one lives. But even so, and even taking into account evaporation and the fact that much of the rain over land quickly runs off into the oceans before it can be captured, there is still a lot of usable rainfall every year. Indeed, there is enough every year to yield 5,700 liters per person—about six times as much as the average person actually consumes. Of course, Mother Nature is not particularly evenhanded in the distribution of this usable rainfall. For example, China gets only 5 percent of it, despite having 20 percent of the world's population. Brazil, Canada, and Russia, which together have 6 percent of the world's population, receive 29 percent of the usable rainfall. And although the United States does pretty well on average, picking up 5 percent of the rain and having about 5 percent of the world's population, there are plenty of differences within our borders. Massive amounts of rain fall in southeastern Alaska and on the mountain slopes of Hawaii, while very little falls in Southern California. But the fact that people routinely choose to locate themselves in places where it does not rain highlights one of the fundamental points of this chapter: Water is an **economic good,** and the distribution and consumption of water are fundamentally economic problems, ones that can be solved in markets, just as other economic problems (such as the provision of food, shelter, and clothing) are solved in markets. To focus clearly on this point, let's examine some of the myths that have grown up around water in recent years.

Myth 1: The planet is drying up. As we have suggested earlier, there is nothing to worry about here. The cheapest (and completely sustainable) source of clean freshwater is rainfall, and roughly 113,000 cubic kilometers (3 quadrillion gallons) of the stuff falls every year on land areas around the world, year in and year out. Although small amounts of this are temporarily stored in plants and animals while they are alive, all of it eventually either recharges groundwater or evaporates, forms clouds, and precipitates—all 113,000 cubic kilometers, year after year. Sometimes, more is in Brazil and less in Sudan, and sometimes more of it inconveniently runs off in floods, but because the earth is a closed system, that water stays with us.

Myth 2: We can save water by flushing less and using less in agriculture. Remember the closed system? That applies to toilets and alfalfa, too. Flushing the toilet does not send the water to the moon. It just sends it through the sewer system to a water treatment plant and eventually into aquifers under the ground or back down on our heads in the form of raindrops. So-called low-flow toilets (and showers) have no effect on the amount of water in existence. (Because they may slightly reduce the amount of water running through water and sewer systems, they may conserve a bit on the amount of resources used in these systems. But there are offsets. Such devices are routinely more costly to produce than regular toilets or shower heads, and they occupy people's time—because of double flushes and longer showers. On balance, besides not "saving" water, there is thus no evidence that such devices conserve resources at all.)

Even agriculture, notorious for consuming an enormous amount of (usually subsidized) water around the world, does not destroy the stuff. Most of the water used by agriculture evaporates or runs off into rivers or soaks into underground aquifers. A small amount is temporarily stored in the crops, but this, soon enough, is consumed by animals or humans and simply returns to the same system that delivers 113,000 cubic kilometers of water onto our heads every year. There is no doubt that all of this use of water in agriculture is costly, because it could be used elsewhere. Moreover, agricultural use of water is generally subsidized by taxpayers. Making farmers pay full market value for water would reduce agricultural use and raise our collective wealth by improving the allocation of resources. But it would not alter the amount of water available.

Having said this, agricultural use of water does present two important economic issues. First, as we just noted, government policies around the world routinely cause water for agriculture to be heavily subsidized. Farmers often pay as little as $10 to $20 per acre-foot (about 325,000 gallons) for water that costs anywhere from $500 to $1,000 per acre to provide to them. Because of this huge subsidy, farmers are no doubt richer, but the losses to society are much greater, meaning that our overall wealth is lower. (For an explanation of why we get such subsidies despite this, see Chapters 2 and 23.)

Second, we not only subsidize water use for agriculture, but we also routinely forbid farmers to sell or lease their water to other users, especially nonagricultural users. This is a particular problem in the relatively arid American West, where farmers effectively own most of the rights to surface and groundwater but must "use it or lose it"—if they don't put it to beneficial use on their crops, they lose their rights to it. But often this water would be much more productively "used" if it were left in the streams to help support the spawning and other essential life activities of downstream species, such as trout or salmon. Laws are slowly changing to recognize environmental uses as being "beneficial" uses, but existing restrictions on the use of water still yield lower overall wealth for us.

Myth 3: Water is different from other goods. Many people seem to think that because it is essential to life, water is somehow different from other goods—or at least that it should be treated differently in some very specific ways. Let's first get rid of the notion that water doesn't obey the laws of demand and supply. In fact, although the demand for water in some uses is relatively inelastic, usage of water in *all* uses responds as predicted by the law of demand—when the price of water goes up, people use less of it. Similarly, although getting water from where it is to where people would like it to be is costly, the law of supply still holds true—when the price of water rises, suppliers of water provide more of it to consumers. Sometimes this process is as simple as diverting a stream or capturing rainfall. Sometimes it is as complicated as using reverse osmosis to convert seawater into freshwater. But even if the production technique is as esoteric as recycling urine into fresh, drinkable water (as is done on the international space station), the fact remains that when water becomes more valuable, people are incredibly ingenious in finding ways to make sure it is available.

Myth 4: Price controls on water protect low-income consumers. Some people claim that water should *not* be treated like other goods, specifically arguing that the price of water received by suppliers and the price paid by consumers should both be kept down by government decree. This, it is said, will protect people, especially those who are poor, from high water prices and will prevent suppliers from earning "excessive" profits. After all, some 1.1 billion people around the world currently do not have ready access to clean water, which makes an inviting target for anyone who might become a monopoly supplier to substantial numbers of these people.

It is true that governments can reduce the profits of the suppliers of water (or anything else) by limiting the prices they charge. But in reality, this does not protect consumers, particularly not the poorest consumers. Price controls on water *reduce* the amount supplied and, especially for the poor, generally make consumers worse off. They end up with less water than if prices were allowed to reach equilibrium levels, and they are forced to undergo nonprice rationing schemes (ranging from limited hours of service to getting no clean water at all). In fact, if we examine places around the world where the poor have little or no access to clean water, we find that government efforts to "protect" people from potential suppliers of water are in fact a key source of this lack of access. In Brazil, for example, government limits on private water rates forced a major international water project company to cease operations there, reducing the supply of clean water. In India, the widespread insistence by many local governments that water be provided free of charge has effectively stalled most efforts to improve water distribution in that country. And in China, government price controls have discouraged water utilities from developing new water supplies and from upgrading water distribution systems. As we see in detail in Chapter 10, government controls on prices make goods *more* scarce, not less, and it is generally the disadvantaged members of society who suffer the most as a result.

Myth 5: The ocean is too salty to drink. As a practical matter, prolonged consumption of saltwater by species not specifically adapted for it is highly deleterious. But the technology for desalination of seawater is advancing rapidly, and the cost of desalination is falling just as rapidly—more than 95 percent over the past twenty years. In relatively arid parts of the earth (including Southern California) desalination has become price-competitive with other sources of supply, and large-scale desalination plants are in operation around the world.

The process yields highly concentrated brine as a by-product. To avoid damage to ocean species that are sensitive to excess salinity, this brine must be dealt with carefully (dispersed widely) when it is returned to the sea. Nevertheless, this is simply a matter of routine care. Moreover, if local conditions make wide dispersal impractical or expensive, the brine can be evaporated, and the resulting solid materials then either used or disposed of in ordinary landfills. The upshot is that with continued technological progress in desalination, water from the ocean will likely become cheaper than collecting rainfall in large portions of the world. Far from running out of water, people everywhere will then find themselves able to secure it as easily as, well, turning on the tap.

DISCUSSION QUESTIONS

1. How much water do people "need"? Is your answer the same if you have to pay their water bills?

2. Evaluate the following: "Although taxpayers foot the bill for federal water sold to farmers at subsidized prices, they also eat the crops

grown with that water. Because the crops are cheaper due to the subsidized water, taxpayers get back exactly what they put in, and so there is no waste from having subsidized water for farmers." Would you give the author of this quote an A or an F in economics? Explain.

3. During the droughts that periodically plague California, farmers in that state are able to purchase subsidized water to irrigate their crops, at the same time that many California homeowners have to pay large fines if they water their lawns. Can you suggest an explanation for this difference in the treatment of two different groups of citizens in the state of California?

4. If allocating water through nonprice means generally harms society, can you suggest why governments often do this?

Chapter 9

THE (DIS)INCENTIVES OF HIGHER TAXES

Politicians always seem to be looking for additional ways to raise tax revenues. And most often, politicians talk (and even act) as though their taxing decisions have no effect on the quantity supplied or the quantity demanded of whatever good or service they wish to tax. Indeed, there is a saying among economists that politicians believe all demand curves and supply curves are **perfectly inelastic.** In such a world, higher taxes would have no effect on either quantity demanded or quantity supplied. What a wonderful world that would be—for politicians.

In the real world, however, changes in taxes cause changes in **relative prices,** and individuals in their roles as consumers, savers, investors, and workers do react to these relative price changes. Consider a truly telling example: the luxury tax enacted by Congress in 1991. Members of Congress were looking for additional revenues to reduce the federal budget deficit. What better way to raise these hoped-for revenues than with new taxes on the purchases of high-priced luxury items, such as big boats, expensive cars, furs, planes, and jewelry. After all, rich people don't really care how much they pay, right? That is why we call them rich. So Congress passed a 10 percent luxury surcharge tax on boats priced over $100,000, cars over $30,000, aircraft over $250,000, and furs and jewelry over $10,000.

The federal government estimated that it would rake in $9 billion in extra revenues over the following five-year period. Yet just a few years later, the luxury tax was quietly eliminated. Why? Because the actual take for the federal government was almost *nothing*.

Rich people, strange as it may seem, react to relative price changes, too. For high-priced new boats, for example, they had alternatives. Some bought used luxury boats instead of new ones. Others decided not to trade in their older luxury boats for new ones. Still others bought their new boats in other countries and never brought them back to the United States to be taxed. The moral of the story for politicians is that the laws of supply and demand apply to everyone, rich and poor, young and old, whatever their description might be.

The discrepancy between the fantasyland of politics and the reality of human behavior can be traced in part to the fact that politicians routinely engage in **static analysis.** They assume that people's behavior is static (unchanging), no matter how the constraints they face—such as higher taxes—might change. If the politicians who had pushed for the luxury tax had used **dynamic analysis,** they would have correctly anticipated that consumers (even rich ones) were going to change their buying decisions when faced with the new taxes.

Dynamic analysis takes into account the fact that the impact of the tax *rate* on tax *revenue* actually collected depends crucially on the **elasticity** of the relevant demand or supply curves. That is, even a high *rate* (measured in tax per item, or as a percentage of the value of the item) can yield relatively little *revenue* (total dollars collected) if consumers are highly responsive to the tax-inclusive price of the good. For example, in the case of the luxury tax, the **elasticity of demand** for new, high-end boats was relatively high: When the tax per boat went up, the quantity demanded fell so far that tax collections were negligible.

Now let's shift from the demand side of this taxing issue to the supply side. Does quantity supplied react to changing relative prices? Yes, but you might not know it from listening to politicians. The first modern federal personal income tax was imposed in 1916. The highest rate was 15 percent. Eventually, the top federal personal marginal income tax rate reached an astounding 91 percent, during the years 1951 to 1964. This marginal tax rate dropped to 70 percent in 1965. In 1980, it was lowered to 50 percent. For much of the 1980s and since, the highest federal marginal income tax rate has ranged from 31 percent to almost 40 percent.

Often politicians (and even some members of the general public) believe that the income tax rates paid by America's richest individuals do not matter to them because they are so rich that even after paying taxes, they are still very rich. The underlying "theory" behind such a belief is that the supply of labor is completely unresponsive to the net after-tax price received by the providers of labor. Stated another way, if you were to draw the **supply curve** of labor, it would be a nearly vertical line for each individual at some fixed number of work hours per year; supposedly, the **elasticity of supply** of labor is low.

To be sure, you might know somebody who loves work so much that she or he will work with the same intensity and for the same number of hours per year no matter what the income tax rate is. But changes occur at the margin in economics (meaning in the real world). If there are *some* individuals who respond to higher federal marginal tax rates by working less, then the overall supply curve of labor is going to be upward-sloping even for the ultrarich—just like all other supply curves for goods and services.

The data seem to confirm our economic predictions. In 1980, the top marginal income tax rate was 70 percent. The highest 1 percent of income-earning Americans paid 19 percent of all federal personal income taxes in that year. In 2007, when the top tax rate was 35 percent, the richest 1 percent paid more than double that share. How can this be explained? The answer is relatively straightforward: Lower marginal income tax rates create an incentive for people to work more and harder, because the rewards of doing so are greater. Also, in their role as risk-taking entrepreneurs, individuals are almost always going to be willing to take bigger risks if they know that success will yield greater net after-tax increases in their incomes.

Data from Europe suggest that exactly the same incentives are at work across a broad spectrum of income earners. Researchers have found that a tax increase of just over 12 percentage points induces the average adult in Europe to reduce work effort by over 120 hours per year—the equivalent of almost four weeks' work. Such a tax change also causes a sharp reduction in the number of people who work at all and causes many others to join the underground economy. Overall, then, higher tax rates cause lower output and higher unemployment and also induce marked increases in efforts devoted to tax evasion.

It is also true that what we have been talking about applies even among people who are at the very bottom of the income distribution. In many countries today, and in many circumstances in the United States, poorer individuals receive benefits from the government. These benefits can be in the form of food stamps, subsidized housing, subsidized health care or health insurance, and direct cash payments (often referred to as "welfare"). Those who receive such government benefits typically pay no income taxes on these benefits. In the case of the United States, they may even receive an **earned-income tax credit,** which is a type of **negative tax** or **tax credit.**

If such individuals were to accept a job (or a higher-paying job, if they are already employed), two things will normally occur. The first is that they will lose some or all of their government benefits. The second is that they may have to start paying federal (and perhaps state) personal income taxes. They understand that the loss of a benefit is the equivalent of being taxed more. And when they also have to pay explicit taxes, they know that the result is effectively double taxation.

Just as at the top end of the income ladder, the quantity of labor supplied by people at the lower end is affected by changes in the marginal income tax rates they face. If taking a good job and getting off the welfare rolls means losing benefits plus paying income taxes, the person on welfare has less incentive to accept a job. A good case in point is Ireland, which for most of the past twenty years was the fastest-growing economy in Europe. Twenty-five years ago, its economy was a disaster, one of the poorest among European countries. One of the problems was that individuals on welfare faced an effective (implicit) marginal income tax rate of about 120 percent if they got off the dole and went back to work. Obviously, they weren't directly taxed at 120 percent, but with the actual income tax that did apply, combined with the loss in welfare benefits, the *implicit* marginal tax rate was indeed 120 percent. Stated differently, their available spendable income would drop by about 20 percent if they went back to work! Needless to say, large numbers of poorer Irish stayed on the welfare roles until the program was completely overhauled.

Interestingly enough, this overhaul of the incentives facing low-income individuals was accompanied by an overhaul of the tax rates (and thus incentives) facing high-income corporations, with much the same results. In the 1990s, the Irish slashed the corporate profits tax to 12.5 percent, the lowest in Europe and only about one-third as high as the U.S. rate of 35 percent. Beginning in 2004, the Irish government also began offering a 20 percent tax credit for company spending on research and development, offering high-tech firms an opportunity to cut their taxes by starting up and expanding operations in Ireland. Almost immediately, Ireland became a magnet for new investment and for successful companies that didn't want to hand over a third or more of their profits to the tax collector.

The combination of lower corporate tax rates and tax breaks on research and development induced hundreds of multinational corporations to begin operations in Ireland. They brought with them hundreds of thousands of new jobs (and this to a nation of only 4 million residents), and Ireland quickly became number one among the European Union's fifteen original members in being home to companies that conduct research and development. And tax revenues of the Irish government? Well, despite the drastic cut in tax rates, tax revenues actually soared to levels never seen before. Indeed, measured as a share of gross domestic product, the Irish collect 50 percent more tax revenues out of corporate profits than Americans do, despite Ireland's lower tax rate.

The lesson of our story is simple. It is true that "nothing in life is certain but death and taxes." But it is equally true that higher tax rates don't always mean higher tax revenues. And that is a lesson that politicians can ignore only at their own peril.

DISCUSSION QUESTIONS

1. If you found yourself in the 91 percent federal personal income tax bracket in 1951, how great would have been your incentive to find legal loopholes to reduce your federal tax liabilities? If you found yourself in the lowest federal personal income tax bracket of, say, 15 percent, would your incentive to find loopholes to reduce your tax bill be the same? Explain.

2. Explain how the incentive effects of each of the following hypothetical taxes would cause people to change their behavior; be sure to explain what people are likely to do *less* of and what they are likely to do *more* of in response to each tax:

   (a) A $1,000,000-per-story tax on all office buildings more than two stories tall

   (b) A $2,000-per-car tax on all red (and only red) cars

   (c) A $100-per-book tax on all *new* college textbooks

3. Suppose that federal marginal personal income tax rates will rise significantly over the next ten years. Explain the ways in which individuals at all levels of income can react over time, not just immediately after taxes are raised. How will the size of the response differ, say, a year after the rise in tax rates compared to a week after the increase? Is it possible that some people will actually change their behavior *before* the higher tax rates go into effect? Explain.

4. How does a country's tax structure affect who decides to immigrate into the nation or emigrate out of the nation? Contrast, for example, nations A and B. Assume that nation A applies a 20 percent tax on every dollar of income earned by an individual. Nation B applies a 10 percent tax on the first $40,000 per year of income and a 40 percent tax on all income above $40,000 per year earned by an individual. Start by computing the tax bill in each country that must be paid by a person earning $40,000 a year and the tax bill that must be paid by a person earning $100,000 per year. Then consider the more general issue: If the language, culture, and climate of the two nations are similar, and if a person can choose to live on one side or the other of a river separating the two nations, who is more likely to choose to live in A and who is more likely to choose to live in B? To what extent does your reasoning apply if an ocean, rather than a river, separates the two countries? Does it apply if the language, culture, or climate in the two nations differs? Explain.

Chapter 10

BANKRUPT LANDLORDS, FROM SEA TO SHINING SEA

Take a tour of Santa Monica, a beachfront enclave of Los Angeles, and you will find a city of bizarre contrasts. Pick a street at random, and you may find run-down rental units sitting in disrepair next to homes costing $800,000. Try another street, and you may see abandoned apartment buildings adjacent to luxury-car dealerships and trendy shops that sell high-fashion clothing to Hollywood stars. Sound strange? Not in Santa Monica—known locally as the People's Republic of Santa Monica—where stringent rent-control laws once routinely forced property owners to leave their buildings empty and decaying rather than even bothering to sell them.

Three thousand miles to the east, rent-control laws in New York City—known locally as the Big Apple—have forced landlords to abandon housing units because the laws imposed on owners huge financial losses. Largely as a result of such abandonments, the city government of New York owns thousands of derelict housing units—empty, except for rats and small-time cocaine dealers. Meanwhile, because the controls also discourage new construction, the city faces a housing gap of two hundred thousand rental units—apartments that could easily be filled at current controlled rental rates if the units were in habitable condition.

From coast to coast, stories like these are commonplace in the two hundred or so American cities and towns that practice some form of **rent control**—a system in which the local government tells building owners how much they can charge for rent. Time and again, the stories are the same: poorly maintained rental units, abandoned apartment buildings, tenants trapped by housing gridlock in apartments no longer suitable for them, bureaucracies bloated with rent-control enforcers, and even homeless families that can find no one who will rent to them. Time and again, the reason for the stories is the same: legal limits on the rent that people may pay for a place to live.

Our story begins in 1943, when the federal government imposed rent control as a temporary wartime measure. Although the federal program ended after the war, New York City continued the controls on its own. Under New York's controls, a landlord generally could not raise rents on apartments as long as the tenants continued to renew their leases. Rent controls in Santa Monica are more recent. They were spurred by the inflation of the 1970s, which, combined with California's rapid population growth, pushed housing prices and rents to record levels. In 1979, the city of Santa Monica (where 80 percent of the residents were renters) ordered rents rolled back to the levels of the year before and stipulated that future rents could go up by only two-thirds as much as any increase in the overall price level. In both New York and Santa Monica, the objective of rent controls has been to keep rents below the levels that would be observed in freely competitive markets. Achieving this goal required that both cities impose extensive regulations to prevent landlord and tenant from evading the controls—regulations that are costly to enforce and that distort the normal operation of the market.

It is worth noting that the rent-control systems in New York and Santa Monica are slowly yielding to decontrol. For a number of years, some apartments in New York have been subject only to "rent stabilization" regulations, which are somewhat less stringent than absolute rent controls. In addition, New York apartments renting for over $2,000 per month are deregulated when a lease ends. In Santa Monica, the state of California mandated that as of 1999, rent for newly vacant apartments could increase. Even so, in both cities, much of the rental market is dominated by rent controls. Accordingly, in this chapter we focus on the consequences of those controls.

In general, the unfettered movement of rental prices in a freely competitive housing market performs three vital functions: (1) It allocates existing scarce housing among competing claimants; (2) it promotes the efficient maintenance of existing housing and stimulates the production of new housing, where appropriate; and (3) it rations usage of housing by demanders, thereby preventing waste of scarce housing. Rent control prevents rental prices from effectively performing these functions. Let's see how.

Rent control discourages the construction of new rental units. Developers and mortgage lenders are reluctant to get involved in building new rental properties because controls artificially depress the most important long-run determinant of profitability—rents. Thus in one recent year, eleven thousand new housing units were built in Dallas, a city with a 16 percent rental vacancy rate but no rent-control statute. In that same year, only two thousand units were built in San Francisco, a city with a 1.6 percent vacancy rate but stringent rent-control laws. In New York City, the only rental units being built are either exempt from controls or are heavily subsidized by the government. Private construction of new apartments in Santa Monica also dried up under controls, even though new office space and commercial developments—both exempt from rent control—were built at a record pace.

Rent control leads to the deterioration of the existing supply of rental housing. When rental prices are held below free market levels, property owners cannot recover through higher rents the costs of maintenance, repairs, and capital improvements. Thus such activities are sharply curtailed. Eventually, taxes, utilities, and the expenses of the most rudimentary repairs—such as replacing broken windows—exceed the depressed rental receipts; as a result, the buildings are abandoned. In New York, some owners have resorted to arson, hoping to collect the insurance on their empty rent-controlled buildings before the city claims them for back taxes. Under rent controls in Santa Monica, the city insisted that owners wishing to convert empty apartment buildings to other uses had to build new rental units to replace the units they no longer rented. At a cost of up to $50,000 per apartment, it is little wonder that few owners were willing to bear the burden, choosing instead to leave the buildings empty and graffiti-scarred.

Rent control impedes the process of rationing scarce housing. One consequence of this is that tenant mobility is sharply restricted. Even when a family's demand for living space changes—due, for example, to a new baby or a teenager's departure for college—there can be substantial costs in giving up a rent-controlled unit. In New York City, landlords often charge "key money" (a large up-front cash payment) before a new tenant is allowed to move in. The high cost of moving means that large families often stay in cramped quarters while small families or even single persons reside in very large units. In New York, this phenomenon of nonmobility came to be known as *housing gridlock*. It is estimated that more than 20 percent of renters in New York City live in apartments that are bigger or smaller than they would otherwise occupy. In Santa Monica, many homeowners rented out portions of their houses in response to soaring prices in the 1970s and then found themselves trapped by their tenants, whom they could not evict even if they wanted to sell their homes and move to a retirement community.

Not surprisingly, the distortions produced by rent control lead to efforts by both landlords and tenants to evade the rules. This in turn leads to the growth of cumbersome and expensive government bureaucracies whose job is to enforce the controls. In New York, where rents can be raised when tenancy changes hands, landlords have an incentive to make life unpleasant for tenants or to evict them on the slightest pretense. The city has responded by making evictions extremely costly for landlords. Even if a tenant blatantly and repeatedly violates the terms of a lease, the tenant cannot be evicted if the violations are corrected within a "reasonable" time period. If the violations are not corrected—despite several trips to court by the owners and their attorneys—eviction requires a tedious and expensive judicial proceeding. For their part, tenants routinely try to sublet all or part of their rent-controlled apartments at prices substantially above the rent they pay the owner. Because both the city and the landlords try to prohibit subletting, the parties often end up in the city's housing courts, an entire judicial system developed chiefly to deal with disputes over rent-controlled apartments.

Strict controls on monthly rents force landlords to use other means to discriminate among prospective tenants. Simply to ensure that the rent check comes every month, many landlords rent only to well-heeled professionals. As one commentator put it, "There is no disputing that Santa Monica became younger, whiter, and richer under rent control." The same pattern occurred under the rent-control laws of Berkeley, California, and Cambridge, Massachusetts.

There is little doubt the bureaucracies that evolve to administer rent-control laws are cumbersome and expensive. Between 1988 and 1993, New York City spent $5.1 billion rehabilitating housing confiscated from private landlords. Even so, derelict buildings continued piling up at a record rate. The overflow and appeals from the city's housing courts clog the rest of New York's judicial system, impeding the prosecution of violent criminals and drug dealers. In Santa Monica, the Rent Control Board began with an annual budget of $745,000 and a staff of twenty people. By the early 1990s, the staff had tripled in size, and the budget was pushing $5 million. Who picked up the tab? The landlords did, of course, with an annual special assessment of $200 per unit levied on them. And even though the 1999 state-mandated changes in the law meant that apartment rents in Santa Monica can be increased when a new tenant moves in, the new rent is then controlled by the city for the duration of the tenancy. Indeed, the Rent Control Board conveniently maintains a Web site where one can go to learn the maximum allowable rent on any of the tens of thousands of rent-controlled residences in Santa Monica.

Ironically, the big losers from rent control—in addition to landlords—are often low-income individuals, especially single mothers. Indeed, many observers believe that one significant cause of homelessness in cities such as New York and Los Angeles is rent control. Poor individuals often cannot assure the discriminating landlord that their rent will be paid on time—or paid at all—each month. Because controlled rents are generally well below free market levels, there is little incentive for apartment owners to take a chance on low-income individuals as tenants. This is especially true if the prospective tenant's chief source of income is a welfare check. Indeed, a significant number of the tenants appearing in New York's housing courts have been low-income mothers who, due to emergency expenses or delayed welfare checks, have missed rent payments. Often their appeals end in evictions and residence in temporary public shelters or on the streets. Prior to the state-mandated easing of controls, some apartment owners in Santa Monica who used to rent one- and two-room units to welfare recipients and other low-income individuals simply abandoned their buildings, leaving them vacant rather than trying to collect artificially depressed rents that failed to cover operating costs. The disgusted owner of one empty and decaying eighteen-unit building had a friend spray-paint his feelings on the wall: "I want to tear this mess down, but Big Brother won't let me." Perhaps because the owner had escaped from a concentration camp in search of freedom in the United States, the friend added a personalized touch: a drawing of a large hammer and sickle, symbol of the former Soviet Union.

It is worth noting that the ravages of rent controls are not confined to the United States. In Mumbai (Bombay), India, rents are still set at the levels that prevailed back in 1940. A two-bedroom apartment near the center of the city may have a controlled rent of as little as $8.50 per month. (Nearby, free market rents for an apartment of the same size can be as much as $3,000 per month.) Not surprisingly, landlords have let their rent-controlled buildings decay, and collapsing apartments have become a regular feature of life in this city of 12 million people. Over the past ten years, about ninety people have been killed in the collapse of more than fifty rent-controlled buildings. The city government estimates that perhaps one hundred more apartment buildings are on the verge of collapse.

Even Communist nations are not exempt from rent controls. In a heavily publicized news conference several years ago, the foreign minister of Vietnam, Nguyen Co Thach, declared that a "romantic conception of socialism" had destroyed his country's economy after the Vietnam War. Thach stated that rent control had artificially encouraged demand and discouraged supply and that all of the housing in Hanoi had fallen into disrepair as a result. Thach concluded by noting, "The Americans couldn't destroy Hanoi, but we have destroyed our city by very low rents. We realized it was stupid and that we must change policy."

Apparently, this same thinking was what induced the state of California to compel changes in Santa Monica's rent-control ordinance.

The result of that policy change was an almost immediate jump in rents on newly vacant apartments, as well as a noticeable rise in the vacancy rate—exactly the results we would expect. Interestingly enough, however, prospective new tenants were less enthusiastic about the newly available apartments than many landlords had expected. The reason? Twenty years of rent controls had produced many years of reduced upkeep and hence apartments that were less than pristine. As one renter noted, "The trouble is, most of this area . . . [is] basically falling apart." And another complained, "I don't want to move into a place that's depressing, with old brown carpet that smells like chicken soup." Higher rents are gradually changing both the ambiance and the aroma of Santa Monica apartments—but only at the same rate that the market is allowed to perform its functions.

DISCUSSION QUESTIONS

1. Why do you think governments frequently attempt to control apartment rents but not house prices?

2. What determines the size of the key-money payments that landlords demand (and tenants offer) for the right to rent a controlled apartment?

3. Who, other than the owners of rental units, loses as a result of rent controls? Who gains from rent controls? What effect would the imposition of rent controls have on the market price of an existing single-family house? What effect would rent controls have on the value of vacant land?

4. Why do the owners of rental units reduce their maintenance expenditures on the units when rent controls are imposed? Does their decision have anything to do with whether they can afford those expenditures?

PART THREE

Labor Markets

Introduction

Almost everyone participates in the labor market, and most of us do so for most of our lives. In one sense, labor (or **human capital,** as it is sometimes called by economists) is no different from any other **economic good.** After all, labor is a **scarce good,** and so the basic tools used by economists can be applied to understanding the markets for it. Nevertheless, special care is sometimes required to understand what appears to be going on in labor markets because not all aspects of these markets are what they seem to be.

As you will see in Chapter 11, "(Why) Are Women Paid Less?" since the middle of the twentieth century, there has been a revolution in the labor market as women have entered in unprecedented numbers. Yet even though women now regularly work in jobs formerly closed to them, the data still suggest that they are being paid less than men. Much of this seeming discrimination in pay is attributable to the occupational choices made by women: They work in less hazardous environments and take jobs that offer greater flexibility and fewer hours of work per week. Safe, flexible employment that demands fewer hours of work per week is desirable; once we correct for these job attributes, the real differences in pay between men and women are much smaller than they appear to be at first glance. Nevertheless, the question remains: Do women select such jobs because that is really their preferred choice, or are they forced into such work because discrimination by male business owners and managers gives women no real alternatives? This is an issue that only further study will resolve.

The issue of discrimination also arises when we examine what happens when the government interferes with the operation of labor markets. We examine this in Chapter 12, "The Effects of the Minimum

Wage." As we shall see time and again in this book, the effects of government actions are not always what they seem, nor are they usually what their proponents claim for them. The chief losers from the **minimum wage**—disadvantaged minority teenagers—are often the very people who can least afford those losses, while those who claim to support the law on altruistic grounds are in fact likely to be the biggest winners. The message of this chapter may well be this simple piece of advice: When someone claims to be doing something *for* you, it is wise to ask what that person is doing *to* you.

The plight of the disadvantaged is the central focus of Chapter 13, "Immigration, Superstars, and Poverty." Over the past forty or fifty years, people at the bottom of the income distribution in America have experienced a rising standard of living. In more recent years, however, this rise seems to have slowed relative to the improving standard of living at the very top of the income distribution. Here we learn that several factors are likely at work, including the rising premium on education, technological changes that have helped top performers ("superstars") earn even more, and high rates of immigration that have depressed wages near the bottom of the income distribution. Sadly, it also appears that some (though not all) government programs directed at improving life for the least fortunate have had the reverse effect. Once again, we see that when it comes to important public issues, things are rarely what they appear to be.

As its title makes clear, Chapter 14, "A Farewell to Jobs," addresses the issues of employment in labor markets—in this case, the claim that American firms are exporting jobs, to the detriment of American workers. In the past decade, many American corporations have begun assigning more service jobs (such as technical and customer support) to workers located in foreign lands. Despite claims regarding the novelty (and supposed harm to the economy) of this activity, **outsourcing** is no different from any other form of trade. When Americans purchase, say, technical support from a company in a foreign land, that service is provided by residents of that country rather than by residents of the United States; to this extent, employment in technical support is lower in America than it otherwise would be. But foreigners only sell us goods in the expectation that they will be able to buy something from us in return. Ultimately, then, **imports** (purchases) of services or goods from abroad must result in more **exports** of goods or services to foreign lands—and this implies more employment in those export industries. Like all voluntary trade, international trade creates wealth for the trading partners. The residents of each land are making the most of their **comparative advantage** in producing different goods and services, and government restrictions on such activities serve only to make us worse off.

Chapter 11

(WHY) ARE WOMEN PAID LESS?

Since the middle of the twentieth century, there has been a revolution in the job market. Women have entered the paid workforce in unprecedented numbers. In 1950, for example, only about one-third of working-age women were in the paid workforce; today, some 61 percent are. And because the male **labor force participation rate** has fallen from 89 percent to 76 percent over this period, women now account for almost half of the paid workforce in America. There has also been an overwhelming change in the nature of paid work done by women. Fifty years ago, professional careers for women outside of nursing or teaching were unusual. Today, women comprise nearly half of the newly minted attorneys and physicians starting work each year. Over the same fifty-year period, there has been a transformation of wages, too. In 1950, median earnings of women were only two-thirds those of men. Today, women earn 80 percent of what men are paid.

Reread that last sentence. On average, for every dollar a man earns, a woman gets paid 80 cents. Can this possibly be true? Consider this fact: Nearly 70 percent of employers' costs are accounted for by labor. An employer who hired only women at 80 cents on the dollar could cut labor costs by 20 percent relative to an employer who hired only men. This would yield added profits of about 14 percent of sales—which would *triple* the **profit** earned by the typical firm. If women are paid 20 percent less than men, how could any employer possibly afford to hire anyone *but* women?

At this point you may be saying to yourself, "Surely, there are differences between men and women other than their sex that can help account for this 'gender gap' in earnings." And you would be correct. Earnings are a reflection of experience, education, marital status, and age, for example. But even when economists control for all of these individual characteristics, using nationwide data, such as from the U.S. Census

Bureau or the Bureau of Labor Statistics, unexplained differences between the pay of men and women persist. Men with the same measured individual characteristics are paid at least 10 percent more than women, and some studies find a difference twice that size.

The widespread opinion of many observers is that the unexplained gap between the pay of men and women is chiefly the result of discrimination against women. The reasoning is simple. Most business owners and senior managers are men, and given a choice between hiring a man or a woman, the "old-boy network" operates in favor of the man. According to this view, women can get the job only if they agree to accept lower wages.

Consider this fact, however: For more than forty years, it has been illegal to discriminate in the workforce on the basis of race or gender. Two major federal agencies, the Equal Employment Opportunity Commission and the Office of Federal Contract Compliance, are wholly or largely devoted to ensuring that this antidiscrimination mandate is enforced. As interpreted by the courts, the law now says that if the statistical *appearance* of lower wages for women (or minorities) is present in a workplace, the employer is *presumed* to be guilty of discrimination and must prove otherwise. No one thinks that federal agencies do a perfect job at enforcing the law here or elsewhere, but it is hard to believe that a persistent 20 percent pay difference could escape the notice of even the most nearsighted federal bureaucrat.

A hint of what might be going on begins to emerge when economists study the payroll records of individual firms, using actual employee information that is specific and detailed regarding location of the firm, type of work, employee responsibilities, and other factors. These analyses reveal that the so-called wage gap between men and women is much smaller—typically no more than 5 percent—and often there is no gap at all. The sharp contrast between firm-level data and economywide data suggests that something may be at work here besides (or in addition to) outright gender discrimination.

That something is actually three things. First, women's pay is extremely sensitive to whether or not they have children. In Britain, for example, where this issue has been studied intensively, the average pay earned by a woman begins to fall shortly before the birth of her first child and continues to drop until the child becomes a teenager. Although earnings begin to revive once the first child passes the age of twenty or so, they never fully recover. The earnings drop associated with motherhood is close to one-third, and only one-third of that drop is regained after the nest is empty. American data suggest that the same pattern is present on this side of the Atlantic.

The parenthood pay declines suffered by women stem from a variety of sources: Some are put on the "mommy track," with reduced responsibilities and hours of work; others move to different employers around the time their first child is born, taking jobs that offer more flexible work schedules but offer correspondingly lower pay as well. Overall, a woman with average skills who has a child at age twenty-four can expect to receive nearly $1 million less compensation over her career, compared to one who remains childless. It is worth emphasizing that no similar effect is observed with men. In fact, there is some evidence that men with children are actually paid *more* than men without children. These findings strongly suggest a fact that will come as no surprise to most people: Despite the widespread entry of women into the labor force, they retain the primary responsibility for child care at home, and their careers suffer as a result.

The second factor at work in explaining male-female wage differences is occupational selection. Compared to women, men tend to be concentrated in paid employment that is dangerous or unpleasant. Commercial fishing, construction, law enforcement, firefighting, truck driving, and mining, to name but a few, are occupations that are much more dangerous than average and are dominated by men. As a result, men represent 92 percent of all occupational deaths. Hazardous jobs offer what is known as a **compensating differential,** extra pay for assuming the differential risk of death or injury on the job. In equilibrium, these extra wages do no more than offset the extra hazards. So even though measured earnings *look* high relative to the educational and other requirements of the jobs, appearances are deceiving. After adjusting for risk, the value of that pay is really no greater than for less hazardous employment—but the appearance of higher pay contributes to the measured gender gap.

The third key factor influencing pay is hours of work. Men are more than twice as likely as women to work in excess of fifty hours a week in paid employment. Overall, the average paid workweek for men is about 15 percent longer than it is for women. Men are also more likely than women to be in full-time, rather than part-time, paid employment, and the wage differences here can be huge. Working an average of forty-four hours per week versus thirty-four hours per week, for example, yields more than twice the pay, regardless of gender. This substantial gender gap in hours of paid work is due in part to the "mommy track" phenomenon, but the question that remains is, does this constitute discrimination on the part of employers, or is it the result of choices by women?

Although we cannot answer that question definitively, there is reason to believe that some differences in occupational choice (and thus in pay) are due to discrimination. For example, the highest-paying blue-collar jobs are typically union jobs, and industrial and crafts unions have had a long history of opposition to women as members. Or consider medicine. Women are becoming much more numerous in specialties such as dermatology and radiology, where schedules tend to be more flexible, hours of work can be limited, and part-time practice is feasible. But many physicians would argue that the noticeable underrepresentation of women in the high-paying surgical specialties is partly the result of discrimination against women, rather than reflecting the occupational choices preferred by women. If this argument is correct, then even if women in a given specialty are paid the same as men in that specialty, the exclusion of women from high-paying slots will lower their average wages and make them worse off.

The extent of gender discrimination in the workplace is unlikely to be definitively settled anytime soon. Measured earnings differences, even those that account for experience, education, and other factors, clearly overstate the true pay gap between equally qualified men and women. Just as surely, however, given the heavier parenting demands typically made on women, even when they receive equal pay, it is not for equal work.

DISCUSSION QUESTIONS

1. Suppose an employer offers a base wage of $20 per hour for the first forty hours of work each week and overtime pay of $30 per hour for any hours beyond forty per week; the employer allows workers to choose their own hours of work. Suppose employee A chooses to work thirty-six hours per week and employee B chooses to work forty-two hours per week. Compute the average weekly earnings for employees A and B, and compute the "earnings gap" (in percentage terms) between them. In your view, does this observed earnings gap constitute discrimination? Justify your conclusion.

2. A recent British study found that married men earned more than unmarried men—but only if their wives did not have full-time paid employment. Suggest an explanation for this finding. (*Hint:* In which case is a man more likely to share in the household responsibilities, including child care?)

3. Women who own their own businesses earn net profits that are only half as large as the net profits earned by men who own their own businesses. First, consider why women would be willing to accept lower profits. Could this reflect poorer options for women as

employees? Alternatively, could it reflect other attributes of self-employment that women might find more advantageous than men do? Then think about why women earn lower profits. Is this evidence of discrimination? If so, by whom? If not, what else might account for the lower profits?

4. Why do you think we have laws that prohibit discrimination in pay based on gender or race but permit employers to discriminate in pay based on education or experience?

Chapter 12

THE EFFECTS OF
THE MINIMUM
WAGE

Ask workers if they would like a raise, and the answer is likely to be a resounding yes. But ask them if they would like to be fired or have their hours of work reduced, and they would probably tell you no. The effects of the minimum wage are centered on exactly these points.

Proponents of the **minimum wage**—the lowest hourly wage firms may legally pay their workers—argue that low-income workers are underpaid and therefore unable to support themselves or their families. The minimum wage, they say, raises earnings at the bottom of the wage distribution, with little disruption to workers or businesses. Opponents claim that most low-wage workers are low-skilled youths without families to support. The minimum wage, they say, merely enriches a few teenagers at the far greater expense of many others, who can't get jobs. Most important, opponents argue, many individuals at the bottom of the economic ladder lack the skills needed for employers to hire them at the federal minimum. Willing to work but unable to find jobs, these people never learn the basic job skills needed to move up the economic ladder to higher-paying jobs. The issues are clear—but what are the facts?

The federal minimum wage was instituted in 1938 as a provision of the Fair Labor Standards Act. It was originally set at 25 cents per hour, about 40 percent of the average manufacturing wage at the time. Over the next forty years, the legal minimum was raised periodically, roughly in accord with the movement of market wages throughout the economy. Typically, its level has averaged between 40 and 50 percent of average manufacturing wages. In response to the high inflation of the late 1970s, the minimum wage was hiked seven times between 1974 and 1981, reaching $3.35 per hour—about 42 percent of manufacturing wages. President Ronald Reagan vowed to keep a lid on the minimum wage, and by the time he left office, the minimum's unchanged level left it at 31 percent of average wages. Legislation passed in 1989 raised the minimum to $3.80 in 1990 and $4.25 in 1991. Five years later, Congress raised it in two steps to $5.15 per hour. Over the period 2007 to 2009, the minimum was hiked in three steps to its current level of $7.25 per hour.

About half a million workers earn the minimum wage; another 1.5 million or so are paid even less because the law doesn't cover them. Supporters of the minimum wage claim that it prevents exploitation of employees and helps people earn enough to support their families and themselves. Even so, at $7.25 per hour, a full-time worker earns only about two-thirds of what the government considers enough to keep a family of four out of poverty. In fact, to get a family of four with one wage earner up to the poverty line, the minimum wage would have to be above $11.00 per hour.

Yet opponents of the minimum wage argue that such calculations are irrelevant. For example, two-thirds of the workers earning the minimum wage are single, and they earn enough to put them above the poverty cutoff. Moreover, about half of these single workers are teenagers, most of whom have no financial obligations, except perhaps clothing and automobile-related expenditures. Thus opponents argue that the minimum wage chiefly benefits upper-middle-class teens who are least in need of assistance at the same time that it costs the jobs of thousands of disadvantaged minority youths.

The debate over the minimum wage intensified a few years ago when research suggested that a change in the New Jersey minimum wage had no adverse short-run impact on employment. Further research by other scholars focusing on Canada reveals more clearly what happens when the minimum wage is hiked. In Canada, there are important differences in minimum wages both over time and across different provinces. These differences enabled researchers to distinguish between the short-run and long-run effects of changes in minimum wages. The short-run effects are indeed negligible, as implied by the New Jersey study. But the Canadian research shows that in the long run, the adverse effects of a higher minimum wage are quite substantial. In the short run, it is true that firms do not cut their workforce by much in response to a higher minimum. But over time, the higher costs due to a higher minimum wage force smaller firms out of business, and it is here that the drop in employment shows up clearly.

The Canadian results are consistent with the overwhelming bulk of the U.S. evidence on this issue, which points to a negative impact of the minimum wage on employment. After all, the number of workers demanded, like the quantity demanded for all goods, responds to price: The higher the price, the lower the number desired. There remains, however, debate over how many jobs are lost due to the minimum wage. For example, when the minimum wage was raised from $3.35 to $4.25, credible estimates of the number of potential job losses ranged from 50,000 all the way up to 400,000. When the minimum was hiked to $5.15, researchers suggested that at least 200,000 jobs were at stake. More recently, some economists have estimated that the hike in the federal minimum wage to $7.25 will ultimately cause up to a million people to lose their jobs. With a workforce of over 150 million persons, numbers like these may not sound very large. But most of the people who don't have jobs as a result of the minimum wage are teenagers; they comprise only about 5 percent of the workforce but bear almost all of the burden of forgone employment alternatives.

Significantly, the youths most likely to lose work due to the minimum wage are disadvantaged teenagers, chiefly minorities. On average, these teens enter the workforce with the fewest job skills and the greatest need for on-the-job training. Until and unless these disadvantaged teenagers can acquire these skills, they are the most likely to be unemployed as a result of the minimum wage—and thus least likely to have the opportunity to move up the economic ladder. With a teen unemployment rate more than triple the overall rate and unemployment among black youngsters hovering around 30 percent, critics argue that the minimum wage is a major impediment to long-term labor market success for minority youth.

Indeed, the minimum wage has an aspect that its supporters are not inclined to discuss: It can make employers more likely to discriminate on the basis of gender or race. When wages are set by market forces, employers who would discriminate face a reduced, and thus more expensive, pool of workers. But when the government mandates an above-market wage, a surplus of low-skilled workers results, and it becomes easier and cheaper to discriminate. As former U.S. Treasury secretary Lawrence Summers noted, the minimum wage "removes the economic penalty to the employer. He can choose the one who's white with blond hair."

Critics of the minimum wage also argue that it makes firms less willing to train workers lacking basic skills. Instead, companies may choose to hire only experienced workers whose abilities justify the higher wage. Firms are also likely to become less generous with fringe benefits in an effort to hold down labor costs. The prospect of more discrimination, less job training for low-skilled workers, and fewer fringe benefits for entry-level workers leaves many observers uncomfortable. As the economist Jacob Mincer noted, the minimum wage means "a loss of opportunity" for the hard-core unemployed.

Despite these adverse effects of the minimum wage, many state and local governments believe that people with jobs should be paid a wage on which they can "afford to live." In fact, some states and localities mandate that minimum wages (sometimes called "living wages") be even higher, at levels ranging up to $9.50 an hour in Santa Fe, New Mexico (an amount that is adjusted up to reflect inflation each year). In some cases, as in Baltimore, Maryland, the local minimum wage applies only to workers at firms that do business with the relevant government entity. But in the case of the Santa Fe minimum wage and all state-determined minimums, the law applies to all but a few firms that are declared exempt because of their very small size or their industry (such as agriculture).

When politicians decide to raise the minimum wage, it is only after heated battles often lasting months. Given the stakes involved—an improved standard of living for some, a loss of job opportunities for others—it is not surprising that discussions of the minimum wage soon turn to controversy. As one former high-level U.S. Department of Labor official said, "When it comes to the minimum wage, there are no easy positions to take. Either you are in favor of more jobs, less discrimination, and more on-the-job training, or you support better wages for workers. Whatever stance you choose, you are bound to get clobbered by the opposition." When Congress and the president face this issue, one or both usually feel the same way.

DISCUSSION QUESTIONS

1. Are teenagers better off when a higher minimum wage enables some to earn higher wages but causes others to lose their jobs?

2. Are there methods other than a higher minimum wage that could raise the incomes of low-wage workers without reducing employment among minority youngsters?

3. Why do you think organized labor groups, such as unions, are supporters of a higher minimum wage, even though their members all earn much more than the minimum wage?

4. Is it possible that a higher minimum wage could ever *increase* employment?

Chapter 13

IMMIGRATION, SUPERSTARS, AND POVERTY

In 1960, the poorest 20 percent of households in the United States received a bit over 4 percent of total income. Today, after nearly five decades of government efforts to relieve poverty, the bottom 20 percent receive a bit less than 4 percent of total income. Almost 40 million Americans lived in poverty in 1960; almost 38 million U.S. citizens *still* live in poverty, despite the expenditure of hundreds of billions of dollars in aid for the poor. In the richest country in the world, poverty seems remarkably resilient.

If we are to understand why, we must begin by getting the facts straight. First, even though the absolute number of Americans living in poverty has not diminished over the past fifty years, population growth has brought a sizable reduction in the *proportion* of impoverished Americans. As conventionally measured, more than 22 percent of Americans lived in poverty in 1960; today a bit over 12 percent of the population is below the poverty line.

Second, traditional methods of measuring poverty may be misleading because they focus solely on the *cash income* of individuals. In effect, government statisticians compute a "minimum adequate budget" for families of various sizes—the "poverty line"—and then determine how many people have a cash income below this line. Yet major components of the federal government's antipoverty efforts come in the form of **in-kind transfers** (transfers of goods and services rather than cash) such as Medicare, Medicaid, subsidized housing, food stamps, and school lunches. When the dollar value of these in-kind transfers is included in measures of *total* income, the standard of living of persons at lower income levels has improved substantially over the years.

There is disagreement over how much of these in-kind transfers should be included in measures of the total income of recipients.[1] Nevertheless, most observers agree that these transfers, plus the **earned-income tax credit** (which gives special tax rebates to low-income individuals), are major sources of income for people at the bottom of the income distribution. Adjusting for these transfers and taxes, it seems likely that over the past fifty years, the proportion of Americans living below the poverty line has been cut roughly in half. Just as important, the standard of living for the poorest 20 percent of the population has more than doubled since 1960. In short, the number of poor individuals in this country has declined significantly, and those who remain poor are generally better off than the poor of fifty years ago.

Whatever measure of income we use, it is crucial to remember that most Americans exhibit a great deal of **income mobility**—they have a tendency to move around in the income distribution over time. The most important source of income mobility is the "life-cycle" pattern of earnings: New entrants to the workforce tend to have lower incomes at first, but most workers can enjoy rising incomes as they gain experience on the job. Typically, annual earnings reach a maximum at about age fifty-five. Because peak earnings occur well beyond the **median age** of the population (now about thirty-seven), a "snapshot" of the current distribution of earnings will find most individuals on the way up toward a higher position in the income distribution. People who have low earnings now are likely, on average, to have higher earnings in the future.

Another major source of income mobility stems from the operation of Lady Luck. At any point in time, the income of high-income people is likely to be abnormally high (relative to what they can expect on average) due to recent good luck—they may have just won the lottery or received a long-awaited bonus. Conversely, the income of people who currently have low incomes is likely to be abnormally low due to recent bad luck, for example, because they are laid up after an automobile accident or have become temporarily unemployed. Over time, the effects of Lady Luck tend to average out across the population. Accordingly,

---

1. There are two reasons for this disagreement. First, a given dollar amount of in-kind transfers is generally less valuable than the same dollar amount of cash income because cash offers the recipient a greater amount of choice in his or her consumption pattern. Second, medical care is an important in-kind transfer to the poor. Inclusion of all Medicaid expenditures for the poor would imply that the sicker the poor got, the richer they would be. Presumably, a correct measure would include only those medical expenses that the poor would have to incur if they were *not* poor and thus had to pay for the medical care (or medical insurance) out of their own pockets.

people with high incomes today will tend to have lower incomes in the future, while people with low incomes today will tend to have higher future incomes; this means that many people living below the poverty line are there temporarily rather than permanently.

The effects of the forces that produce income mobility are strikingly revealed in studies examining the incomes of individuals over time. During the 1970s and 1980s, for example, among the people who were in the top 20 percent (quintile) of income earners at the beginning of the decade, less than half were in the top quintile by the end of the decade. Similarly, among the people who were in the bottom quintile at the beginning of the decade, almost half had moved out of that bracket by the end of the decade. Despite news stories that suggest otherwise, income mobility remains robust. From 1996 to 2005 (the decade most recently studied), more than half of the people who were in the bottom 20 percent income bracket in 1996 had moved out of that bracket by 2005.

Nevertheless, there are several forces that have either increased income inequality in the United States or have given the appearance of such an increase, so it is best to be clear on the nature of these. Consider first that a rising proportion of the population is *far* above the poverty line. In 1969, for example, only about 4 percent of all people in America had incomes seven times greater than the poverty level. Today, about 20 percent of Americans have incomes that high (above $150,000 for a family of four). Much of this jump in incomes at the top of the income distribution has come at the very top. Thirty years ago, for example, people in the top 10 percent of earners in America pulled in about 31 percent of total income; today they garner 37 percent. And most of this jump is in even more rarified company. The top 1 percent of earners used to account for 9 percent of total income; today they take in 16 percent of income. Thus although inflation-adjusted incomes are rising across the board, they appear to be rising the fastest at the very top. This pattern, which first became apparent during the 1990s, is one that economists are seeking to explain. Much work remains to be done, but a few answers are emerging.

First, some key demographic changes are occurring. America is aging, and an older population tends to have more income inequality than a young population, because older people have had more time to experience rising or falling fortunes. Americans are also getting better educated, and this tends to increase income inequality. People with little education have incomes that tend to cluster together, while the incomes of well-educated people spread out: Some choose to convert their human capital into much higher incomes, while others convert it into added leisure time. Taken together, these two demographic changes (aging and education) can account for more than 75 percent of the *appearance* of greater income inequality.

Second, a substantial part of the rapid income growth at the top has really been a matter of accounting fiction, rather than reality. Until the late 1980s, there were substantial tax advantages for the very wealthy to have a large portion of their incomes counted as corporate rather than personal income; in effect, a big chunk of income for the wealthy used to be hidden, not from the tax authorities, but from the policymakers who worry about the distribution of income. Subsequent changes in the tax laws have since encouraged people to report this income as personal rather than corporate income: Their incomes haven't really changed; it just looks to policymakers like they have.

Nevertheless, it is clear that there are more people in the rarified upper reaches of the income distribution, in part due to the so-called superstar effect. Technological changes have vastly expanded the size of the economic market that top performers can serve. Because of cell phones, videoconferencing, and e-mail, for example, top business managers can effectively direct far larger enterprises than used to be the case. Sports and entertainment stars can now use cable TV and the Internet to reach audiences of tens (or hundreds) of millions, far more than the tens of thousands who can attend a live performance. And these additional customers are each willing to pay for these services, so the incomes of those at the very top have multiplied correspondingly.

So much for incomes at the top; what about those at the bottom? Well, between 1990 and 2005, there was a huge influx of immigrants to the United States. New immigrants typically earn far less than long-term residents. When large numbers of them are added to the mix of people whose incomes are being measured, *average* income can fall, even when the incomes of all individuals are rising. Thus immigration has created downward pressure on *measured* incomes at the bottom of the distribution. But new immigrants have also added to competitive pressures in labor markets for less-skilled individuals. On balance, it appears that immigration has probably lowered the wages of high school dropouts in America some 4 percent to 8 percent. And although this seems small, remember that it is occurring among people whose incomes are already low. Both of these effects are likely to lessen, perhaps even reverse, due to the recession of 2007–2009: Deteriorating economic conditions in America caused many recent immigrants to return to their homelands.

Public policy has also taken its toll on the incomes of people at the bottom. The war on drugs, for example, has saddled literally millions of

individuals with criminal records, and the impact has been disproportionately greatest on African Americans, whose incomes were lower to
begin with. For example, since 1990, more than 2 million African American males have served time in jail on serious (felony) drug charges. Once
they return to the workforce, they find that their felony records exclude
them from most jobs—and not just jobs in the middle or at the top. Often
convicted felons cannot find positions that pay more than $8 per hour.
The result is that the incomes of such individuals are sharply diminished,
which means more poverty.

The expansion of Social Security Disability Insurance (SSDI) has
also likely contributed to income stagnation at the bottom. Originally
established in 1956 as a program to help individuals under age sixty-five
who are truly disabled, SSDI has become the federal government's
fastest-growing transfer program. It now accounts for about $110 billion
in federal spending per year. It allows even those who are not truly disabled to receive payments from the government when they do not work.
Since 1990, the number of people receiving disability payments from the
Social Security Administration has almost tripled to about 8 million. This
is not surprising when you consider that the real value of the monthly
benefits a person can collect has gone up 60 percent in the last thirty-five
years, and eligibility requirements have been eased. The federal government spends more on disability payments than it does on food stamps or
unemployment benefits.

What does this mean? Simply that people who might have worked
through chronic pain and temporary injuries—particularly those without
extensive training and education—now choose to receive a government
disability benefit instead. The average Social Security disability payment
is over $1,000 a month, tax-free. For many at the lower echelon of the job
ladder, $1,000 a month seems pretty good. For the truly disabled, SSDI
and related federal disability programs have definitely made life better.
But experts believe that many disability recipients are now being drawn
out of higher-paying jobs by the tax-free status of disability pay, combined with the fact that it enables them to spend more time with family
and friends. This development also means that measures of income
inequality have risen because even though disability recipients are clearly
better off as a result of the program, their incomes as measured by government statisticians are markedly lower.

There is one definite bright spot on the poverty policy front: the
"welfare reform" program undertaken in 1996. Previously, low-income
families had been eligible to receive—for an unlimited duration—federal
payments called Aid to Families with Dependent Children. The program
was converted in 1996 to Temporary Assistance to Needy Families. Limits

were placed on the length of time individuals could receive payments, and all recipients were given additional **incentives** and assistance to enhance their job skills and enter or reenter the labor force. The full impact of this policy change is still being studied, but it now appears that it has modestly raised incomes among individuals at the bottom of the income distribution.

Although the resilience of poverty in America is discouraging to the poor and to analysts who study their plight, it is useful to consider these issues in an international context. In other industrialized nations, such as Japan and most countries in Europe, people at the bottom of the income distribution sometimes (but not always) fare better than the poor in America. Although the poor typically receive a somewhat larger *share* of national income than in America, the national income in which they are sharing is lower. Thus compared to America, the poorest 10 percent of the population has a higher average income in Japan and Germany but a lower average income in the United Kingdom and Italy.

In developing nations—which is to say, for the vast majority of people around the world—poverty has a completely different meaning than it does in America. In Africa and much of Asia, for example, it is commonplace for people at the bottom of the income distribution to be living on the equivalent of $400 per *year* or less—in contrast to the $10,000 to $15,000 per year they would earn in America. As we noted in Chapter 4, "The Mystery of Wealth," this staggering difference in living standards is due to the vast differences in legal and economic **institutions** that are observed around the world. In America, as in many other industrialized nations, these institutions both give people the incentives to put their talents to work and protect them from having their assets expropriated by the government. Thus the best antipoverty program anyone has ever seen is the creation of an institutional environment in which human beings are able to make maximum use of the talents with which they are endowed.

DISCUSSION QUESTIONS

1. Why do most modern societies try to reduce poverty? Why don't they do so by simply passing a law that requires that everybody have the same income?

2. How do the "rules of the game" help determine who will be poor and who will not? (*Hint:* How did the Civil Rights Act of 1964, which forbade discrimination on the basis of race, likely affect the

incomes of African Americans compared to the incomes of white Americans?) Explain your answer.

3. Which of the following possible in-kind transfers do you think raises the true income of recipients the most: free golf lessons, free transportation on public buses, or free food? Why?

4. Consider three alternative ways of helping poor people get better housing: government-subsidized housing that costs $6,000 per year, a housing **voucher** worth $6,000 per year toward rent on an apartment or a house, or $6,000 per year in cash. Which would you prefer if you were poor? On what grounds might you make your decision?

Chapter 14

A FAREWELL TO
JOBS

Let's take a trip back to the late 1980s. The foremost problem on some economists' minds is the merciless competition that American firms face from Asian manufacturers. "Japan, Inc." and its neighbors, for example, have started turning out computer memory chips at ever-lower prices. The result is sharply declining profits for U.S. chipmakers and—according to chipmakers and their political supporters—a dire threat to U.S. jobs. The issue of looming job losses in this and other industries dominates the political scene. Chip industry leaders try to persuade members of Congress that the United States will lose its technological edge unless the federal government steps in to protect U.S. chipmakers. Experts are even prophesying that without government protection and help, U.S. microelectronics will be "reduced to permanent, decisive inferiority within ten years."

Now flash forward twenty years, when the most frequently recurring issue in domestic-policy debates has been much the same. To be sure, the details—which country is "stealing" jobs from which industry—have changed, but not by much. Indeed, as early as the presidential election of 2004, so-called foreign **outsourcing** of **white-collar jobs** had become as un-American as desecrating our flag. A well-known TV business analyst on CNN, Lou Dobbs, even began a listing of all of the "unpatriotic" U.S.-based companies that were "sending this country's jobs overseas." The House of Representatives tried to pass measures to prevent any type of outsourcing for the Department of State and the Department of Defense. Representative Don Manzullo (R., Ill.) said, "You just can't continue to outsource overseas time after time after time, dilute the strategic military base, and then expect this Congress to sit back and see the jobs lost and do nothing."

According to Craig Barrett, chair of the board at Intel (the world's largest chipmaker), American workers today face the prospect of "300 million well-educated people in India, China, and Russia who can do effectively any job that can be done in the United States." In a similar vein, Forrester Research has predicted that 3.3 million service jobs will "move offshore" by 2015. Five hundred thousand of those jobs will supposedly be in computer software and services. The 2004 Democratic presidential nominee, John Kerry, had a name for the leaders of companies that "export" such jobs: "Benedict Arnold CEOs." When he was campaigning for president in 2008, Barack Obama said we had to stop "shipping jobs" to China and India. And when the chair of the Council of Economic Advisers publicly stated that foreign outsourcing of service jobs wasn't such a bad idea, numerous politicians lambasted him, arguing that foreign outsourcing of domestic service jobs was the biggest plague ever to hit the U.S. economy.

To understand the hot-button issue of outsourcing service employment to workers located abroad, you have to go back to our chapter-opening scenario. What actually happened after the "Asian invasion" of computer chips and other high-tech items in the late 1980s? The result was not the demise of Silicon Valley. Rather, American high-tech companies responded to the challenge by identifying the things at which they were best and leaving the rest to their foreign competitors. They became innovative. They led the way in personal computing and the development of the Internet. They became the engine of job creation throughout the 1990s. Indeed, we can look back through American business history and find numerous other periods in which foreign competition has threatened a particular sector of the economy. In spite of that competition—and regardless of the outcome for the sector involved—the American economy has continued to prosper.

This was not the first time the resilience of the labor market surprised people. Beginning around 1960, for example, numerous experts predicted that the rise of the computer and robots for use in businesses was going to lead to mass joblessness and poverty. Instead, computers and automation have produced staggering **productivity** increases throughout nearly every industry. They have helped make possible the 82 million jobs created over the past fifty years and the tripling of **real per capita income** over that span. This is hardly the outcome predicted by experts in the 1960s, but then, predicting the future of the labor market has never been easy. Consider the track record of the Bureau of Labor Statistics (BLS), recognized as America's foremost source of information and expertise on the labor market. Twenty years ago, the BLS predicted that the number of gas station attendants and travel agents in America would rise sharply; in fact, employment in both occupations has fallen. And of the twenty occupations that the BLS predicted would suffer the greatest job losses over those twenty years, fully half of them have *grown*, often robustly.

What we have witnessed is a continual testing of a concept that is central to all of economics: **comparative advantage.** The economist David Ricardo got it right two centuries ago, and no one has disproved him since—although U.S. corporate executives facing stiff foreign competition try to do so all the time. In a nutshell, the principle of comparative advantage says that if an individual, firm, or nation is singularly good at doing one thing (has low **costs** of doing it), it must, *by definition,* be less good at doing other things (face higher costs of doing them). Comparative advantage implies that there is a niche for everyone and that those niches can best be filled (and our wealth increased the most) if we permit unfettered freedom of trade, both domestically and internationally, and allow all participants to focus on what they do best.

Consider the current situation: Like their counterparts in the United States, engineers and technicians in India have the capacity to provide both computer programming and innovative new technologies. Indian programmers and high-tech engineers earn one-quarter of what their counterparts earn in the United States. Consequently, India is able to do both jobs at a lower dollar cost than the United States: India has an **absolute advantage** in both. In other words, it can produce a unit of programming for fewer dollars than the United States, and it can also produce a unit of technology innovation for fewer dollars. Does that mean that the United States will lose not only programming jobs but innovative technology jobs too? Does that mean that our standard of living will fall if the United States and India engage in international trade?

David Ricardo would have answered no to both questions—as we do today. While India may have an absolute advantage in both activities, that fact is *irrelevant* in determining what India or the United States will produce. India has a comparative advantage in doing programming in part because such activity requires little **physical capital.** The flip side is that the United States has a comparative advantage in technology innovation partly because it is relatively easy to obtain capital in this country to undertake such long-run projects. The result is that Indian programmers will do more and more of what U.S. programmers have been doing in the past. In contrast, American firms will shift to more and more innovation. The United States will specialize in technology innovation; India will specialize in programming. The business managers in each country will opt to specialize in activities in which they have a comparative advantage. As in the past, the U.S. economy will continue to concentrate on what are called the "most best" activities.

The principle here is no different from what we regularly observe among world-class athletes. Typically, they have the physical and mental skills that would enable them to beat virtually anyone else in any of several sporting activities. They have an absolute advantage in athletics. Yet they invariably end up specializing in *one* sport, the one in which they have a comparative advantage. They do this because they are so good in that sport *relative* to other sports that their earnings would be lower if they "wasted" their time in those other sports. Exactly the same thing is happening with the Indian engineers and technicians, just as it happens in all other endeavors.

Let's return to the general issue of outsourcing services to foreign workers. Computer programming is just one area in which such outsourcing is occurring. This outsourcing also extends, somewhat amazingly, to U.S. income tax return preparation. The fact is that accounting firms small and large use workers in India to prepare returns for U.S. clients. At least a quarter of a million returns each year are being prepared by Indians in Bangalore and Mumbai. Moreover, U.S. hospitals are sending (via the Internet, of course) computer-image X-rays to India for physicians and medical technicians there to prepare before the images are resent to the United States for a final diagnosis.

Sending overseas white-collar jobs that are labor-intensive—answering simple complaints, taking orders over the phone, explaining basic computer setup, and reading simple medical-test results—is no different from what we did when we bought lower-priced computer chips from Japan and other Asian countries in the 1980s. Nor is it fundamentally different from what we did when we started importing more labor-intensive textiles in the 1980s and 1990s. Because of foreign competition, specific industries throughout time have been forced to be more innovative and cost-conscious, but overall, the number of jobs in the United States has consistently grown, decade after decade. Indeed, at least for the high-tech industrial sector, the aftermath of the "Asian invasion" of the 1980s was a productivity boom.

The fact is that there is little evidence that well-paying jobs are being "sent overseas." Unemployment among college-educated workers is lower than among all other workers. Moreover, although the unemployment rate for college graduates rises in recessions and falls in economic expansions, the overall trend in the unemployment rate for this group of workers is actually slightly downward over the past thirty years. And employment has grown much more rapidly for college graduates than for people of other educational levels.

Jobs disappear in this economy and everywhere else—normally, because of **technological change.** (Actually, jobs disappear in the U.S.

economy at the rate of 1 million per *week* as workers quit or are fired; but in a typical year, slightly more than a million jobs per week are created as workers accept new employment.) It is also true that manufacturing employment in America continues to shrink. But the decline in manufacturing jobs is not unique to the United States. Indeed, despite talk of "losing" manufacturing jobs to China and elsewhere, the number of manufacturing jobs in foreign countries such as China is shrinking *faster* than it is in the United States!

Wealth-enhancing technological change is relieving human beings of the necessity of performing mind-numbing, repetitive, dangerous factory jobs. It is making us more productive, and we are collectively better off as a result, even though some individuals may be worse off. But the only way to protect *everyone* from the effects of technological change is to prevent all technological change. Not only would this impoverish us if we tried it, but we would fail in our attempts because other nations would gleefully step into the technology-leading shoes we had vacated.

Indeed, the reason that U.S. companies can outsource service jobs to India, China, and elsewhere is *because* of technological change—dramatic improvements in telecommunications and computing. One thing you can be absolutely certain of is this: The political brouhaha over "exporting" jobs will eventually die out, but technological change will never stop. We don't know what the next great innovation cycle will be or which sectors will be affected. When they are affected, though, some politicians will jump on the bandwagon and declare that a new threat to the American economy has emerged. You'll then hear much pontification about how foreigners are destroying the U.S. economy. But remember this: For the past 250 years, technological change is what has enabled us to become richer as a nation; indeed, in the United States, every generation over this span has been roughly 50 percent richer than the one that preceded it. It is true that along the way, some people in the whale blubber–rendering and buggy-whip industries have had to move on to other employments. But as long as humans can think, technology will change, and jobs will change along with them. Our only option is to decide whether we want to get rich by embracing these changes or get poor by rejecting them.

DISCUSSION QUESTIONS

1. What is the difference between buying automobiles, clothes, and DVD players from abroad and buying low-cost labor services, such as call-center services, from abroad?

2. Given the possibility of continued outsourcing of programming services abroad, what do you think will happen to the demand for degrees in computer sciences in the United States over time?

3. In what way can immigration be thought of as "insourcing" jobs, that is, bringing people into America to do the jobs here? Suppose we had decided a century ago (as many politicians advocated at the time) to stop this "insourcing" threat to Americans by eliminating all immigration. Would our nation be better or worse off? Would you even be an American?

PART FOUR

Market Structures

Introduction

The competitive model employed in our discussion of **demand** and **supply** assumes that firms on both sides of the market satisfy the conditions of **pure competition.** For sellers of goods, this means the **demand curve** they face is **perfectly elastic:** Suppliers must take the market price as given because any attempt by them to raise their price above the market price will result in the loss of *all* of their sales. Similarly, purchasers in the competitive model face a **supply curve** that is also perfectly elastic. The market price is given, and any attempt by them to purchase at less than that price will be unsuccessful—no one will sell to them.

The conditions of pure competition imply that buyers and sellers have no effect individually on market prices. Even a casual glance at the world suggests that the conditions of pure competition are not always met. Sometimes, as is the case for major corporations, the firms are large enough relative to the market that significant changes in their purchase or sale decisions will have an effect on prices. In other cases, buyers or sellers are "unique," in that no other buyer or seller offers exactly what they do. (Classic examples include the superstars of sports and entertainment, who will sell less of their services if they raise their prices but will still sell some.) Sometimes firms that would otherwise be pure competitors join to form a **cartel,** acting as a single decision-making unit whose collective output decisions affect the market price.

When a seller's decisions affect the price of a good, economists usually call the firm a **monopoly.** Literally, this means "single seller," but what is actually meant is that the firm faces a downward-sloping demand curve for its output, so that its decisions affect the price at which its output is sold. When a buyer's decisions affect the market price, we term the firm a **monopsony,** or "single buyer." This means that the firm faces a positively sloped supply curve, so that its purchasing decisions affect the price at which it buys goods. (Some economists use the term **price searcher** to mean any firm, buyer or seller, whose decisions affect market prices and who must therefore search for—or decide on—the price that maximizes the firm's profits. Following this terminology, a pure competitor would be called a **price taker,** for such a firm takes the market price as given.)

The starting point for our examination of market structures is Chapter 15, "Big Oil, Big Oil Prices." Crude oil plays a key role in many aspects of our lives, as the basis for products ranging from jet fuel to gasoline to heating oil. It is no surprise, then, that people worry about the price of oil. And when the price surges, as it did in 2007–2008, plenty of people think that big oil companies are the culprits. Make no mistake, the big oil companies are definitely price searchers: They can raise their price above their **marginal cost** and still sell plenty of oil. But their absolute size (measured in billions of dollars of sales or hundreds of billions in assets) is no sure guide to *how much* they are able to raise their prices. In the case of petroleum products, such as gasoline, that ability seems to be limited to something like pennies per gallon, rather than the far larger sums often attributed to big oil. Those pennies per gallon that oil companies squeeze out of us are enough to make for big **profits,** but they aren't enough to explain the oil and gasoline price surges of the 1970s or the 2000s. To begin to do that, we need to move on to our next chapter.

As you will see in Chapter 16, "Contracts, Combinations, and Conspiracies," the rigors (and low profits) of competition are such that firms often try to devise ways to avoid competing. One of the most popular is the cartel, which is simply a collective agreement by many or all firms in an industry to reduce total output so that the price of the product—and thus the profits of the cartel's members—can be increased. Cartels are generally illegal in the United States, but the National Collegiate Athletic Association (NCAA) is a cartel that is both legal and flourishing. Cartels are more commonly observed in international markets. Here we examine three international cartels, in the markets for oil, diamonds, and caviar. In each case, we find that although the **incentives** to form cartels are great, even greater are the incentives to cheat on the cartels almost as soon as they are formed. The overriding message of this chapter is that despite their enormous profit potential, competitive pressures make cartels inherently unstable and thus generally short-lived.

Whatever the degree of competition, firms are always seeking ways to raise profits. Often this means developing new products and striving to offer superior service. But sometimes, as you will see in Chapter 17,

"Coffee, Tea, or Tuition-Free?" it simply means adjusting prices on existing products. The practice of charging prices that differ among customers in ways not due to differences in the marginal costs of supplying them is called **price discrimination.** Although technically illegal in the United States, it is routinely observed in markets ranging from airline travel to college financial aid. In the case of air travel, you are almost certainly the beneficiary of price discrimination, paying a lower price than you would if price discrimination were completely eliminated. But don't feel too smug: By the time you start traveling for business rather than pleasure, you are likely to be on the wrong end of the price discrimination, paying plenty so that the college kid in the seat next to you can enjoy spring break in a sunny clime.

Speaking of college, you may have noticed that it has gotten pretty expensive, a topic we investigate in Chapter 18, "College Costs (. . . and Costs and Costs)." The market structure in which colleges operate is called **monopolistic competition:** Sellers (in this case, colleges) are offering similar products for sale but using advertising to differentiate their products from those offered by other sellers. Chapter 17 made clear that colleges have enough market power to price-discriminate among students. Nevertheless, there is enough competition among colleges that the structure of this market does not seem capable of explaining the high *average* price of a college education these days. To do that, we must look at a host of other factors that have come into play in this market in recent years, most notably, a rising demand for college education.

As Chapter 19, "Keeping the Competition Out," demonstrates, enlisting the government to hamstring or exclude competitors is probably the most reliable means of ensuring that you are protected from the rigors of competition. Perhaps for this reason, the array of markets in which the government stifles competition is nothing short of remarkable. Here we examine just a handful, ranging from taxicabs to hair braiding, but the list could have gone on and on. In each case, the method is the same: Usually under the guise of "consumer protection," the government prevents entry by some firms into a market, thereby reducing supply in that market. The effect is much the same as that produced by a fully enforced cartel. Firms thus protected by the government enjoy both a higher price for their product and a larger **market share.** The consumers, supposedly "protected" by their government, are usually the big losers due to higher product prices and reduced selection among suppliers.

Chapter 15

BIG OIL, BIG OIL
PRICES?

The milk crates began disappearing at an unprecedented rate. Berkeley Farms in Northern California started "losing" about fourteen hundred crates a day, 30 percent more than the company had been losing in an average year. Velda Farms in Winter Haven, Florida, reported a similar increase in missing milk crates. About the same time, police investigators in Southern California noticed an increase in the number of large SUVs that were being abandoned in the Los Angeles River bed and set on fire.

What do these seemingly unrelated events—missing milk crates and burning SUVs—have in common? The answer is the high price of oil and petroleum-based products. Consider first the sudden outbreak of flaming SUVs. When the price of gasoline soared, the resale value of used SUVs plummeted. Many owners of those cars found themselves "upside down," meaning they owed more on their car loans than the cars were worth. So arson seemed like a good solution to this financial problem. Pay someone to steal the car and set it on fire; then collect from the auto insurance company and start over again, presumably with a smaller car.

As for the missing milk crates, well, the thieves who stole them knew exactly where they were. As oil prices climbed, the prices for petroleum-based resin climbed too. Milk crates are made of such resin. At the same time that drivers were paying record **nominal prices** for gas, petroleum-based resin prices were hitting nominal-price peaks also. Resin can be recycled. At higher resin prices, there were greater **incentives** for thieves to steal milk crates to sell them to recyclers. And so they did.

Not long after gas prices peaked at over $4 per gallon in the summer of 2008, they swiftly plunged back to less than half that level. Just as quickly, the public and political outcry over high gasoline prices subsided. But you can be sure that the next time gas prices jump, the outcry will return with a vengeance. As the title of this chapter suggests, there is a common view that big oil—multibillion-dollar oil companies—is behind big oil prices, which translate into higher prices for gas at the pump. Let us first look at the notion of what "big" means.

To be sure, today's oil companies are huge. They have to be, because exploring for oil is a costly and risky venture. But certainly, you may think, an oil company worth many billions of dollars must have plenty of **monopoly power** in the marketplace. After all, in 2008, the market valuation of ExxonMobil hit $480 billion. Shell and BP were both worth $280 billion at that time, while Chevron was valued at "only" $200 billion.

As it turns out, however, the absolute size of a corporation is rarely a good indicator that it is a monopoly. For a company to be effective in raising prices much above the competitive level, it has to have a large *share* of the total market. To put things in perspective, the three largest privately owned oil companies in the world are ExxonMobil, Shell, and BP. *Added together,* they are smaller than the Saudi Arabian Oil Company. And none of the three private firms is as big as any of the national oil companies of Mexico, Venezuela, or China.

Make no mistake, the big oil companies in America can and do influence the price you pay at the pump. One example of this is found in **zone pricing,** varying prices to take advantage of local market conditions. For example, they might charge a nickel or a dime a gallon more at stations near an upscale university, where the SUV-driving students won't bother to drive an extra mile to save a buck on a tankful of gas. A nickel here and a dime there pretty soon adds up to real money when you are selling billions of gallons a year. But it doesn't add up to the price swings in petroleum products that America witnessed in the 2000s.

In fact, those price swings are worth a look. All of the headlines about the price of a barrel of oil reaching historic highs—over $140 per barrel—meant less than you might think because prices were always presented *uncorrected for inflation.* It is true that oil and gasoline prices in 2008 hit levels that were high by modern standards. But after correcting for inflation, they were only about 50 percent above levels reached in the early 1980s. And as we noted in Chapter 7, a rising standard of living had actually made oil and gas more affordable than thirty years earlier. The fact is that when placed in a larger historical context, oil and gas were still remarkably cheap at $140 a barrel and $4 per gallon.

Consider, by contrast, the price of oil and gasoline in the 1800s. In 1859, when Colonel Edwin Drake struck oil in Pennsylvania, you could buy a barrel of oil for $4. Of course, if you adjust that $4 for changes in the price level and in the standard of living between then and now, it would be the equivalent of $1,200 per barrel today. As you might imagine, there was a surge in oil drilling and discoveries after word of Drake's discovery spread, which pushed prices ever downward. By 1896, when

Henry Ford's first quadricycle went on sale, the price of gasoline at the pump was, in terms comparable to today's income, about $10 a gallon. (This may help explain why Ford designed his vehicle to run on ethanol.) In the years since, the prices of crude oil and its derivatives have gone up and down (actually, mostly down) in response to global **demand** and **supply,** just as the prices of all other resources, products, and services vary in response to demand and supply over time.

About thirty-five years ago, the Organization of Petroleum Export-ing Countries (OPEC) curtailed oil production sharply; this pushed the price of oil up by a factor of 5 (from $18 per barrel in 2009 prices to about $90 per barrel). In response, oil users in developed countries, espe-cially the United States, became more energy-efficient, just as we would expect under the **law of demand.** Today, we use only 50 percent as much energy for every dollar of production as we did in 1973. Moreover, since 1980, the share of consumer spending that goes for energy has been slashed by over a third. So when the **real price** of oil soared between 2003 and 2008, it was a lot less painful than it had been in the 1970s.

Nevertheless, many people have been claiming that the latest spike in oil prices is different. We have had energy crises in the past, but noth-ing like what awaits us, they say. All you have to do is look at the titles of some recent books on the energy problem: *The Empty Tank, Out of Gas,* and *The Coming Economic Collapse: How You Can Thrive When Oil Costs $200 a Barrel.* As it turns out, experts from the federal govern-ment have been telling Americans that we are running out of oil for quite a long time. In 1914, for example, the Interior Department announced that there was only a ten-year supply of oil left. That same department told us in 1939 that there was a thirteen-year supply. Then in 1951, we were told that oil wells would run dry in the mid-1960s. President Jimmy Carter in the 1970s said that we would use up all **proven reserves** of oil in the world by the end of the 1980s.

Something is wrong here. The economy of every developed country in the world depends critically on oil to keep it going. If the world is running out of oil, we would expect the real price of oil to rise over time under these circumstances. But it hasn't—because global oil reserves are increasing, not decreasing. In 1970, Saudi Arabia had about 90 bil-lion barrels of proven reserves. Since then, Saudi Arabia has pumped and sold over 100 billion barrels of oil. The wells should have run dry in the desert there, but they did not. In fact, Saudi Arabia now says that there are still 260 billion barrels left under the ground. And the proven oil reserves in Canada, which were tiny in 1970, are now bigger than those of any nation *except* Saudi Arabia. The explanation is that every time there is a sustained jump in oil prices, exploration for oil increases.

So far, this has paid off with improved technology for finding and extracting oil and with more oil reserves. For example, oil companies now routinely extract oil from the bottom of the ocean at the same real cost they spent four decades ago drilling just a hundred feet down into the earth in Texas. Over the long haul, the result of this process is that real prices have trended downward.

Hysteria over the possibility of running out has occurred with other resources, too. At the end of the nineteenth century, there were numerous articles about industry grinding to a halt because we were running out of coal. Yet today there is a five hundred years' supply. What is happening with oil, coal, and many other resources is that the lure of profits induces companies to invest in better technology to create and sell more of these commodities.[1]

This process of exploration and discovery takes place over many years, even decades—it is a long-run process. In the short run, which can last several years, the **elasticity of supply** of oil and many other natural resources is relatively low: A large percentage increase in price will call forth only a small percentage increase in quantity supplied in the short run. Hence it is possible for economic or political developments to cause large changes in market prices. In the 2000s, hurricanes temporarily slashed supply from U.S. sources, and political upheaval in the Middle East and Africa cut supplies there too. Moreover, demand was elevated by the Chinese government, which was trying to acquire large amounts of oil to ensure that its rapidly growing economy would remain well lubricated. Reduced supplies combined with the added demand from China produced the price spike. Then came the financial crisis and ensuing recession of 2007–2009, which quickly brought the demand for oil and gas—and thus their prices—right back down.

Consumers were relieved by the lower prices, but oddly enough, in the case of oil, outrage can sometimes arise when prices fall. In the weeks leading up to the congressional elections of 2006, the price of gasoline fell 20 percent. Many people complained that the drop was the result of a conspiracy between big oil and the government to alter the outcome of the elections. What people overlooked was that gas prices *typically* fall between Labor Day and the first week of November because the end of the summer vacation season reduces the demand for gasoline well before the onset of winter increases the demand for heating fuel.

---

1. This assumes that the **property rights** to these resources are well defined, enforceable, and transferable. As we discuss in Chapter 27, "Bye-Bye, Bison," if such conditions are not met, this process of conserving existing resources and expanding new sources of them cannot be expected to occur.

Make no mistake, big oil companies take big risks and make big **profits.** And they are extremely good at squeezing that last nickel or dime a gallon out of us—income we might get to keep if this market were more competitive. But even though a nickel here and a nickel there soon adds up to big profits, it does not add up to price swings of $2 per gallon of gas or $80 per barrel of oil. To understand that, you have to go back to the old familiar forces of demand and supply.

DISCUSSION QUESTIONS

1. In the 1970s, during different periods, Americans had to line up and wait to get gas. Today, even when there are periodic disruptions in the oil market, we rarely, if ever, have to wait a long time to fill up. Why? (*Hint:* During the 1970s, the federal government imposed wage and price controls.)

2. If the size of proven oil reserves keeps going up, what can you say about the term *proven* as it is used by geologists? How would an economist define "proven reserves"?

3. The price at the pump for gasoline, whether it is $2 or $3 or $4, certainly seems higher than it was, say, fifteen years ago. Nonetheless, Americans have not switched in great numbers to small, lightweight cars that consume less gas. Indeed, we remain a nation of large cars. Americans do love big cars, but what might be some other reasons for not downsizing?

4. When big oil companies make big profits, where do those profits go? (*Hint:* Over 50 percent of adult Americans own shares in American corporations, either directly or indirectly.)

CONTRACTS, COMBINATIONS, AND CONSPIRACIES

The Sherman Act of 1890 outlaws any "contract, combination, . . . or conspiracy, in restraint of trade or commerce" in the United States. Translated from the legalese, this means that firms in America cannot lawfully join with competitors to form a **cartel** to raise prices above the competitive level.[1] Because successful cartels have the potential for great **profits,** there are strong **incentives** to form them. Usually, however, if the government discourages them, or even if it does not actively encourage them, cartels are difficult to keep together. This is because a cartel must meet four requirements if it is to be successful:

1. *Share.* It must control a large share of actual and potential output, so that other producers of the good it sells will not be able to depress prices by expanding output significantly.

2. *Substitutes.* Consumers must regard alternatives to the cartel's product as relatively poor substitutes, and these substitutes must be few in number and relatively inelastic in supply; such factors all reduce the **elasticity of demand** facing the cartel, helping it raise prices.

3. *Stability.* There must be very few outside factors that tend to disturb **cost** or **demand** conditions in the industry, so that the cartel is not continually having to make new price and output decisions in response to changing conditions.

---

1. Despite this, many American agricultural producers are legally permitted to collectively agree to raise their prices on products ranging from almonds to oranges. They do so under the umbrella of "marketing orders," which are effectively cartels approved and enforced by the U.S. Department of Agriculture.

4. *Solidarity.* It must be relatively easy for the cartel to maintain solidarity by identifying and punishing members who cheat on the cartel agreement with price cuts.

All successful cartels have been able to meet these requirements to some extent. Conversely, a breakdown in one or more of these factors has been the downfall of each one that has failed. In general, successful cartels are international. They are either effectively beyond (or exempt from) national laws forbidding them or encouraged by or made up of governments themselves.

One of the most famous and most successful cartels has been the Organization of Petroleum Exporting Countries (OPEC). Formed in 1960, its members have included many major oil-producing countries, such as Algeria, Indonesia, Iran, Iraq, Kuwait, Libya, Nigeria, Saudi Arabia, and Venezuela. OPEC had little impact on the price of oil until the outbreak of the Middle East war in 1973 provided the impetus for cohesive action. Saudi Arabia, Kuwait, and several other Arab nations sharply reduced their production of oil; because the **demand curve** for oil is downward-sloping, this reduction in supply pushed oil prices—and thus the profits of OPEC members—up sharply. On January 1, 1973, one could buy Saudi Arabian crude oil for about $10 per barrel (in 2009 dollars). Within one year, the price of crude had risen to $32 per barrel; by the next year, to $41, and by the end of the decade, to $80 per barrel with no end in sight.

Several forces combined to send oil prices in the opposite direction by the mid-1980s. At least partly in response to the high prices charged by OPEC, worldwide output of oil from other sources began to grow, led by rising production on Alaska's North Slope and by aggressive marketing of the oil flowing out of the Norwegian and British fields located in the North Sea. Eventually, this additional production significantly reduced the **market share** controlled by OPEC members and thus helped reduce their stranglehold on price.

The most important problem for OPEC, however, as for so many cartels, has been cheating on the cartel agreement by its members. Whenever there are numerous firms or countries in a cartel arrangement, there will always be some that are unhappy with the situation, perhaps because they think they are not getting enough of the profits. They cheat by charging a slightly lower price than the one stipulated by the cartel, a move that will result in a very large increase in the cheater's revenues (and thus profits). The potential for cheating is a constant threat to a cartel's existence, and when enough of a cartel's members try to cheat, the cartel breaks up.

In the case of OPEC, war between the member nations of Iran and Iraq during the 1980s precipitated a major outbreak of cheating as those two nations expanded production beyond their **quotas,** using the extra sales to finance heavy military expenditures. Expressed in 2009 dollars, the price of crude oil plunged to less than $20 per barrel in 1986, when cheating on output quotas spread throughout the cartel. Saudi Arabia, the world's largest producer of crude, finally restored order when it threatened to double its output if other OPEC members did not adhere to their quotas. Crude oil prices hovered around $25 to $30 per barrel from then until early 2004, when they started a sharp climb due to rising world demand. After peaking at over $140 per barrel in 2008, prices subsequently dropped back to around $40 in response to worldwide recession.

The difficulties faced by cartels are also illustrated in the diamond market, where DeBeers, the famous diamond company, once controlled as much as 80 percent of the world supply but now can claim only a 40 percent market share. DeBeers itself produces about 25 percent of the world's diamond output and controls the marketing of another 15 percent through a cartel called the Diamond Trading Company (DTC). Under the direction of DeBeers, the DTC has long restricted the sale of rough-cut diamonds to keep their prices at levels that maximize the profits of its members. After many years of profitable success, however, the diamond cartel has hit rough times. Cartel profits spurred searches for new sources of supply, and major discoveries have been made in Australia and Canada. Moreover, Russia, which accounts for about one-fourth of world output, has defected from the DTC cartel to market its diamonds through the Lev Leviev Group, the top DTC competitor. The combined effect of increased supplies and cartel defections has been to push the inflation-adjusted price of top-quality diamonds down to less than half the levels of thirty years ago.

The Russians have had troubles with their own historically successful cartel, the one that controls—or controlled—the supply of fine caviar. The principal source of some of the world's best caviar is the Volga River delta, where Kazakhstan and Russia (both former members of the Soviet Union) share a border at the northern end of the Caspian Sea. Both the temperature and the salinity of the water in the delta make it the ideal spawning ground for sturgeon, the long-nosed prehistoric fish whose eggs have for centuries been prized as the world's finest caviar. Originally, the Russian royal families ran the show, eating what they wanted of the harvest and then controlling the remaining supplies to their advantage.

When the Russian Revolution disposed of the Romanov dynasty in 1917, the new Communist regime quickly saw the potential profits to be had from cornering the market on caviar. Hence, for the next seventy-five years or so, a Soviet state-dominated cartel controlled the nation's caviar business from top to bottom. Although the Soviet sturgeon were considerate enough to produce an annual catch of some 2,000 tons of caviar, the Communist cartel allowed only 150 tons out of the country. As a result, a state-supplied kilogram (2.2 pounds) of top-grade black caviar costing $5 or less on the Moscow black market commanded $1,000 or more in New York.

The demise of the Soviet Union spawned trouble, however, for **competition** reared its ugly head. As it turns out, the largest sturgeon fisheries fell under the jurisdictions of two different autonomous republics—Russia and Kazakhstan—each of which wanted to own and operate its own lucrative caviar business. Moreover, a variety of individuals, including enterprising Caspian Sea fishermen from these republics, staked private claims and in some cases set up their own **export** channels (behavior officially termed "black market piracy"). The effect of this capitalist behavior was a 20 percent drop in the official caviar export price during the first year of autonomy, plus an escalation of competition since then.

Caviar consumers were pleased at this turn of events, but old-line suppliers were not so happy. "We don't need this kind of competition," complained one. "All of these small rivals mean that prices will fall and the market will be ripped apart. This is a delicacy—we need to keep it elite." Recent years have seen a sharp upswing in world caviar prices, although not because Russia and Kazakhstan have managed to get competition under control. Instead, it turns out that pollution from leftover Soviet industry in the area has sharply reduced the region's sturgeon population. The resulting decline in the amount of harvestable caviar drove costs and prices up and profits even lower. Adding insult to injury, firms in America (whose costs are not affected by the Soviet pollution) have entered the caviar market in response to the higher prices, intensifying the price-cost squeeze that the former Soviet republics are suffering. And so just as Soviet citizens found that communism wasn't all that it was cracked up to be, it appears some of them are now learning that capitalism may be more than they bargained for—but perhaps no less than Karl Marx warned them about.

Oddly enough, despite the Sherman Act and other tough antitrust laws, one of the longest-running cartels can be found right here in the United States. The National Collegiate Athletic Association (NCAA), which operates under a special exemption from the antitrust laws, sets the rules not only for how intercollegiate sports competition takes place but also for how athletes are recruited and paid. And under NCAA rules, college athletes are not paid much. Indeed, as a practical matter, compensation for collegiate athletes is limited to the cost of room, board, books, and tuition at their university or college, an amount that typically ranges from $25,000 to $50,000 per year. This might sound like pretty good pay to you, and indeed, for a field hockey player or college wrestler, it probably is. But for the so-called revenue sports of college athletics, most notably football and basketball, such sums amount to a pittance compared to what these athletes would bring on the open market. (This, of course, is exactly the point: Universities are joined together in the NCAA in part simply to keep down the costs of college athletics.) In the case of football, this issue has been studied quite intensively, so we actually have a good idea of what top college players are worth. Over a four-year college career, a player who ends up getting drafted by a professional team is underpaid by about $2 million. And while lesser players are underpaid by lesser amounts, numbers like these make it clear that despite encouraging open competition on college playing fields, when it comes to competition in the marketplace, the NCAA is guilty of unsportsmanlike conduct.

DISCUSSION QUESTIONS

1. Why are all cartels inherently unstable?

2. Would it be easier to form a cartel in a market with many producers or one with few producers?

3. What happens to the producers of caviar made from other types of fish eggs (such as salmon, whitefish, and trout) when the price of the finest sturgeon caviar changes? Would these firms ever have an incentive to help the governments of Russia and Kazakhstan reestablish the caviar cartel?

4. If the members of your class were to attempt to form a study-reduction cartel in which everyone agreed to study less, which individuals would have the most to gain from the cartel? Which ones would have the greatest incentive to cheat on the cartel?

Chapter 17

COFFEE, TEA, OR TUITION-FREE?

A few years ago, the Internet retailing giant Amazon.com received some unwanted publicity when it was revealed that the company was charging different prices for movies sold to different customers. Amazon insisted that the price differences were random and amounted to an effort to simply test the market. But some customers complained that Amazon was using the practice to tailor prices to customer characteristics, charging more to people who were likely to be willing to pay more. The flap over Amazon's "market test" soon died out, but as time passes, Internet firms and other companies are finding it almost impossible to resist regularly charging different prices to different customers. The reason is simple: By tracking people's buying habits, firms can get a pretty good idea of how to engage in **price discrimination** among their customers and thus increase their **profits.**

Shouldn't price discrimination be illegal? Actually, it *is* illegal, at least under some circumstances. Nevertheless, it is routinely practiced by businesses of all descriptions—and perhaps even by the college you attend. Interestingly, although price discrimination definitely benefits the firms (or colleges) that engage in it, you may benefit, too. Let's see how.

First things first: Price discrimination is defined as the existence of price differences across customers for the same good that are not due to differences in the **marginal costs** of supplying the customers. Thus price discrimination can occur when marginal costs are the same across customers but prices are different or when prices are the same despite differences in marginal costs. An example of the former occurs when pharmacies or movie theaters charge lower prices to "senior citizens" than to other customers. An example of the latter can be found at "all you can eat" buffets, where the price is the same for all diners, even though some eat much more food than others.

Three conditions must exist for a firm to engage in price discrimination. First, the firm must be, at least to some extent, a **price searcher**— it must be able to raise price above marginal cost without losing all of its sales to rivals. Second, there must be identifiable differences across customers in their willingness (or ability) to pay different prices for the same good. Third, the firm must be able to prevent customers who pay lower prices from reselling the good to customers who otherwise would be charged higher prices—or else customers eligible for the lowest price will buy on behalf of all customers.

The objective of price discrimination is, of course, higher profits for the firm that engages in it. To see how this might work, consider a firm selling to two identifiable groups of customers, say, retirees and working people. Also suppose that the retirees have lower income and so perhaps have a higher **price elasticity of demand** for the good—that is, they tend to be more sensitive to changes in price. In this case, it may be possible for the firm to reallocate sales among customer groups, lowering prices slightly to retirees and raising them somewhat to working people, thereby getting more revenue at the same costs, and so earning higher profits. Of course, to be able to accomplish this, the firm must be able to distinguish between the two groups. (This ability is often approximated by offering the lower prices only to persons who can prove they are older and thus more likely to be retired.) Moreover, the firm must be able to prevent resale from low-price buyers to other customers; in the case of prescription medicines, pharmacies are aided by federal and state laws that forbid such resale, while in the case of movie theaters, the person getting the lower price generally must attend the movie personally to get the lower price. (This helps explain why movie rental companies like Blockbuster are less likely than movie theaters to offer senior-citizen discounts: It would be too easy for seniors to rent movies on behalf of younger people who wish to avoid the higher prices applicable to them.)

If you have ever traveled on an airplane, you are likely to have been a beneficiary of price discrimination (although your parents—or their employers—may have been victims of such discrimination if they fly on short-notice business trips). Prior to 1978, the fares charged by airlines in the United States were regulated by the federal government, so all airlines offered the same government-approved fares; discounts were rare beyond late-night ("red-eye") or weekend flights.[1] Once deregulation

---

1. Those fares were also considerably higher on average than they are today because the federal government agency responsible for regulating the airlines also prevented them from competing on the basis of price.

occurred, airlines quickly discovered that there were large differences in the price elasticity of demand across customers. Business travelers typically had a lower price elasticity of demand and hence were willing to pay higher fares than leisure travelers. Fares charged business travelers are now higher than they used to be, even though leisure fares are significantly lower than they were in the days of government regulation.

The precision and effectiveness with which the airlines engage in price discrimination have been rising steadily over time, thanks to a process known as "yield management." Combining sophisticated statistical techniques and massive historical databases, together with computerized up-to-the-minute bookings, the airlines can predict with almost pinpoint accuracy how many business customers will want seats on a given flight and how much they'll be willing to pay. As a result, says one industry insider, "high fares get higher and low fares get lower."

The process begins months before a flight ever departs, as the airline divides the seats on a plane into as many as seven or more different fare classes, or categories. Initial fares on a flight are established for each of the categories, and the yield-management computers begin the process of monitoring the reservations, comparing them to historical patterns. If advance bookings are slow, the airline will move seats to low-fare categories. But if business travelers buy higher-priced, unrestricted tickets sooner than expected, the yield-management computer removes seats from discount categories and holds them for last-minute business passengers that are predicted to show up.

A host of techniques are used to optimize the blend between filling the seats on a plane and getting the highest possible fare for each seat. In the weeks leading up to a flight, the level of fares assigned to each category may be adjusted up or down based on the latest moves by competitors, and as the flight date approaches, lower-priced categories are likely to be closed out altogether. Moreover, some people seeking reservations may be told a given flight is "sold out" even though passengers using that flight as a connector to another of the airline's routes may find ample seating—for a price, of course. The result of all this fine-tuning is that passengers on the same flight from, say, Chicago to Phoenix, may pay round-trip fares that vary by a factor of 5—ranging, say, from $280 for the lowest-priced seats to $1,400 for the top fares.

Interestingly, the same yield-management techniques refined by the airlines are now being used by universities when they decide on financial-aid packages offered to students. After all, given the nominal tuition at a university, a more generous financial-aid offer can be thought of as a lower price, and students, like everyone else, behave according to the **law of demand.** Universities have found, for example, that they can offer less generous aid packages to students who apply for early admission because such students are more eager to attend; as one financial-aid consultant notes, "Those who have the most interest in the school are going to be less price sensitive." In a similar vein, some colleges have found that people who come for campus interviews are more interested in attending; the response has been to offer slightly less generous aid packages to such students, even though the colleges routinely recommend that students come for interviews.

In addition to these regular features of price discrimination in financial-aid offers, universities also monitor their enrollment figures each year, just as the airlines watch bookings by fare category. If a school is getting, say, too many premed students and not enough in the humanities, financial-aid offers will be adjusted accordingly, with bigger than usual aid offers being made to the students the school is trying to attract. Schools that are noted for excellence in one area but are trying to maintain a balanced mix of majors have become particularly adept at the financial-aid game. As the enrollment vice president for Carnegie Mellon University notes, without sophisticated adjustments to the blend of aid packages offered, "I'd have an institution full of engineers and computer scientists and I wouldn't have anybody in arts and design." Carnegie Mellon also recognizes the importance of competition in determining the prices it charges: After admitted students are notified of their aid offers in the spring, they are invited to fax the school any better offers they receive from other colleges. Using funds from a special account set aside for the purpose, the university generally meets competing offers received by desirable students.

Price discrimination can even be practiced on a worldwide scale. Most major pharmaceutical companies price-discriminate based on the nationality of the people buying their drugs. Partly because incomes in other nations are lower than in the United States, people in other nations have higher elasticities of demand than American citizens. Consequently, pharmaceutical companies sell prescription drugs elsewhere at lower prices than they do in the United States. But one of these other nations is Canada, and American senior citizens have found that by getting on a bus (or even just visiting the Web site of a Canadian pharmacy), they can save a bundle on their prescriptions.[2] Although this practice is technically illegal, neither the United States nor Canada has stopped it. In fact,

---

2. Another reason for lower prices in Canada is that it has a nationalized health-care system, meaning that the government buys drugs on behalf of all Canadians. This practice makes the Canadian government a **monopsonist** (literally, "single buyer"), with the power to force drug prices down below what they otherwise would be.

by the time you read this, Congress may have legalized the importation of prescription drugs from other nations.

Price discrimination certainly profits the firms that practice it, but there is an entirely different question—one that cannot be answered by economics—as to whether it is fair. Most student travelers who can stay over a Saturday night or make reservations a month in advance probably don't mind the lower fares made possible by price discrimination. But business travelers are far from pleased with the high fares they must pay to get where they want, when they want, usually on short notice. "They've got you, and they know it," says one executive. The flip side, of course, is that without the extra revenue generated by price discrimination, some companies or colleges would be hard-pressed to survive. Indeed, when asked about the equity of fine-tuning aid packages to willingness to attend rather than ability to pay, one financial-aid official noted he had little choice in the matter: "I could make it very fair—and be out of business."

DISCUSSION QUESTIONS

---

1. First-class passengers generally pay higher fares than coach passengers, even when they take advantage of advance-purchase discounts. Is this price discrimination? (*Hint:* Seats in first class are generally leather rather than fabric and are about 50 percent wider than coach seats. Also, there are more flight attendants per passenger in the first-class section.)

2. Is it price discrimination when a professional football team charges, say, $150 per ticket for 50-yard-line tickets in the lower deck and $50 per ticket for upper-deck tickets overlooking the end zone?

3. What factors other than income are likely to affect willingness to pay? How will differences in these factors among its customers affect the likelihood that a firm will engage in price discrimination?

Chapter 18

COLLEGE COSTS
(... AND COSTS
AND COSTS)

There is an old saying that "you get what you pay for." The implication of this aphorism is that if you want higher quality, you must pay a higher price. If that were true in higher education, college students today should be receiving triple the education quality they received three decades ago. For that is how much college costs have risen (after correcting for inflation). Few of you reading this book will have had any firsthand knowledge of the quality of higher education that long ago. Your authors do, however. We can tell you (although unscientifically) that the quality of a college education on average today is not three times better than it was thirty years ago. So what is happening here?

First, it must be noted that the rapid pace of technological change and the explosion of new sources of information have both put a premium on individuals with top skills. And this gets translated in part into a demand for people who are better educated. Thus, according to the College Board and other sources, the economic returns to college education have risen. Thirty years ago, male college graduates earned 19 percent more than men with a high school diploma. Female college graduates earned 35 percent more. Today, male college graduates earn 63 percent more and female college graduates 70 percent more. Moreover, the unemployment rate for college graduates is half the unemployment rate for the general population. Consequently, a college education is worth more now than before in the market, so people are willing to pay more for it.

Still, the rise in the annual cost of college has been staggering, and it has been accompanied by an increase in the number of years it takes to finish a degree. Thirty years ago, at both public and private colleges, it took just a little over four years for the typical student to graduate. These days, the average student in a private college takes 5.3 years to graduate. The average public university student takes 6.2 years to complete his or her studies. Someone going to a private university who does not receive any form of financial aid ends up paying about $200,000 for that degree. Hence many people are now arguing that college costs can't be fully justified by the economic returns.

There are literally thousands of colleges and universities in the United States. The existence of so many competitors would seem to qualify the industry structure in higher education as perhaps not perfect competition but at least **monopolistic competition.** In a monopolistically competitive industry, producers and sellers are offering similar products for sale, albeit ones with slight variations in features or quality. And in such an industry, there are not tens of thousands of producers, as there might be in a perfectly competitive one, but there are a large number. Monopolistic competition is characterized by advertising and **product differentiation**—and so is higher education. In a monopolistically competitive industry, though, prices and quality are, at least in the long run, related—higher prices can only be obtained by providing higher quality. Why? Because of intense **competition** among firms, which means that in the long run, businesses in monopolistically competitive industries cannot make **economic profits.** We should also add that because consumers patronizing the typical firm in such an industry are each paying the full cost of whatever they purchase, they are careful to keep tabs on those costs and to switch their patronage when they can cut their costs by doing so. This obviously adds to the competition among firms and helps keep prices in line with product quality.

How well does the model of monopolistic competition seem to apply to higher education? There is one way in which it clearly does not: Virtually all colleges and universities are not for profit. You can buy and sell the shares of Apple, Microsoft, and Google, and as a shareholder, you can extract the profits out of the companies via the dividends they pay. You can do neither for Harvard, Yale, MIT, or any of the state-financed higher education institutions. In the for-profit world, businesses that are well run and have consequently higher profits see their share values go up. Managers and employees in the best-run businesses are often rewarded with higher paychecks. Nothing of this nature resembles the "marketplace" for higher education. There is no "bottom line." It is difficult to measure workers' (staff, faculty, and administrators') **productivity.** Consequently, there are reduced **incentives** for those who run universities to use their **resources** more efficiently. This means that costs are higher for any given level and quality of output. (This is not to say that people who work in higher education are less capable than anyone else; rather, the incentive structure is different.)

But colleges have been not-for-profit for a long time, so we really need to look elsewhere to see what has changed recently that might affect their costs or the prices they charge relative to those costs. Let's look first at the "superstar" phenomenon discussed in Chapter 13. Because of changing technology, the economic returns to those in the very highest echelons of performance have risen relative to the returns for the typical performer. Among colleges, this has intensified competition for superstar faculty and for (potential) superstar students—especially students who might eventually become very rich and subsequently donate large sums to their alma mater.

This competition gets translated into higher average costs. For example, salaries of the very best faculty and administrators are far above the average. In this circumstance, even if the salary of a typical professor doesn't budge, average salaries will rise, and this must be paid for somehow. Similarly, to help attract superstar faculty, the university must offer them the best labs and computer facilities. Again, this raises costs and must be paid for by someone, probably you.

The scramble for superstars has also been translated into a new pricing policy by universities, which have learned by watching major companies (such as airlines) about charging what the market will bear. As we note in Chapter 17, because of cheaper and more powerful computing capacity, private firms have been able to set up algorithms that estimate the maximum amount they can charge customers, depending on the time of day, the time of year, and so forth. When costs are the same but a different price is charged to different people for the same good or service, we call this **price discrimination**—and it is something that institutions of higher learning are getting increasingly good at doing. Via an elaborate analysis of information on family incomes, colleges give discounts in the form of scholarships and other ways to potential and actual students that have a higher **price elasticity of demand.** Because competition is greatest for the best students, the big discounts are being used to attract those—the ones with high SAT scores who will improve the college's position in the *U.S. News & World Report* rankings of the country's best colleges. At the same time prices are cut for top students (via lucrative scholarships), prices are hiked for most other students, the merely very good or average ones, via higher tuition. And because the "list prices" for tuition that get reported in the press don't reflect the discounts given to top students, costs appear to be higher than they actually are.

This quest for the best students also gets translated into **nonprice competition** among universities. Students are interested in academic quality, to be sure. But even the brightest won't turn up their noses at luxurious dormitories, elegant dining facilities, spa-quality recreational centers, and winning athletic programs. All of these are expensive to provide, and so measured costs go up even further. Now, once we adjust for the quality of the offerings, it is possible that the **constant-quality price** is not in fact changing due to these improvements. But the news media don't report prices adjusted for quality, and so the headlines tell us only that prices are up.

Over the past decade, one additional factor has entered into the college cost equation. Numerous states have instituted lotteries that earmark all or part of their net proceeds for education. In at least fifteen states, an important part of the lottery funding is channeled through students in the form of scholarships. These scholarships are typically based on high school performance and are then continued (or not) based on the student's ensuing college performance. Such scholarships increase the demand to go to college, which in turn puts upward pressure on tuition.

Many students (up to two-thirds at some universities) who use the scholarships to start college don't make grades good enough to keep the scholarships after their first or second year. Meanwhile, they have finished part of their education and also have come to "know the ropes" at their college and accumulated a host of friends. This reduces their **elasticity of demand** at that school. As a result, many students who lose their scholarships stay on in school, even some who would not initially have started the process without the scholarship. When their financial-aid funds get recycled to bring in new students, the upward press on tuition continues, because existing students are staying around, too. So the next time you see a billboard advertising the "millions" that your state's lottery has channeled into education, keep in mind that unless you are a superstar, not much of it may have gone toward *your* education.

DISCUSSION QUESTIONS

1. In recent years, some state governments have changed the way they allocate state funds to public universities. Instead of handing the funds directly to the universities, they are handing them to the students (in the form of scholarships) and allowing the students to use those scholarships at any public university they wish to attend within that state. How does this change in allocation methods affect the incentives of universities to compete for students? Is this change likely to be beneficial or harmful for students? If retention of the scholarships is dependent on student performance in college, how does this

affect student incentives to go to class, allocate time between studying and leisure, and so forth? Explain your answers.

2. According to one study, the salaries of full professors at the most prestigious American universities have risen more than 50 percent (corrected for inflation) in the past twenty-five years. What causes universities to offer such high salaries? What benefits do prestigious universities receive from "superstar" faculty members?

3. According to researcher Richard Vedder, only 21 cents of every added dollar that universities have spent over the past twenty-five years has gone to student instruction. Where did the other 79 cents go? If you are an undergraduate today, what tangible benefits of these increased university resources can you see around you?

4. Why do universities discount their fees to attract superstar athletes?

Chapter 19

KEEPING THE COMPETITION OUT

Most competitors hate **competition.** And who can blame them? After all, if a firm can keep the competition out, **profits** are sure to rise. How high they will rise obviously varies by industry, but the lowly taxicab market gives some indication of what is at stake.

In New York City, the number of taxicabs is limited by law—limited, in fact, to one cab for every six hundred people, in a town where many people don't own cars. To legally operate a taxi in New York, one must own a taxi medallion, a city-issued metal shield affixed to the cab's hood. Although the number of taxi medallions in New York is fixed by law, you are free to buy one from a current owner, assuming that you can come up with the prevailing market price, about $500,000. That price, we should note, does not include the taxi itself, although it does entitle you to the right to work a seventy-hour week, subject to robbery, rude customers, and the erratic driving habits of other cabbies. And lest you think New York taxi drivers are crazy to pay such sums, keep this in mind: Because the city keeps the competition out, the taxi business is so lucrative that the medallions can be used as collateral to borrow at favorable interest rates, and any cabbie who wants to leave the business can immediately find a buyer for his or her medallion, usually at a price that will bring even more profit. In fact, the long-run **rate of return** on New York taxi medallions compares favorably with the long-run rate of return on stocks listed on the New York Stock Exchange.

Keeping the competition out works this way: Reducing the number of firms in an industry decreases the **supply** of the good, thus driving up its price. Firms that remain thus enjoy both a higher price for their product and a larger **market share.** Consumers lose, however, suffering not only from higher prices but also from fewer alternative sources of supply from which to choose. Another group of losers are the firms that are excluded. They are forced to go into lower-paying pursuits for which they are not as well suited. The higher profits enjoyed by the firms that are protected from competition thus come at the expense of consumers and excluded competitors; the net result is also an overall loss to society as a whole, because the limit on competition reduces the total extent of mutually beneficial exchange.

Note that we said that the number of taxi medallions in New York is limited by the government. This is typical. Even though many government agencies (for example, the Federal Trade Commission and the Department of Justice at the federal level) are supposed to promote competition, getting the government involved is usually the most effective way to *stifle* competition. Consider telephones. It used to be that both long-distance and local telephone markets were regulated by the federal government. In 1984, the long-distance market was deregulated, and AT&T had to begin competing with MCI and Sprint for customers. The result was a 40 percent drop in inflation-adjusted long-distance rates. Local telephone service continued to be regulated by the Federal Communications Commission (FCC), however, and over the same period of time, local phone rates *rose* 40 percent in real terms—chiefly because the FCC has kept competition out of the local phone service market.

Keeping the competition out seems to be growing in popularity across America. As the economy has moved from manufacturing to services, the number of people working in licensed professions has risen sharply. Thirty years ago, there were about eighty occupations for which one or more state governments required a license. Today, there are eleven hundred occupations, ranging from secretaries in Georgia to wallpaper hangers in California, which require a license in at least one state. Some 28 percent of U.S. workers, about 43 million individuals, now belong to a licensed profession. Officially, of course, this is all done to protect the consumer from unscrupulous or incompetent practitioners. In fact, such licensing requirements serve chiefly—if not solely—to keep the competition out and raise the earnings of those who manage to get licensed.

Many of the decision makers who work for the government agencies that limit competition are lawyers, so it is not surprising that competition among lawyers is limited. For example, in every state but one (California), the number of law schools is capped by state law, thereby restricting entry into the profession and driving up earnings. Real estate agents are also well represented among the members of state legislatures, and so it may come as no surprise that they, too, have been successful in keeping the competition out. In addition to having to pass examinations to be licensed, real estate agents are prohibited—at their own request— from engaging in all sorts of competitive behavior. In a dozen states, agents are prohibited from discounting their prices even if they perform less than the usual amount of services for their customers. In eight states, real estate agents are not permitted to perform fewer services than the local realty association specifies, even if the customer does not want those services. These crimps on competition make life both comfortable and profitable for real estate agents, but it's not such a good deal for home buyers and sellers. In the United States, the average real estate agent's commission is 5.1 percent of the sale price of the home; the average commission in other countries is 3.6 percent. Thus by keeping the competition out, real estate agents in America are able to charge about one-third more for their services than people providing the same services in other nations.

Sometimes the government gets involved in some unlikely markets in its efforts to prevent the ravages of competition from taking their toll. Consider hair braiding. Some African Americans like to have their hair straightened in beauty shops, a procedure that requires a touch-up every four weeks, for an average monthly cost (excluding cutting and styling) of about $100. An alternative is to get one's hair braided at a braiding salon. There are now about ten thousand of these salons across the country. Braids need maintenance only once every ten weeks, cutting the cost to $50 per month. The same low cost and convenience that make braiding salons attractive to consumers also make them threatening to the conventional beauty shops that straighten hair, especially in fashion-conscious California. Claiming that they are seeking to protect consumers, agents of the California Barbering and Cosmetology Board regularly raid the salons of unlicensed hair braiders. Not surprisingly, the hair braiders think the state is actually trying to protect state-licensed cosmetologists at beauty shops, who must spend $6,000 for sixteen hundred hours of training to get their licenses. Indeed, one of the braiders, Ali Rasheed, argues that the marketplace is better than state licensing boards at protecting consumers. "It's simple," he says. "If I mess up your hair, you don't come back. You spread the word. And very quickly I'd be out of business." Perhaps so, but it looks like the state of California doesn't want to give consumers that option.

Back in New York, there is an example of the fact that the government likes to protect itself from competition, too. New York City is well known for its massive public transit system, comprising both subways and bus lines. What is not so well known is that mass transit in New York City started off as private enterprise. The first horsecars and elevated trains in the city were developed by private companies. Moreover, even though New York's first subway was partly financed by a loan from the city, it was otherwise a private operation, operated profitably at a fare of a nickel (the equivalent of less than a dollar today).

New York's politicians refused to allow fares to rise during the inflation of World War I, yielding financial losses for the private transit companies. Promising to show the private sector how to run a transit system efficiently while simultaneously offering to protect the public from the "dictatorship" of the transit firms, the city took over the subway, merged it with the bus line, and promptly started raising fares. Despite fare increases double the inflation rate, however, costs have risen even faster, so that today, even though the basic fare is $2, the city *loses* $2 a passenger because fares don't cover costs.

Enter the jitneys, privately owned vans that operate along regular routes, like buses, but charge as little as $1 a passenger and make detours for pickups and dropoffs on request. Actually, we should have said "attempted entry" by the jitneys, because the New York City Council—at the insistence of the public transit system—has denied operating permits to almost all jitney operators who have applied. The council says it is only seeking to prevent the vans from causing accidents and traffic problems, but even fully insured drivers who have met federal requirements for operating interstate van services are routinely denied permits. Thus most of the hundreds of jitneys operating in New York City are doing so illegally. Even the few jitneys that have managed to get licensed are forbidden from operating along public bus routes—in the name of public safety, of course.

Transportation economists such as Daniel Klein have argued that public transit systems could once more be profitable—instead of losing an average of 50 cents on the dollar—if the jitneys were given a chance. "Government has demonstrated that it has no more business producing transit than producing cornflakes. It should concentrate instead on establishing new rules to foster competition," says Klein. Unfortunately for the jitneys and their customers, however, that competition would come at the expense of New York's public transit system. Thus for the foreseeable future, it seems the jitneys will have to compete only by breaking the laws, because, like most competitors, the New York City mass transit system just hates competition.

DISCUSSION QUESTIONS

1. Consider two different ways of beating your competition. One way is to offer your customers lower prices and better service. The other is to get a law passed that raises your competitors' costs—for example, by imposing special operating requirements on them. Can you see any difference between these two methods, assuming that both succeed in keeping your competition out?

2. Although governments at all levels sometimes act to prevent some individuals from competing with others, the federal government is probably the most active in this role, state governments are less active, and local governments are the least active. Can you explain this pattern?

3. Is there any difference between prohibiting entry by a group of firms and levying a special tax on those firms?

4. Manicurists and pedicurists are required to be licensed in both California and Florida. In California, people practicing these occupations must take 600 hours of classroom training; in Florida, they must take only 240 hours of classroom training. *Ceteris paribus* (that is, holding other factors constant), in which state would you expect pedicures and manicures to be more expensive? Explain. How could you use per capita consumption of pedicures and manicures in the two states to help you decide whether the classroom training requirement was chiefly designed to improve the quality of pedicures and manicures or to keep the competition out?

PART FIVE

Political Economy

Introduction

The chief focus of economics has always been on explaining the behavior of the private sector. Yet dating back at least to the publication of Adam Smith's *Wealth of Nations* in 1776, economists have never missed an opportunity to apply their theories to additional realms of behavior. For the past fifty years or so, much of this effort has been devoted to developing theories that explain the actions of governments, as well as the consequences of those actions. This undertaking is often referred to as the study of **political economy,** for it often involves a mixture of politics and economics. As the selections in Part Five hint, economists do not yet have a unified theory of government. Nevertheless, they are making progress and are sometimes able to offer surprising insights.

Our first venture into the realm of political economy entails a look at a crucial sector of the American economy—housing—in Chapter 20, "Mortgage Meltdown." Between 1995 and 2009, the United States housing market went on the wildest ride in its history: House prices soared and then swiftly crashed. Similarly, home ownership and construction first rose dramatically and then even more quickly sank precipitously. The result, by 2009, was chaos in credit markets and misery and hardship for millions of Americans. Although many people were initially mystified by this series of events, it turns out that the principal culprit was none other than our own Congress. Operating under a banner promoting "affordable housing," Congress implemented policies that caused mortgage lenders to dramatically reduce the financial standards expected of home buyers who wished to obtain a mortgage. These lower standards enabled many more people to qualify for mortgages, increasing the demand for housing and thus leading to the housing boom of 1995–2005.

But these same lower standards meant that people in weaker financial shape were heavily represented among home buyers—which played a central role in the housing crash and mortgage meltdown of 2006–2009. The congressional objective of "affordable housing" was temporarily achieved, but at a long-term cost that will be heavily borne by many of the same people who were supposed to be helped. Once again, we see that in politics as elsewhere, there is no free lunch.

This principle applies just as fully to roads, bridges, dams, and other key parts of our infrastructure. Oddly, however, as we see in Chapter 21, "The Political Economy of Collapsing Bridges," Congress appears able to appreciate the costs in some contexts but not in others. For example, Congress seems happy to authorize plenty of spending on *new* construction, perhaps spurred by the opportunities to name bridges, highways, and dams after former colleagues. But when it comes to infrastructure *repairs,* Congress seems more interested in ignoring the problem. This is perhaps understandable, because the act of patching potholes doesn't present terribly good naming opportunities but does offer the prospect of plenty of traffic congestion—and thus plenty of irritation for constituents. But whether or not this is the cause of the neglect of our nation's infrastructure, one point is abundantly clear: If politicians aren't willing to finance maintenance and repairs with higher taxes today, we will surely pay for the lack of maintenance in reduced safety and convenience for years to come.

Paying for political decisions is again our theme in Chapter 22, "Is Your Bank Manager Headed to Vegas with Your Money?" For quite sensible reasons, the federal government guarantees commercial bank deposits against loss up to high limits. This effectively eliminates the prospect of widespread bank failures like those that helped make the Great Depression of the 1930s so disastrous. But the same insurance that protects bank customers also induces bank managers to behave in much riskier ways than they otherwise would—behavior that can impose substantial costs on taxpayers. Such costly behavior could be reduced if the owners of commercial banks had to pay prices for their deposit insurance that reflected the risks of their behavior. The appropriate pricing of risk is a concept that is well understood by the suppliers (and consumers) of private auto, fire, and life insurance. When insurance prices reflect relative risks, the result is a much more efficient and productive market for insurance. Applying such pricing in the market for deposit insurance would be politically costly for the members of Congress who voted for it, however, and so they don't. Thus we see once again that although nothing in life is free, politicians often act as though this principle doesn't apply to their choices with our money.

Shifting our attention to rural America, it is fair to say that farmers have exploited the nuances of political economy as well as anyone in this nation, a point we elaborate on in Chapter 23, "Raising Less Corn and More Hell." More than seventy years ago, American farmers convinced the federal government to guarantee that farmers receive prices for their crops well above the **equilibrium prices** and that taxpayers and consumers of food should bear the costs of making these high prices stick. Ever since, consumers have faced higher prices for many crops because of various **target prices** and **price-support programs,** and taxpayers have faced higher tax bills as well. Indeed, the average American household pays about $500 a year in higher food prices and higher taxes due to federal programs benefiting "farmers"—even though most of this money actually ends up in the pockets of shareholders in giant agribusiness corporations. Moreover, as the experience of New Zealand reveals, government farm programs are *not* necessary to protect the vitality or **productivity** of the farm sector. Thirty years ago, New Zealand brought a halt to all of its efforts to protect farmers from **competition.** The result was innovation, cost cutting, and aggressive international marketing by New Zealand farmers, who are now stronger and more productive than ever before.

All governments devote some resources to law enforcement, and so crime rates that won't go down, coupled with criminals who seem impervious to law enforcement, have led many people to ask a simple disturbing question: Is there any effective way to fight crime? Although economic theory says the answer to this question is yes, many empirical estimates obtained by economists have said, well, "maybe." Yet as you will see in Chapter 24, "Crime and Punishment," new evidence is shedding light on the answer to this question. Indeed, it is increasingly clear that the two central tools of traditional law enforcement—police to apprehend the criminals and prisons to punish them—may be every bit as effective as their proponents claim in discouraging criminal activity. Two lessons that emerge from this chapter are that politicians are likely to continue pouring more money into law enforcement and that those resources are going to have a growing impact in reducing crime in America.

For thirty years, the nation struggled with the baby boom generation as it graduated from bassinets to BMWs. For the next thirty years, we will have to grapple with the problems that arise as the boomers progress from corporate boardrooms to nursing homes. As we note in Chapter 25, "The Graying of America," the United States is aging at the fastest rate in its history. As the nation ages, two major problems in political economy are emerging. First, there is the matter of paying the Social Security and Medicare bills of the rapidly growing elderly portion of the population. Second, as increasing numbers of people retire, there will be fewer workers capable of bearing the growing tax burden. America must learn new ways of harnessing the productive capabilities of the elderly and accept that as much as we may wish otherwise, the elderly may largely have to fend for themselves.

Chapter 20

MORTGAGE MELTDOWN

Between 1995 and 2009, the United States housing market went on the wildest ride in its history. Over the years 1995 to 2005, median real (inflation-adjusted) house prices soared 60 percent nationwide and then crashed, falling 40 percent in just four years. Over the same period, the proportion of Americans who owned homes, normally a variable that changes quite slowly, leapt from 64 percent to 69 percent and then quickly dropped back to 66 percent. Meanwhile, the number of new houses built each year soared from 1.4 million to 2.2 million and then plunged to below 500,000 per year.

But what really got people's attention—and created huge pressures on financial markets here and abroad—was the fact that just as quickly as people had snapped up houses during the boom years of 1995–2005, they simply *abandoned* their houses beginning in 2006, refusing to make any more payments on their mortgages. In a typical year, about 0.3 percent of homeowners (fewer than one out of three hundred) stop making mortgage payments each year and thus have their houses go into **foreclosure,** a process in which the borrower must give up ownership in a home because of a failure to meet payment obligations. The foreclosure rate doubled to 0.6 percent in 2006, doubled again in 2007, and rose yet again in 2008. In some hard-hit states, such as Nevada, foreclosures exploded to more than *ten times* the normal nationwide rate, with one home out of thirty going into foreclosure each year.

Across the country, people were literally walking away from their homes, leaving them in the hands of banks and other lenders. These lenders then took huge financial losses when forced to sell the abandoned properties in a market in which house prices were already falling. The result was further downward pressure on prices, which gave more owners the incentive to walk away from their homes, which raised foreclosures, and so forth. Within just a few years, the housing market was more depressed than it had been any time since, well, the Great Depression of the 1930s.

What happened? To answer this, we need to examine why, over this fifteen-year period, the housing market first exploded and then imploded, causing financial chaos on a worldwide scale. Although numerous factors played a role, the principal culprit was none other than our own Congress. Operating under a banner promoting "affordable housing," Congress first amended key mortgage-lending legislation and then put considerable implicit and explicit pressure on government-sponsored mortgage agencies to make more loans to potential home buyers. These actions encouraged mortgage lenders to dramatically reduce the financial standards expected of home buyers who wished to obtain mortgages. These lower standards enabled many more people to obtain mortgage funding, increasing the demand for housing and leading to the housing boom of 1995–2005. But these same lower standards meant that people in weaker financial shape were heavily represented among home buyers, which in turn played a central role in the housing crash and mortgage meltdown of 2006–2009. To see how this evolved, we are going to have to do some digging in the history books.

Prior to World War II, most home mortgages were of short duration, such as a year or two (as opposed to fifteen to thirty years, which is common now). During the Great Depression, many risk-weary lenders refused to renew mortgages when they came due. The state of the economy was such that most borrowers were unable to pay the balance immediately, and so their homes were foreclosed. In response, the U.S. government in 1934 created the Federal Housing Administration (FHA) to guarantee some home mortgages from default and in 1938 created the Federal National Mortgage Association (FNMA, known as Fannie Mae) to purchase mortgages from the FHA, enabling the latter to guarantee still more mortgages. In 1968, Congress authorized Fannie Mae to buy mortgages from virtually all lenders, and in 1970, Congress created Freddie Mac (the Federal Home Mortgage Loan Corporation) to offer competition to Fannie Mae. Both Fannie Mae and Freddie Mac are referred to as "government-sponsored enterprises" (GSEs); both are technically independent of the federal government, but both are subject to congressional oversight and, it turns out, to political pressure to do what Congress wants them to do.

The next key congressional action came in 1977 when the Community Reinvestment Act (CRA) was passed, a law that required banks to lend in all neighborhoods of the geographic areas where they operated, even areas where risks were likely to be much higher than the banks would normally undertake. In 1995, the CRA was amended so that banks were, in effect, *compelled* to ignore their lending standards when making loans in low-income and minority neighborhoods or else face the wrath of government regulators. Not long thereafter, Congress began putting considerable pressure on Fannie Mae and Freddie Mac to buy up the low-quality mortgages being made under the CRA, in the hopes that this would encourage lenders to make still more low-quality loans. And indeed it did: The banks soon recognized that with the two GSEs standing ready to take the worst of their mortgages off their hands, they could earn hefty fees for originating the mortgages and then dump the risks of default off onto Fannie Mae and Freddie Mac. At this point, many potential lenders, including banks, savings and loans, and mortgage brokers, concluded that if Fannie Mae and Freddie Mac were happy to buy up risky mortgages at the drop of a hat, so to speak, then it was OK to hold on to some of the risky mortgages they were making. After all, these mortgages (called subprime mortgages) fattened profits with their above-average interest rates; and if the market turned sour, the GSEs would presumably stand ready to take them off lenders' hands.

Thus we see that it was regulatory and legislative pressure from the federal government (spearheaded by Congress) that pushed mortgage lenders to cut their lending standards in truly remarkable ways. For example, lenders have historically insisted on down payments ranging from 5 percent to 20 percent on home loans. This gives borrowers an incentive to keep making monthly payments (or else they lose their down payment upon foreclosure), and it provides a cushion for the lender (to ensure it gets all its money back upon foreclosure). Under pressure from federal regulators, however, lenders were induced to cut required down payments and even to make so-called piggyback loans, giving borrowers a *second* mortgage on top of the first whose sole function was to provide cash for the down payment. In effect, down payments were driven to zero or close thereto.

But there was more. Federal regulators pushed banks to ignore mortgage applicants' credit histories if they were less than stellar; to forgo confirmation of applicants' current or past employment or income levels; to permit applicants to have lower income-to-loan ratios; and to count as part of income such sources as unemployment insurance and welfare payments, despite the temporary nature of such payments. Banks that had never before offered loans under such conditions soon made them routinely, pushed by the requirements of the CRA and pulled by the willingness of Fannie Mae and Freddie Mac to acquire the loans as soon as the ink was dry. And because the GSEs were so active in making the market for loans, many lenders felt comfortable in making and holding on to such loans, even buying more loans from other lenders.

Congress's avowed intention in this process was to "help promote affordable housing," especially for low-income and minority individuals. Congress claimed to be particularly interested in making home ownership possible for people who had been renters all their lives. And indeed, low-income and minority individuals were for the first time able to own their homes—at least for a while. But once banks became comfortable with making and disposing of high-risk loans, they quickly became amenable to making such loans to anyone who showed up, first-time buyer or not. And if the loan was to buy a house in a low-income or minority neighborhood, it became that much more attractive, because of the possibility that it would keep the bean-counting regulators happy. Thus beginning in the late 1990s and accelerating rapidly in 2002 (when the house price trajectory shot up), speculators—people buying a second or third house in the hopes of selling it quickly for a profit—became an increasingly important part of the market. Indeed, it is now estimated that one-quarter of all borrowers over this period were making speculative purchases of this sort.

Not surprisingly, speculators wanted to make low down payments and to obtain **adjustable-rate mortgages (ARMs).** Not only did ARMs offer slighter lower initial interest rates and payments (because borrowers absorbed the risk of higher rates in the future), but they also gave lenders the flexibility to offer low "teaser" interest rates (and thus ultra-low payments) during the first few years of the mortgage. Such mortgages were considerably riskier for borrowers because of the risk of higher payments later, when the mortgages "popped" (automatically adjusted their interest rates to full long-run levels). But by then, of course, speculators hoped to have sold for a profit and paid off the mortgage. The spread of ARMs, especially those with low teaser rates, was accelerated by people who bought homes hoping to refinance at a low fixed rate later, after rising home prices built equity for them in their houses.

All went well until 2005, when many of the early ARMs began to pop (with payments adjusting upward sharply). Some borrowers found that they were unable to make the higher payments and were thus forced to sell their homes. This slowed the rise in house prices by 2006, making housing less attractive as an investment, which in turn reduced the speculative demand and put further downward pressure on prices. In markets such as Arizona, California, Florida, and Nevada, where speculative activity had been the greatest, house prices started to *fall,* and growing numbers of individuals (especially those who put up low or no down payments) found themselves "upside down," owing more on their mortgages than their houses were worth. By the middle of 2006, the prudent financial course for such people was to stop making payments (especially on

ARMs that had popped) and to simply walk away when the lender began foreclosure proceedings.

Many accounts of this process in the popular press have claimed that it is exclusively high-risk, subprime mortgages that are at the root of the crisis. This sounds sensible enough, because subprime mortgages have always had relatively high foreclosure rates; indeed, the subprime foreclosure rate has historically been about eight times as high as the rate on prime mortgages (1.6 percent per year versus 0.2 percent per year). Hence subprime mortgages now, as in normal times, are disproportionately represented among foreclosures. But a closer look at the data also reveals that foreclosures on *both* types of mortgages shot upward in the middle of 2006, with foreclosures on subprime mortgages soon reaching 4 percent and those on prime mortgages hitting 0.5 percent. Thus it appears that both types of borrowers began to get in trouble at the same time; not just subprime mortgages were affected.

The data also reveal that it is chiefly borrowers who obtained adjustable-rate mortgages who have been at the root of the meltdown. Prior to 2006, foreclosures on ARMs and on fixed-rate mortgages were occurring at about the same rate. But beginning in early 2006, even as the foreclosure rate on fixed-rate mortgages hardly budged, the rate on ARMs exploded: on prime ARMs, the rate leapt by a factor of 5, while the foreclosure rate on subprime ARMs tripled. Moreover, it was on ARMs that foreclosures started up first (at the very beginning of 2006). Forced sales on these homes started the downward pressure on house prices, which gave more owners the incentive to walk away from their homes, which raised foreclosures, and so forth. Soon enough, the entire market had begun to implode.

By the time you read this, we expect (and hope!) that the housing market will have shown signs of recovery. But we also hope that the lesson of this episode will not be forgotten. The road to the mortgage meltdown of 2006–2009 was paved by our very own U.S. Congress, which sought to subvert the market to achieve its political goals. The methods used are perhaps little different than Congress usually employs when it hopes to achieve politically popular social objectives. But the very real difference of this episode is the enormous social cost that it has brought on Americans of all races and all income levels. Literally millions of Americans had their hopes of home ownership first artificially raised and then cruelly dashed. The financial losses and emotional stresses inflicted on individuals, the blighted neighborhoods littered with abandoned houses, and the turmoil felt throughout the states most affected are all costs that will imprint the American scene for years to come.

DISCUSSION QUESTIONS

1. It seems likely that members of Congress, even the strongest supporters of the CRA and those who put the most pressure on the GSEs to buy high-risk mortgages, will likely escape being held responsible for any part of the mortgage meltdown. Can you suggest why?

2. Many large lenders, along with Fannie Mae and Freddie Mac, obtained funding for their activities by selling bonds that offered as collateral the mortgages that were made using those funds. These bonds are often referred to as "mortgage-backed securities." Many billions of dollars of these mortgage-backed securities were purchased by citizens and governments of foreign lands. Explain how this fact helped the financial crisis in America spread to other nations.

3. In light of the fact that foreclosure rates have been much higher on ARMs than on fixed-rate mortgages, what do you predict will happen in the future to the proportion of mortgages that are of each type? Explain.

4. In effect, the CRA and the actions of Fannie Mae and Freddie Mac acted to subsidize home purchases by people who otherwise would not have purchased houses. All subsidies must be financed by taxes, implicit or explicit, on someone. Who is paying the "taxes" in this case? Explain.

Chapter 21

THE POLITICAL ECONOMY OF COLLAPSING BRIDGES

On August 1, 2007, in the middle of Minneapolis rush hour traffic, the 1,907-foot-long I-35W bridge over the Mississippi River collapsed. Thirteen people died; another hundred were injured. That this tragedy occurred on this specific day was, of course, wholly unexpected. But bridge collapses are commonplace. In fact, about 150 of them occur every year in America. Most are small bridges, and few of the collapses kill anyone. Even so, about one-third of the 40,000 traffic fatalities in the United States every year are attributed to substandard road conditions, bridges included. One might expect to hear numbers like these associated with a developing nation, not the world's richest nation. Yet America's infrastructure—our roads, bridges, sewer and water systems, airports, and dams—are in bad shape, and for many years, we have done little to fix the problem.

Consider our highways. The American Society of Civil Engineers (ASCE) estimates that one-third of major roads in the United States are in substandard condition. Of the 600,000 bridges in America that tie our highway system together, nearly one-quarter are officially designated as structurally deficient or obsolete. More than 1,500 miles of our 46,000-mile-long interstate system are judged by engineers to be in "poor" condition. Bringing America's bridges up to standard would cost about $188 billion, and there are currently $68 billion worth of backlogged repairs just on the interstate highway system.

The crumbling infrastructure stretches far and wide. There are 80,000 dams in the United States, for example, and more than 30 percent of them are over fifty years old. About 12,000 of these are considered high-hazard dams, meaning that authorities predict loss of life if they were to fail. Only about twenty-five dams fail every year in America, but that number is expected to rise significantly in coming years because more than 17,000 dams will soon reach the end of their design lives. And although most dams are subject to periodic inspection, even the dams with the highest potential hazard ratings are typically inspected no more than once every five years.

America's sewer and water systems are aging rapidly too, especially in the major cities of the Northeast and upper Midwest. In many cities, for example, the same aged system of pipes is used for both rainwater and sewage, with the mix treated in the sewage system treatment plants. But rain can fill the pipes quickly, and when they reach capacity, the befouled overload must be released directly into the waterways. In one recent year, the swimming leg of the New York City Triathlon was called off because of excess sewage in the Hudson River after an overnight rain. In other cities, aging pipes leak untreated sewage directly into the surrounding soils and possibly groundwater systems.

In 2005, the ASCE issued a report on America's infrastructure, ranging from roads to airports to waterworks; it handed out grades of C or D in fourteen of fifteen categories. Repairs and maintenance on so much of the system have been put off for so long that the ASCE now estimates it would cost at least $160 billion a year over the next five years to fix the existing problems. That works out to $2,000 per year for a family of four, a sizable tax bill increase.

At first blush, it might seem as though it is indeed the high cost of maintenance that is responsible for our collective neglect. But this notion is difficult to reconcile with our willingness to build in the first place. The construction of our interstate highway system, for example, cost $425 billion in today's dollars. And that doesn't include the tens of thousands of miles of other federal, state, and local roads constructed over the same period. Moreover, we weren't just building roads. Since World War II, we have built dozens of major airports, expanded water and sewer systems, and constructed nearly a thousand new dams every year. If we can build these things, why can't we maintain them?

The answer lies at the heart of **political economy**—the study of the causes and consequences of political decision making. Politicians have relatively short time horizons, compared to business owners. As a rough approximation, most politicians rarely look much beyond their next reelection bid when making decisions about what to support or oppose. This leads to a bias in decision making that favors projects or programs with relatively high immediate payoffs to voters; indeed, simply handing out cash to constituents may be best of all. As we discuss in Chapter 23, this helps explain why agricultural subsidies are so popular with Congress.

It is likely that the only reason capital projects such as buildings, roads, and other infrastructure get undertaken at all is that it is easy for Congress to justify borrowing the funds for them and thus putting off the taxes, hopefully until after the next election. And of course, such projects offer plenty of "naming" opportunities, as when buildings, highways, dams, or interchanges are named after or on behalf of politicians and their friends and supporters. A politician may fondly contemplate the proposed "Bill Smith interstate highway," but who would back passage of the "Sally Jones pothole rehabilitation project"? The lack of interest in such repair and maintenance activities is likely to be amplified by the fact that almost all such projects involve considerable disruption and inconvenience to current voters. No one wants to be remembered on Election Day as the person responsible for adding thirty minutes to the daily commute of constituents.

Then there is the matter of paying for the repairs, which ultimately means collecting funds from someone. We all use the basic public infrastructure of the economy, but some of us use it much more intensively than others. Some people drive only a few thousand miles a year, while others drive more than twenty thousand miles per year. Similarly, roads carry 75 percent of all freight in the United States, some 92 percent by value, but we each consume widely varying amounts of what is carried. Hence a sensible way to pay for things like roads is to have something approximating **user fees,** charges to individuals based on some measure of the amount or intensity of their usage. The gasoline taxes levied by federal and state governments try to do this. When people pay a tax of 42 cents per gallon, for example, if they drive twelve thousand miles a year and their car gets twenty miles to the gallon, their tax bill is $252 a year, whereas if they drive twenty thousand miles per year in the same car, they pay $420 in federal gas taxes.

But here is the problem Congress and even the states face: When gas taxes are increased, current voters see the costs immediately at the pumps, whereas the benefits might not show up for many years. And if the funds are spent on maintenance or a repair project, what is likely to show up first is traffic congestion and aggravation. This helps explain why the federal gas tax gets changed only about once every ten years. But because there is inflation most years, the purchasing power of that tax is eroding steadily between increases. For example, the federal gas tax was held at 18.5 cents per gallon from 1993 to 2009, which meant that its purchasing power fell by over one-third during that period. And less real funding means less real maintenance.

There are two ways that the financing obstacles to infrastructure maintenance might be reduced. The first of these is to apply user fees more widely—for example, by implementing more toll roads, on which people effectively pay by the mile. Technology has so advanced that it is cheap to attach transponders to vehicles, devices that automatically record passage of a car or truck beneath an overhead monitoring device (even at full highway speeds), and then bill the owner monthly for the charges. These devices are coming into use on newer roads in the United States, Europe, and Asia, and they have two salutary effects: They provide funding for construction and maintenance of the roads on which they are used, and they help reduce road congestion because they discourage frivolous trips. Tolls are widely recognized as having improved traffic flows in London, Singapore, Southern California, and many places in between.

A second reform that could be implemented is to index user fees to a measure of the price level, such as the **consumer price index.** For example, because the government knows it will be making Social Security payments year after year, these payments are currently indexed (automatically increased) to keep their value from eroding due to inflation. Similarly, the wage base on which Social Security taxes is levied is also automatically adjusted upward each year, because this is understood to be an ongoing program, which must be paid for. In the case of infrastructure, it is widely known that once a road, dam, or comparable structure is built, it is generally efficient to conduct regular maintenance on it over time—costs that will steadily escalate at roughly the rate of inflation. Linking gas taxes and other user fees to the overall price level is a simple way for legislators to provide regular increments to maintenance funding for infrastructure without having to propose large, politically dangerous changes in taxes.

Although private owners of capital goods (such as homes and office buildings) sometimes defer repair and maintenance expenditures, especially during periods of slack economic activity, this behavior is less prevalent than with publicly owned capital goods. The reason for the difference is simple. Homeowners will bear the full cost of their negligence if they fail to maintain their homes, because the market value of those houses will decline to reflect that failure. But if a road falls into disrepair, no such market forces are automatically brought to bear on a member of Congress or a state legislator. Indeed, a politician who cuts corners on maintenance may be publicly lauded for the savings thereby made possible. In the meantime, that bridge in Minneapolis has been replaced with a new one, but if the bridge you cross on the way to work or school is not quite so new, you might want to think of speeding up a bit as you traverse it—just to be on the safe side.

DISCUSSION QUESTIONS

1. What political forces help prevent the more widespread implementation of user fees? (*Hint:* Are the costs of such fees dispersed among many voters or concentrated on a few?)

2. Currently, it is difficult to sue the federal government unless it agrees to be sued. If the law were changed so that lawsuits (such as by victims of the collapse of the I-35W bridge) were easier, how would this change the **incentives** of the government to properly maintain bridges, roads, and dams? How likely is the government to agree to such a legal change?

3. Based on the arguments of this chapter, do the incentives of U.S. senators (who serve six-year terms) differ from those of the members of the House of Representatives (who serve two-year terms) when it comes to engaging in long-term planning of construction and maintenance projects? Would the imposition of term limits, which constrain politicians in the number of years they can serve, improve or impair their long-term incentives?

4. Explain the difference between the incentives of the owner of a house and a renter of a house to undertake expenditures designed to improve or maintain the house. For example, are renters more likely to replace light bulbs or wall-to-wall carpets when they wear out? When renters spend funds on a new bookcase, is it likely to be built-in or portable? What are the parallels between incentives here and the incentives of Congress when it comes to current expenditures versus capital expenditures?

IS YOUR BANK MANAGER HEADED TO VEGAS WITH YOUR MONEY?

Incentives shape human behavior. We see this around us every day. Higher gas prices spur sales of fuel-efficient cars. "Two for one" specials on food or drink encourage people to eat and drink more. Prospects for promotion and higher pay induce employees to work harder. The loom of an upcoming exam encourages students to spend less time in the fitness center and more time in the library. These and other obvious examples of the importance of changing incentives are everywhere. But sometimes changes in incentives are far more subtle.

Consider the fact that during the Panic of 2008, the federal government announced a key new policy: It was insuring against loss all bank deposits up to $250,000 per account. So if your depository institution happened to be holding some toxic (possibly even worthless) mortgage-backed bonds, you were home free. The bank could suffer terrible losses or even go out of business, and yet your accounts, up to $250,000 each, would be guaranteed by the full faith and credit of the United States government—which is to say, the U.S. taxpayer.

For reasons we'll soon see, this policy has had the beneficial effect of promoting confidence in the country's financial system and thus worked to stabilize the economy. But government insurance of bank deposits also changes the incentives of bank managers and customers in ways that may not be obvious but are nevertheless both important and costly to society. Bank managers now have *increased* incentives to undertake risky investments with your money, and you have *reduced* incentives to stop them from doing so. Hence government insurance of deposits can actually *add* to the risks in our financial system. To see how this can happen, we must go back to the 1930s, before the notion of deposit insurance had been conceived.

A **bank run** is the simultaneous rush of bank depositors to convert their deposits into currency. Here is the essence of a bank run: regardless of the true state of the bank's financial condition, rumors or fears that a bank is in trouble can cause depositors to suddenly attempt to withdraw all of their funds. But many **assets** of a bank are typically in the form of loans that cannot immediately be converted into cash. Even if **solvent,** with total assets that exceed **liabilities,** the bank is said to be **illiquid** because it doesn't have enough cash on hand to meet the immediate demands of fearful depositors. And when it attempts to get that cash by selling some assets, any resulting decline in the market value of those assets can quickly turn a solvent bank into an **insolvent** one, causing it to fail. There are many famous old black-and-white pictures of hordes of depositors trying to get into banks during the Great Depression in order to withdraw their deposits in the form of currency.

When the number of bank failures hit four thousand in 1933, at the bottom of the Depression, the federal government decided to act to prevent further bank runs. So that year, Congress passed, and the president signed into law, legislation creating the Federal Deposit Insurance Corporation (FDIC) and the next year created the Federal Savings and Loan Insurance Corporation (FSLIC). Many years later, in 1971, the National Credit Union Share Insurance Fund (NCUSIF) was created to insure credit union deposits, and in 1989, the FSLIC was replaced with the Savings Association Insurance Fund (SAIF). To make our discussion simple, we will focus only on the FDIC, but the general principles apply to all of these agencies.

When the FDIC was formed, it insured against loss each account in a commercial bank, up to $2,500. That number has been increased on seven different occasions, reaching $250,000 in 2008. The result of federal deposit insurance is that there has not really been a bank run in the United States since the Great Depression, despite numerous bank failures in the interim. Even during the Panic of 2008, when confidence in many financial institutions collapsed, federally insured depository institutions continued to operate; indeed, total deposits in them actually rose. The good news about federal deposit insurance is that it has prevented bank runs. But this has come at a significant cost, arising largely due to the unintended consequences of deposit insurance.

To see these, let's begin by supposing that someone offers you what he or she claims is a great investment opportunity. That person tells you that if you invest $50,000, you will make a very high rate of return, say, 20 percent per year, much higher than the 3 percent your funds are currently earning elsewhere. No matter how much you trusted the person offering you this deal, you would probably do some serious investigation of the proposed investment before you handed over fifty thousand hard-earned dollars. You, like other people, would carefully evaluate the risk factors involved in this potential opportunity.

For example, if you use part of your savings to buy a house, you will undoubtedly have the structural aspects of the house checked out by an inspector before you sign on the dotted line. Similarly, if you planned to purchase an expensive piece of art, you surely would have an independent expert verify that the artwork is authentic. Typically, the same is true every time you place your accumulated savings into any potential investment: You look before you leap. In circumstances such as these, there is initially **asymmetric information**—in this case, the seller knows much more than the potential buyer. But with diligence, the buyer can eliminate much of this gap in knowledge and make a wise decision.

Now ask yourself the following question: When is the last time you examined the financial condition or lending activities of the depository institution at which you have your checking or savings account? We predict that the answer is never. Indeed, why should you investigate? Because of federal deposit insurance, you know that even if the depository institution that has your funds is taking big risks, you are personally risking nothing. If that depository institution fails, the federal government will—with 100 percent certainty—make sure that you get 100 percent of your deposits back.

So here we have it, the first unintended consequence of deposit insurance. Depositors like you no longer have any substantial incentive to investigate the track record of the owners or managers of banks. You care little about whether they have a history of risky or imprudent behavior because at worst you may suffer some minor inconvenience if your bank fails. So unlike in the days before deposit insurance, the marketplace today does little to monitor or punish the past performance of owners or managers of depository institutions. As a result, we tend to get **adverse selection**—instead of banks being owned and operated by individuals who are prudent at making careful decisions on behalf of depositors, many of them end up being run by people who have a high tolerance for taking big risks with other people's funds—and are good at persuading them to take those risks.

Now let's look at bank managers' incentives to act cautiously when making loans. You must first note that the riskier the loan, the higher the interest rate the bank can charge. For example, if a developing country with a blemished track record in paying its debts wishes to borrow from a U.S. depository institution, that country will have to pay a much higher interest rate than a less risky debtor nation would. The same is true when a risky company comes looking for a loan: If it gets one at all, it will be at a higher-than-average interest rate.

When trying to decide which loan applicants should receive funds, bank managers must weigh the trade-off between risk and return. Poor credit risks offer high profits if they actually pay off their debts, but good credit risks are more likely to pay off their debts. The right choice means higher profits for the bank and likely higher salaries and promotions for the managers. The wrong choice means losses and perhaps insolvency for the bank and new, less desirable careers for the managers.

To understand how bank mangers' incentives are changed by deposit insurance—even for managers who would otherwise be prudent and conservative—consider two separate scenarios. In the first scenario, the bank manager is told to take $50,000 of depositors' funds to Las Vegas. The rules of the game are that she can bet however she wants, and the bank will share the winnings *and losses* equally with the deposit holders whose funds she has in trust. In the second scenario, the same bank manager with the same funds is given a different set of rules. In this case, the bank doesn't have to share in any of the losses, but it will share in any of the gains from betting in Las Vegas.

Under which set of rules do you think the bank officer will take the higher risks while betting in Las Vegas? Clearly, she will take higher risks in the second scenario, because her bank will not suffer at all if she loses the entire $50,000. Yet if she hits it big, say, by placing a successful bet on double-zero in roulette, her bank will share the profits, and she is likely to get a raise and a promotion.

Well, the second scenario is exactly the one facing the managers of federally insured depository institutions, especially since the fall of 2008. If they make risky loans, thereby earning, at least in the short run, higher profits, they share in the "winnings." The result for them is higher salaries. If, in contrast, some of these risky loans are not repaid, what is the likely outcome? The bank's losses are limited, because the federal government (which is to say, you, the taxpayer) will cover any shortfall between the bank's assets and its liabilities. Thus federal deposit insurance means that banks get to enjoy all of the profits of risk without bearing all of the consequences.

So the second unintended consequence of deposit insurance is to encourage **moral hazard.** Specifically, bank managers of all types (risk lovers or not) have an incentive to take higher risks in their lending policies than they otherwise would. Indeed, when the economy turned down in the early 1980s, we got to see the consequences of exactly this change in incentives. From 1985 until the beginning of 1993, some 1,065 depository institutions failed, at an average rate of more than ten times that for the preceding forty years. The losses from these failures ran to billions of dollars—paid for in large part by you, the taxpayer.

What, then, might be expected from the 2008 insurance hike to $250,000? In the short run, confidence in banks was renewed and depositors were encouraged to keep more funds in banks. This was good news, for it helped the economy adjust to the financial shocks of 2008 and 2009. But the bad news will be forthcoming in the long run: The higher deposit insurance limits will encourage both adverse selection (more risk-loving bank managers) and moral hazard (more risk-taking by bank managers of all stripes). Eventually, the lending standards of banks will deteriorate to the point that losses mount once again—paid for in large part by you, the taxpayer.

So the moral of this story is simple. While your banker is headed to Vegas, you'd better plan on staying at home to work. Sooner or later, as a U.S. taxpayer, your bill for deposit insurance will come due.

DISCUSSION QUESTIONS

---

1. Who pays when an insured depository institution fails and its depositors are nonetheless reimbursed for the full amount of their deposits? How does your answer depend on how much the institutions are charged for the insurance provided by the government?

2. In a world without deposit insurance, what are some of the mechanisms that would arise to "punish" bank managers who acted irresponsibly? (*Hint:* There are similar types of mechanisms for consumer goods and in the stock market.)

3. Explain how "experience rating" of insurance—charging higher premiums to higher-risk customers—affects the incidence of both adverse selection and moral hazard.

4. If the professor in one of your courses "insured" student grades by guaranteeing that no one in the course would receive less than a B+, how would this policy change the number and type of students who enroll in the course and their study habits in the course? Explain.

Chapter 2 3

RAISING LESS
CORN AND MORE
HELL

When politician Mary Lease stumped the Kansas countryside in 1890, she urged the farmers to raise "less corn and more hell," and that is just what they have been doing ever since.

The two decades before World War I witnessed unparalleled agricultural prosperity in the United States. This "golden age of American farming" continued through the war as food prices soared. The end of the war, combined with a sharp recession in 1920, brought the golden age to a painful halt. Even the long economic recovery from 1921 to 1929—the Roaring Twenties—did little to help American farmers. European countries were redirecting their resources into agricultural production, and new American **tariffs** on foreign goods severely disrupted international trade. Because food **exports** had been an important source of farmers' incomes, the decline in world trade reduced the **demand** for American agricultural products and cut deeply into food prices and farm income.

The sharply falling food prices of the 1920s led farmers to view their problem as one of overproduction. Numerous cooperative efforts were made, therefore, to restrict production, but virtually all of these efforts failed. Most crops were produced under highly competitive conditions, with large numbers of buyers and sellers dealing in products that were largely undifferentiated: One farmer's corn, for example, was the same as any other farmer's corn. Thus producers were unable to enforce collective output restrictions and price hikes on a voluntary basis. But what farmers failed to do by voluntary means in the 1920s, they accomplished via government directives in the 1930s. An effective farm **price-support program** was instituted in 1933, marking the beginning of a policy of farm **subsidies** in the United States that continues today.

We can understand the results of price supports and other government farm programs by first examining the market for agricultural commodities in the absence of government intervention. In that competitive market, a large number of farmers supply any given commodity, such as corn. The sum of the quantities that individual farmers supply at various prices generates the **market supply** of a commodity. Each farmer supplies only a small part of the market total. No one farmer, therefore, can influence the price of the product. If one farmer were to raise the price, buyers could easily purchase from someone else at the **market-clearing,** or **equilibrium, price.** And no farmers would sell below the market-clearing price. Thus every unit of output sold by farmers goes for the same price. The price received for the last (*marginal*) unit sold is exactly the same as that received for all the rest. The farmer will produce corn up to the point that if one more unit were produced, its production cost would be greater than the price received. Notice that at higher prices, farmers can incur higher costs for additional units produced and still make a **profit.** Because all farmers face the same basic production decision, all farmers together will produce more at higher prices. Indeed, no farmer will stop producing until he or she stops making a profit on additional units. That is, each farmer will end up selling corn at the market-clearing price, which will equal the costs of production plus a normal profit.[1]

Now, how has the price-support program worked? Under such a program, the government has to decide what constitutes a "fair price." Initially, this decision was linked to the prices farmers received during "good" years—such as during agriculture's golden age. Eventually, the government-established price was determined through intense negotiations between members of Congress from farm states and those from nonfarm states. The key point here is that except for the years of World War II, the "fair" price decreed by the government has generally been well above the equilibrium price that would have prevailed in the absence of price supports. This has encouraged farmers to produce more, which ordinarily would simply push prices back down.

How has the government made its price "stick"? There have been two methods. For the first several decades of farm programs, it agreed to buy the crops, such as corn, at a price, called the **support price,** that was high enough to keep farmers happy but not so high as to enrage too many taxpayers. As a practical matter, these purchases have been disguised as "loans" from a government agency—loans that never need to be repaid. The government then either stored the crops it purchased, sold them on the world market (as opposed to the domestic market) at prices well below the U.S. support price, or simply gave them away to foreign nations under the Food for Peace program. In each instance, the result

---

1. For society as a whole, normal profit is actually a **cost** of production, because it is required to keep the farmer growing corn instead of changing to an alternative occupation.

was substantial costs for taxpayers and substantial gains for farmers. Under the price-support system, the American taxpayers routinely spent more than $10 billion *each year* for the benefit of corn farmers alone. Smaller but still substantial subsidies were garnered by the producers of wheat, peanuts, soybeans, sorghum, rice, and cotton, to name but a few.

In an effort to keep the size of the **surpluses** down, the government has often restricted the number of acres that farmers may cultivate. Under these various **acreage-restriction programs,** farmers wishing to participate in certain government subsidy programs have been required to keep a certain amount of land out of production. About 80 million acres, an area the size of New Mexico, have at one time or another been covered by the agreements. Enticed by high support prices, farmers have found ingenious ways to evade acreage restrictions. For example, soybeans and sorghum are both excellent substitutes for corn as a source of livestock feed. So farmers agreed to cut their corn acreage and then planted soybeans or sorghum on the same land. This action increased the corn surplus and forced the government to extend acreage restrictions and price supports to soybeans and sorghum. Similarly, faced with limitations on the amount of land they could cultivate, farmers responded by cultivating the smaller remaining parcels of land far more intensively. They used more fertilizers and pesticides, introduced more sophisticated methods of planting and irrigation, and applied technological advances in farm machinery at every opportunity. As a result, agricultural output per man-hour is now *twelve times* what it was sixty years ago.

There were a couple of problems with the original price-support system. First, because it kept crop prices high, it kept consumers' food bills high as well. People were spending an extra $10 billion or more on food each year. Another problem with the price-support system was that the surplus crops piled up year after year in government warehouses. Not only was storing the surpluses expensive, but it also eventually became politically embarrassing. For example, at one point, the federal government had enough wheat in its storage bins to make seven loaves of bread for every man, woman, and child *in the world*.

In the early 1980s, the federal government switched to a second system, in which it set a **target price** that was guaranteed to farmers but let the price paid by consumers adjust to whatever lower level it took to get consumers to buy all of the crops. Then the government simply sent a check to farmers for the difference between the target price and the **market price**. This brought consumers' food bills down and eliminated government storage of surplus crops, but it also meant that the cost to taxpayers—up to $25 billion per year—was painfully clear in the huge checks being written to farmers.

The original price-support program hid its subsidies by making it appear as though the crop surpluses were the result of American farmers' simply being "too productive" for their own good. With the direct payments made under the target-price system, however, it became apparent that the government was taking cash out of taxpayers' pockets with one hand and giving it to farmers with the other. Moreover, the target-price system, like our other agricultural programs, geared the size of the subsidies to the amount of output produced by the recipients. Thus small farmers received trivial amounts, while giant farms—agribusinesses—collected enormous subsidies. The owners of many huge cotton farms and rice farms, for example, received payments totaling more than $1 million apiece.

This fact illustrates who actually benefits from federal farm programs. Although these programs have traditionally been promoted as a way to guarantee decent earnings for low-income farmers, most of the benefits have in fact gone to the owners of very large farms, and the larger the farm, the bigger the benefit. In addition, *all* of the benefits from price supports ultimately accrue to *landowners* on whose land price-supported crops are grown.

In 1996, Congress made what turned out to be a futile attempt to reduce agricultural subsidies, enacting the seven-year Freedom to Farm Act. The reforms were supposed to increase farmer flexibility and remove market distortions by moving away from price-support payments for wheat, corn, and cotton. In their place, farmers would receive "transition payments." The taxpayer was supposed to save billions of dollars.

It was not to be. Beginning in 1998, Congress passed large farm "supplemental bills" each year, each costing billions of dollars per year that go directly from your paycheck to the bank accounts of the largest agribusiness corporations in America. Then, in 2002, Congress passed what was then the most expensive farm bill in the history of the United States, with an advertised price tag of over $191 billion for a ten-year period. President Bush said, when he signed the bill, "This nation has got to eat." He further said, "Our farmers and ranchers are the most efficient producers in the world . . . . We are really good at it."

Congress got even better at subsidizing farmers in 2008 when, despite a veto by President Bush, it passed the Food, Security and Bioenergy Act—with an advertised ten-year cost of more than $300 billion. The new legislation gave the growers of many crops a choice of federal subsidy programs. Depending on the crop, they can select a mix of what amount to target-price or support-price programs, or they can choose a program offering guaranteed revenues. If crop prices are high, farmers get to sell at those prices, but if prices are low, they get a check that increases their earnings to the guaranteed level.

One of the claims often used to promote farm subsidies is that farming earns its practitioners relatively low incomes. In fact, farmers' household incomes have been averaging 20 percent *above* household incomes for nonfarm families over the past decade, and given the size of the subsidies, it is not hard to see why. In one recent year, when farm profits were $72 billion, the federal government handed out $25 billion in subsidies to farmers, almost 50 percent more than it spent on welfare payments for poor families. Millionaires such as Ted Turner and David Rockefeller receive hundreds of thousands of dollars a year in taxpayer-financed agricultural subsidies. When we add the billions in direct subsidies to the billions in higher food prices that result from the farm program, we find that the average American household will pay more than $5,000 in higher food prices and taxes under the latest farm bill. And still, two-thirds of all farm subsidies will go to the top 10 percent of farms, most which earn over $250,000 annually. Thus large agribusinesses continue to be the chief beneficiaries of our generous agricultural policy.

Farmers can now receive payments for *not* growing crops they used to grow. In fact, if they sell their land to someone else, the right to receive these payments goes with the land. So in many cases, even if the land is subsequently carved up into lots on which people build homes, the happy homeowners are eligible for these "direct payments," made because years ago the land was used to grow, say, rice. The price tag in one recent year: $1.3 billion. Farmers also receive payments to compensate them for losses they don't actually incur. To see how this works, let's suppose the government's target price for corn is $2.60 per bushel and that a farmer manages to sell his crop for $3.00 per bushel during a period of the year when prices were a bit higher than usual. If at any time during the year the price per bushel fell below $2.60, say, to $2.00, the farmer can claim a "deficiency payment" from the government. In this case, the farmer would be eligible for 60 cents per bushel ($2.60 – $2.00) for every bushel produced, even though the corn actually sold for $3.00.

Perhaps we should not complain too much about farm programs in the United States, for at least we don't have Japanese farm programs. In Japan, a combination of subsidies for domestic farmers and tariffs on imported food have pushed farm incomes to a level roughly *double* the average income in the country as a whole. They also have driven up the price of an ordinary melon to $100 (yes, one hundred dollars). Even the Europeans seem to find lavishing largesse on farmers irresistible. In recent years, Americans have been shelling out about $40 billion a year for farm subsidies. The European Union (EU) has been spending more than $130 billion a year on farm subsidies. To be sure, the EU is about 50 percent more populous than the United States, but even adjusting for this, the huge spending there means that the average EU citizen is spending twice as much subsidizing farmers as we spend here.

Politicians from the farming states argue that we cannot abandon our farmers because the United States would end up with too many bankrupt farms and not enough food. But there is evidence from at least one country that such a scenario is simply not correct. In 1984, New Zealand's government ended all farm subsidies of every kind, going completely "cold turkey" without any sort of transition to the new era of free markets for food. Agricultural subsidies in New Zealand had accounted for more than 30 percent of the value of agricultural production, even higher than what has been observed in the United States. The elimination of subsidies in New Zealand occurred rapidly, and there were no extended phaseouts for any crops. Despite this, there was no outbreak of farm bankruptcies. Indeed, only 1 percent of farms have gone out of business in New Zealand since 1984. Instead, the farmers responded by improving their techniques, cutting costs, and aggressively marketing their products in export markets.

The results have been dramatic. The value of farm output in New Zealand has increased by more than 40 percent (in constant-dollar terms) since the subsidy phaseout. The share of New Zealand's total annual output attributed to farming has increased from 14 percent to 17 percent. Land **productivity** has increased at about 6 percent per year. Indeed, according to the Federated Farmers of New Zealand, the country's experience thoroughly debunked the myth that the farming sector cannot prosper without government subsidies.

Are any members of the U.S. Congress listening?

DISCUSSION QUESTIONS

1. American corn farmers receive billions of dollars in taxpayer subsidies each year. These subsidies allow them to sell their grain at prices below what it costs to produce it, particularly for export markets. How do U.S. corn subsidies hurt Mexican farmers?

2. If it is so obvious that farm subsidies hurt consumers, why do such subsidies continue to be voted in by Congress? (*Hint:* Revisit the discussion of **rational ignorance** in Chapter 2, "Ethanol Madness.")

3. What groups would be the major beneficiaries if farm subsidies in the United States were eliminated?

4. Why do you suppose that farmers, rather than economists, receive subsidies from the federal government? (*Hint:* If you are tempted to answer that there are more farmers than economists, ask yourself, what would happen to the number of self-proclaimed economists if the federal government started offering subsidies to economists?)

Chapter 24

CRIME AND PUNISHMENT

The city of Detroit, Michigan, has twice as many police per capita as Omaha, Nebraska, but the violent crime rate in Detroit is four times as high as in Omaha. Does this mean that police are the source of violent crime? If that sounds like an odd question, consider this: During one recent twenty year period, the number of Americans in prison tripled as a share of the population, while the violent crime rate doubled and the property crime rate rose 30 percent. Does sending people to prison actually encourage crime?

Few people would answer either question in the affirmative, yet there is still widespread concern that crime pays and that there is little that policymakers can do about it. In a nation in which about 20 percent of households can expect to be victimized by a serious crime in any given year, it is little wonder that people are asking some tough questions about law enforcement. Do harsher penalties discourage people from committing crimes? Will longer prison sentences reduce the crime rate? Are more police the answer? Crime costs its victims more than $200 billion every year in America, even as we are spending about the same amount in public funds to prevent it, so answers to questions such as these are clearly important.

There is one thing we can be sure of at the start: Uniformly heavy punishments for all crimes will lead to a larger number of *major* crimes. Let's look at the reasoning. All decisions are made at the margin. If theft and murder will be punished by the same fate, there is no marginal deterrence to murder. If a theft of $5 is met with a punishment of ten years in jail and a theft of $50,000 incurs the same sentence, why not go all the way and steal $50,000? There is no marginal deterrence against committing the bigger theft.

To establish deterrents that are correct at the margin, we must observe empirically how criminals respond to changes in punishments.

This leads us to the question of how people decide whether to commit a crime. Here we might look to Adam Smith, the founder of modern economics, who observed:

> The affluence of the rich excites the indignation of the poor, who are often both driven by want, and prompted by envy, to invade his possessions. It is only under the shelter of the civil magistrate that the owner of that valuable property, which is acquired by the labour of many years, or perhaps by many successive generations, can sleep a single night in security. He is at all times surrounded by unknown enemies, whom, though he never provokes, he can never appease, and from whose injustice he can be protected only by the powerful arm of the civil magistrate continually held up to chastise it. The acquisition of valuable and extensive property, therefore, necessarily requires the establishment of civil government.[1]

Thus, Smith concluded, theft will be committed in any society in which one person has substantially more property than another. If Smith is correct, we can surmise that the individuals who engage in theft are seeking income. We can also suppose that before acting, a criminal might look at the anticipated **costs** and returns of criminal activity. These could then be compared with the net returns from legitimate activities. Hence individuals engaging in crimes may be thought of as doing so on the basis of an assessment in which the benefits to them are perceived to outweigh their costs. The benefits of the crime of theft are clear: loot. The costs to the criminal would include, but not be limited to, apprehension by the police, conviction, and jail. The criminal's calculations are thus analogous to those made by an athlete when weighing the cost of possible serious injury against the benefits to be gained from participating in a sport.

If we view the supply of offenses in this manner, we can devise ways in which society can lower the net expected benefit for committing any illegal activity. That is, we can figure out how to reduce crime most effectively. Indeed, economists have applied this sort of reasoning to study empirically the impact of punishment on criminal activity. The two areas on which they have focused are (1) the impact of increasing the probability that criminals will be detected and apprehended by, for example, putting more police on the street, and (2) the role of punishment by, for example, imprisonment.

---

1. Adam Smith, *An Inquiry into the Nature and Causes of the Wealth of Nations,* 1776, bk. 5, ch. 1.

Surprisingly, at least to an economist, the early empirical answers to these questions came back rather mixed. The impact of imprisonment on crime rates appeared quite small, often little different from zero. Moreover, most of the early studies that attempted to estimate the impact of police on the crime rate found either no relationship or that a larger police force appeared to *increase* the crime rate!

The problem researchers have encountered in estimating the impact of police or prison terms on criminal activity is simple in principle but difficult to correct: Because people who live in areas with higher crime rates will want to take measures to protect themselves, they are likely to have larger police forces and to punish criminals more severely. Thus even if more police and more severe penalties actually do reduce crime, this true effect may be masked or even seem to be reversed in the data because high-crime areas will tend to have more police and higher prison populations.

Economic research has begun to unravel these influences, however, offering us the clearest picture yet of the likely effects of police and imprisonment on the crime rate. The key is to find factors that strongly influence the number of police in a community or the size of a state's prison population but do not otherwise affect the crime rate. For example, it turns out that election cycles tend to have a strong independent effect on the size of police forces. Because crime is such a hot political issue, both mayors and governors have strong **incentives** (and the ability) to push for more police funding in election years. So even though police forces in major cities tend to remain constant in nonelection years, they grow significantly in election years. These increases in policing, in turn, have clearly detectable effects in reducing crime.

The strongest deterrent effect of police appears to be on violent crimes such as murder, rape, and assault. In fact, the **elasticity** of violent crime with respect to police is about -1.0. Accordingly, a 10 percent increase in a city's police force can be expected to produce about a 10 percent decrease in the violent crime rate in that city. With regard to property crimes, such as burglary, larceny, and auto theft, the impact of having more police is smaller but still significant. In this case, the estimated elasticity is about -0.3, meaning that a 10 percent increase in the police force will yield about a 3 percent reduction in property crimes. The implications for a city like Detroit are quite striking. Increasing the police force by 10 percent would mean adding about 440 officers. These estimates imply that as a result, the city could expect to suffer about 2,100 fewer violent crimes each year and about 2,700 fewer property crimes.

Researchers have also been able to isolate the role of imprisonment on deterring crime. Once again, the effects are strongest for violent crime. A 10 percent decrease in a state's prison population can be expected to increase the violent-crime rate in that state by about 4 percent. In the case of property crime, a 10 percent decrease in prison population will yield about a 3 percent rise in burglaries, larcenies, and auto thefts in the state. Perhaps not surprisingly, many states have been constructing new prisons.

Separate research has found that juvenile criminals respond to incentives, just as their adult counterparts do. From the mid-1970s to the mid-1990s, juvenile crime soared relative to adult crime, which has led many commentators to worry about a generation of juveniles who are seemingly undaunted by the threat of imprisonment. In fact, it appears that soaring juvenile crime was largely the result of changes in the incentives juveniles faced: Over this same period of time, violent-crime imprisonment rates for juveniles fell 80 percent relative to those for adults. Hence the chances of violent young criminals being jailed dropped to only about half those of violent adult criminals. Moreover, the change in penalties that occurs as youths become subject to adult laws (usually at age eighteen) has a strong effect on their behavior. In states tough on youth but easy on adults, violent-crime rates rise 23 percent at age eighteen, but in states that are easy on juveniles and tough on adults, such crime drops 4 percent at age eighteen. Incentives, it seems, still matter.

Are the growing expenditures on crime prevention worthwhile? According to what we know now, the answer is yes. Adding another person to the prison population costs about $30,000 per year but can be expected to yield benefits (in terms of crime prevention) of more than $50,000 per year. Although adding an officer to the police force has an expected cost of about $80,000 per year, that officer can be expected to produce crime-prevention benefits of almost $200,000. These numbers suggest that we can expect further increases in spending on crime prevention in the years to come and perhaps even more reductions in the crime rate.

DISCUSSION QUESTIONS

1. The analysis just presented seems to make the assumption that criminals act rationally. Does the fact they do not necessarily do so negate the analysis?

2. In many cases, murder is committed among people who know each other. Does this mean that raising the penalty for murder will not affect the number of murders committed?

3. Consider the following prescription for punishments: "Eye for eye, tooth for tooth, hand for hand, foot for foot." Suppose our laws followed this rule, and further suppose we spent enough money on law enforcement to apprehend everyone who broke the law. What would the crime rate be? (*Hint:* If the penalty for stealing $10 was $10, and if you were certain you would be caught, would there be any expected gain from the theft? Would there be an expected gain from the theft if the penalty were only, say, $1, or if the chance of being caught were only 10 percent?)

4. In recent years, the penalty for selling illegal drugs has been increased sharply. How does that affect the incentive to sell drugs? For the people who decide to sell drugs anyway, what do the higher penalties for dealing do to their incentive to commit other crimes (such as murder) while they are engaged in selling drugs?

THE GRAYING
OF AMERICA

America is aging. The 78 million baby boomers who pushed the Beatles and the Rolling Stones into stardom are nearing retirement. In twenty years, roughly 20 percent of all Americans will be sixty-five or older. Just as the post–World War II baby boom presented both obstacles and opportunities, so does the graying of America. Let's see why.

Two principal forces are behind America's "senior boom." First, we're living longer. Average life expectancy in 1900 was forty-seven years; today, it is seventy-eight and is likely to reach eighty within the next decade. Second, the birthrate is near record low levels. Today's mothers are having far fewer children than their mothers or grandmothers had. In short, the old are living longer, and the ranks of the young are growing too slowly to offset that fact. Together, these forces are pushing up the proportion of the population over age sixty-five; indeed, the number of seniors is growing at twice the rate of the rest of the population. In 1970, the **median age** in the United States—the age that divides the older half of the population from the younger half—was twenty-eight; it is now thirty-eight and rising. Compounding these factors, the average age at retirement is low by historical standards. The result is more retirees relying on fewer workers to help ensure that their senior years are also golden years.

Why should a person who is, say, college age be concerned with the age of the rest of the population? Well, old people are expensive. In fact, people over sixty-five now consume over one-third of the federal government's budget. Social Security payments to retirees are the biggest item, now running over $500 billion a year. Medicare, which pays hospital and doctors' bills for the elderly, costs around $350 billion a year and is increasing rapidly. Moreover, fully a third of the $300 billion annual budget for Medicaid, which helps pay medical bills for the poor of all ages, goes to people over the age of sixty-five.

Under current law, the elderly will consume 40 percent of all federal spending within fifteen years: Medicare's share of the gross domestic product (GDP) will double, as will the number of very old—those over eighty-five and most in need of care. Within twenty-five years, probably *half* of the federal budget will go to the old. In a nutshell, senior citizens are the beneficiaries of an expensive and rapidly growing share of all federal spending. What are they getting for our dollars?

To begin with, today's elderly are already more prosperous than any previous generation. Indeed, the annual discretionary income of Americans over sixty-five averages 30 percent higher than the average discretionary income of all other age groups. Each year, inflation-adjusted Social Security benefits paid to new retirees are higher than the first-year benefits paid to people who retired the year before. In addition, for the past thirty-five years, cost-of-living adjustments have protected Social Security benefits from inflation. The impact of Social Security is evident even at the lower end of the income scale: The poverty rate for people over sixty-five is much lower than for the population as a whole. Retired people today collect Social Security benefits that are two to five times what they and their employers contributed in payroll taxes plus interest earned.

Not surprisingly, medical expenses are a major concern for many elderly. Perhaps reflecting that concern, each person under the age of sixty-five in America currently pays an average of more than $1,600 a year in federal taxes to subsidize medical care for the elderly. Indeed, no other country in the world goes to the lengths that America does to preserve life. Some 30 percent of Medicare's budget goes to patients in their last year of life. Coronary bypass operations, costing over $40,000 apiece, are routinely performed on Americans in their sixties and seventies. For those over sixty-five, Medicare picks up the tab. Even heart transplants are now performed on people in their sixties and paid for by Medicare for those over sixty-five. By contrast, the Japanese offer no organ transplants. Britain's National Health Service generally will not provide kidney dialysis for people over fifty-five. Yet Medicare subsidizes dialysis for more than one hundred thousand Americans, half of them over age sixty. The cost: more than $4 billion a year. Overall, the elderly receive Medicare benefits worth five to twenty times the payroll taxes (plus interest) they paid for this program.

The responsibility for the huge and growing bills for Social Security and Medicare falls squarely on current and future workers, because both programs are financed by payroll taxes. Thirty years ago, these programs were adequately financed with a payroll levy of less than 10 percent of the typical worker's earnings. Today, the tax rate exceeds 15 percent of median wages and is expected to grow rapidly.

By the year 2020, early baby boomers, born in the late 1940s and early 1950s, will have retired. Late baby boomers, born in the early 1960s, will be nearing retirement. Both groups will leave today's college students, and their children, a staggering bill to pay. For Social Security and Medicare to stay as they are, the payroll tax rate may have to rise to 25 percent of wages over the next fifteen years. And a payroll tax rate of 40 percent is not unlikely by the middle of the twenty-first century.

One way to think of the immense bill facing today's college students and their successors is to consider the number of retirees each worker must support. In 1946, the burden of one Social Security recipient was shared by forty-two workers. By 1960, nine workers had to foot the bill for each retiree's Social Security benefits. Today, roughly three workers pick up the tab for each retiree's Social Security and Medicare benefits. By 2030, only two workers will be available to pay the Social Security and Medicare benefits due each recipient. Thus a working couple will have to support not only themselves and their family but also someone outside the family who is receiving Social Security and Medicare benefits.

Congress and the executive branch have seemed unwilling to face the pitfalls and promises of an aging America. Although the age of retirement for Social Security purposes is legislatively mandated to rise to sixty-seven, the best that politicians in Washington, D.C., appear able to do is appoint commissions to "study" the problems we face. And what changes are our politicians willing to make? We got a sample of this in 2003, with new legislation promising taxpayer-funded prescription drug benefits for senior citizens. Even people in favor of the new program called it the largest expansion in **entitlement programs** in forty years. Before passage of the law, President Bush claimed it was going to cost $35 billion a year, but within a couple of months, that estimate had been hiked to over $50 billion. In fact, the benefits of the program will be less than claimed, and the costs will be even higher, because more than three-quarters of senior citizens had privately funded prescription drug plans *before* the new law took effect. These private plans are already disappearing, leaving seniors with fewer choices and sticking younger taxpayers with a larger tax bill.

By now you may be wondering how we managed to commit ourselves to the huge budgetary burden of health and retirement benefits for senior citizens. There are three elements to the story. First, the cause is worthy: After all, who would want to deny the elderly decent medical care and a comfortable retirement? Second, the benefits of the programs are far more concentrated than the costs. A retired couple, for example, collects more than $25,000 per year in Social Security and consumes another $15,000 in subsidized medical benefits. In contrast, the typical working couple pays only about half of this each year in Social Security and Medicare taxes. Hence the retired couple has a stronger **incentive** to push for benefits than the working couple has to resist them. And finally, senior citizens vote at a far higher rate than members of any other age group, in no small part because they are retired and thus have fewer obligations on their time. They are thus much more likely to make it clear at the ballot box exactly how important their benefits are to them.

It is possible for government to responsibly address the crisis in funding programs for senior citizens. Chile, for example, faced a national pension system with even more severe problems than our Social Security system. Its response was to transform the system into one that is rapidly (and automatically, as time passes) converting itself into a completely private pension system. The result has been security for existing retirees, higher potential benefits for future retirees, and lower taxes for all workers. Americans could do exactly what the Chileans have done—if we chose to do so.

In the meantime, if Social Security and Medicare are kept on their current paths and older workers continue to leave the workforce, the future burden on today's college students is likely to be unbearable. If we are to avoid the social tensions and enormous costs of such an outcome, the willingness and ability of older individuals to retain more of their self-sufficiency must be recognized. To do otherwise is to invite a future in which the golden years are but memories of the past.

DISCUSSION QUESTIONS

1. How do the payroll taxes levied on the earnings of workers affect their decisions about how much leisure they consume?

2. When the government taxes younger people to pay benefits to older people, how does this affect the amount of assistance *that* younger people might voluntarily choose to offer older people?

3. When the government taxes younger people to pay benefits to older people, how does this affect the size of the bequests that older people are likely to leave to their children or grandchildren when they die?

4. In general, people who are more productive earn higher incomes and thus pay higher taxes. How would change in the immigration

laws that favored more highly educated and skilled individuals affect the future tax burden of today's American college students? Would the admission of better-educated immigrants tend to raise or lower the wages of American college graduates? On balance, would an overhaul of the immigration system benefit or harm today's college students?

PART SIX

Property Rights and the Environment

Introduction

You saw in Part Four that **monopoly** produces outcomes that differ significantly from the outcomes of **competition** and yields gains from trade that fall short of the competitive ideal. In Part Six, you will see that when **externalities** are present—when there are discrepancies between the **private costs** of action and the **social costs** of action—the competitive outcome differs from the competitive ideal. Typically, the problem in the case of externalities is said to be *market failure,* but the diagnosis might just as well be termed *government failure.* For markets to work efficiently, **property rights** to **scarce goods** must be clearly defined, cheaply enforceable, and fully transferable, and it is generally the government that is believed to have a **comparative advantage** in ensuring that these conditions are satisfied. If the government fails to define, enforce, or make transferable property rights, the market will generally fail to produce socially efficient outcomes, and it becomes a moot point as to who is at fault. The real point is, what might be done to improve things?

As population and per capita income both rise, consumption rises faster than either, for it responds to the combined impetus of both. With consumption comes the residue of consumption, also known as plain old garbage. Many of us have heard of landfills being closed because of fears of groundwater contamination or of homeless garbage scows wandering the high seas in search of a place to off-load; all of us have been bombarded with public service messages to recycle everything from aluminum cans to newspapers. The United States, it seems, is becoming the garbage capital of the world. This is no doubt true, but it is also true that the United States is the professional football capital of the world—and yet pro football teams seem to have no problem finding cities across the country willing to welcome them with open arms. What is different about garbage? You are probably inclined to answer that football is enjoyable and garbage is not. True enough, but this is not why garbage sometimes piles up faster than anyone seems willing to dispose of it. Garbage becomes a problem only if it is not priced properly—that is, if the consumers and businesses that produce it are not charged enough for its removal and the landfills where it is deposited are not paid enough for its disposal. The message of Chapter 26, "The Trashman Cometh," is that garbage really is no different from the things we consume in the course of producing it. As long as the trashman is paid, he will come, and as long as we have to pay for his services, his burden will be bearable. We will still have garbage, but we will not have a garbage problem.

We noted that the property rights to a scarce good or resource must be clearly defined, fully enforced, and readily transferable if that resource is to be used efficiently—that is, in the manner that yields the greatest net benefits. This is true whether the resource in question is space in a landfill, water in a stream, or as you will see in Chapter 27, "Bye-Bye, Bison," members of an animal species. If these conditions are satisfied, the resource will be used in the manner that benefits both its owner and society the most. If these conditions are not satisfied—as they were not for American bison on the hoof or passenger pigeons on the wing—the resource will generally not be used in the most efficient manner. And in the case of animal species that are competing with human beings, this sometimes means extinction. What should be done when a species becomes endangered? If our desire is to produce the greatest net benefit to humanity, the answer in general is not to protect the species at *any* possible cost, for this would be equivalent to assigning an infinite value to the species. Instead, the proper course of action is to devise rules that induce people to act as though the members of the species were private property. If such rules can be developed, we won't have to worry about spotted owls or African elephants becoming extinct any more than we currently worry about parakeets or cocker spaniels becoming extinct.

In Chapter 28, "Smog Merchants," property rights are again the focus of the discussion as we look at air pollution. We ordinarily think of the air around us as being something that we all own. The practical consequence of this is that we act as though the air is owned by none of us, for no one can exclude anyone else from using "our" air. As a result, we overuse the air in the sense that air pollution becomes a problem. This chapter shows that it is possible to define and enforce property rights to air, which the owners can then use as they see fit, which includes selling the rights to others. Once this is done, the users of clean air have the **incentive** to use it just as efficiently as they do all of the other **resources** (such as land, labor, and capital) used in the production process.

Air—or more generally, the atmosphere as a whole—reappears as the topic of Chapter 29, "Greenhouse Economics." Evidence is growing that human action is responsible for rising concentrations of so-called greenhouse gases in the earth's atmosphere and that left unchecked, this growth may produce costly increases in the average temperature of our planet. Given the nature of the problem—a **negative externality**—private action taken on the individual level will not yield the optimal outcome for society. Thus the potential gains from government action, in the form of environmental regulations or taxation, are substantial. The key word here is *potential,* for government action, no matter how well intentioned, does not automatically yield benefits that exceed the **costs.** As we seek solutions to the potential problems associated with greenhouse gases, we must be sure that the consequences of premature action are not worse than those of delaying action until the problem can be examined further. If we forget this message, greenhouse economics may turn into bad economics—and worse policy.

Chapter 26

THE TRASHMAN COMETH

Is garbage really different? To answer this question, let us consider a simple hypothetical situation. Suppose a city agreed to provide its residents with all the food they wished to consume, prepared in the manner they specified, and delivered to their homes for a flat, monthly fee that was independent of what or how much they ate. What are the likely consequences of this city food-delivery service? Most likely, people in the city would begin to eat more, because the size of their food bill would be independent of the amount they ate. They would also be more likely to consume lobster and filet mignon rather than fish sticks and hamburger because, again, the cost to them would be independent of their menu selections. Soon the city's food budget would be astronomical, and either the monthly fee or taxes would have to be increased. People from other communities might even begin moving (or at least making extended visits) to the city just to partake of this wonderful service. Within a short time, the city would face a food crisis as it sought to cope with providing an ever-increasing amount of food from a city budget that can no longer handle the financial burden.

If this story sounds silly to you, just change "food delivery" to "garbage pickup"; what we have just described is the way most cities in the country have historically operated their municipal garbage-collection services. The result during the 1990s was the appearance of a garbage crisis, with overflowing landfills, homeless garbage barges, and drinking-water wells said to be polluted with the runoff from trash heaps. This seeming crisis—to the extent it existed—was fundamentally no different from the food crisis just described. The problem was not that almost nobody wants garbage or that garbage can have adverse environmental effects or even that we had too much garbage. The problem lay in that we often do not put prices on garbage in the way we put prices on the goods that generate the garbage and that a strange assortment of participants used a few smelly facts to make things seem worse than they were.

First things first. America produces plenty of garbage each year—about 255 million tons of household and commercial solid waste that has to be burned, buried, or recycled. (That works out to 1,600 pounds per person.) About 33 percent of this is paper; yard waste (such as grass trimmings) accounts for another 13 percent. Plastic accounts for about 20 percent of the volume of material that has to be disposed of, but because plastic is relatively light, it makes up only about 12 percent of the weight. More than 85 million tons of this trash is recycled.

Landfills are the final resting place for most of our garbage, although incineration is also widely used in some areas, particularly in the Northeast, where land values are high. Both methods began falling out of favor with people who lived near these facilities (or might eventually), as NIMBY ("not in my backyard") attitudes spread across the land. Federal, state, and local regulations also made it increasingly difficult to establish new waste disposal facilities or even to keep old ones operating. The cost to open a modern 100-acre landfill rose to an estimated $70 million or more, and the permit process needed to open a new disposal facility soared to seven years in some states. Meanwhile, environmental concerns forced the closure of many landfills throughout the country and prevented others from ever beginning operations. By the early 1990s, all but five states were exporting at least some of their garbage to other states. Today, most of the garbage from some densely populated states in the Northeast ends up in other people's backyards: New Jersey ships garbage to six other states, and New York keeps landfill operators busy in nine states. Across the country, some Americans have wondered where all of the garbage is going to go.

Although the failure of America's cities to price garbage appropriately led to an inefficient amount of the stuff, much of the appearance of a garbage crisis has been misleading. Rubbish first hit the headlines in 1987 when a garbage barge named *Mobro,* headed south with New York City trash, couldn't find a home for its load. As it turns out, the barge operator wanted to change his disposal contract after he sailed; when he tried to conduct negotiations over the radio while under way, operators of likely landfills (mistakenly) suspected he might be carrying toxic waste rather than routine trash. When adverse publicity forced the barge back to New York with its load, many people thought it was a lack of landfill space, rather than poor planning by the barge operator, that was the cause. This notion was reinforced by an odd combination of environmental groups, waste-management firms, and the Environmental Protection Agency (EPA).

The Environmental Defense Fund wanted to start a major campaign to push recycling, and the *Mobro* episode gave things the necessary push.

As one official for the organization noted, "An advertising firm couldn't have designed a better vehicle than a garbage barge." Meanwhile, a number of farsighted waste-management companies had begun loading up on landfill space, taking advantage of new technologies that increased the efficient minimum size of a disposal facility. Looking to get firm contracts for filling this space, the trade group for the disposal industry started pushing the notion that America was running out of dump space. State and local officials who relied on the group's data quickly bought into the new landfills, paying premium prices to do so. The EPA, meanwhile, was studying the garbage problem but without accounting for the fact that its own regulations were causing the efficient scale of landfills to double and even quadruple in size. Thus the EPA merely counted landfills around the country and reported that they were shrinking in number. This was true enough, but what the EPA failed to report was that because landfills were getting bigger much faster than they were closing down, total disposal capacity was *growing* rapidly, not shrinking.

For a while, it seemed that recycling was going to take care of what appeared to be a worsening trash problem. In 1987, for example, old newspapers were selling for as much as $100 per ton (in 2009 dollars), and many municipalities felt that the answer to their financial woes and garbage troubles was at hand. Yet as more communities began putting mandatory recycling laws into effect, the prices for recycled trash began to plummet. Over the next five years, 3,500 communities in more than half the states had some form of mandatory curbside recycling; the resulting increase in the supply of used newsprint meant that communities were soon having to pay to have the stuff carted away. For glass, the story is much the same. The market value of the used material is below the cost of collecting and sorting it. Numerous states have acted to increase the demand for old newsprint by requiring locally published newspapers to have a minimum content of recycled newsprint. Because of these mandates, the recycling rate for newsprint has doubled over the past twenty years, but the current rate of 70 percent is thought by many experts to be about the practical maximum.

Recycling raises significant issues that were often ignored during the early rush to embrace the concept. For example, the production of 100 tons of de-inked fiber from old newsprint produces about 40 tons of sludge that must be disposed of somehow. Although the total volume of material is reduced, the concentrated form of what is left can make it more costly to dispose of properly. Similarly, recycling paper is unlikely to save trees, for most virgin newsprint is made from trees planted expressly for that purpose and harvested as a crop; if recycling increases, many of these trees simply will not be planted. In a study done for Resources for the Future, A. Clark Wiseman concluded, "The likely effect of [newsprint recycling] appears to be smaller, rather than larger, forest inventory." Moreover, most virgin newsprint is made in Canada, using clean hydroelectric power. Makers of newsprint in the United States (the primary customers for the recycled stuff) often use higher-polluting energy such as coal. Thus one potential side effect of recycling is the switch from hydroelectric power to fossil fuels.

Some analysts have argued that we should simply ban certain products. For example, Styrofoam cups have gotten a bad name because they take up more space in landfills than paper hot-drink cups and because Styrofoam remains in the landfill forever. Yet according to a widely cited study by Martin B. Hocking of the University of Victoria in British Columbia, Canada, the manufacture of a paper cup consumes 36 times as much electricity and generates 580 times as much wastewater as the manufacture of a Styrofoam cup. Moreover, as paper degrades underground, it releases methane, a greenhouse gas that may contribute to global climate change. In a similar vein, consider disposable diapers, which have been trashed by their opponents because a week's worth generates 22.2 pounds of post-use waste, whereas a week's worth of reusable diapers generates only 4 ounces. Because disposable diapers already amount to 1 percent of the nation's solid waste, the edge clearly seems to go to reusable cloth diapers. Yet the use of reusable rather than disposable diapers consumes more than three times as many BTUs (British thermal units) of energy and generates ten times as much water pollution. It would seem that the trade-offs that are present when we talk about "goods" are just as prevalent when we discuss "bads" such as garbage.

It also appears that more government regulation of the garbage business is likely to make things worse rather than better, as may be illustrated by the tale of two states, New Jersey and Pennsylvania. A number of years ago, to stop what was described as price gouging by organized crime, New Jersey decided to regulate waste hauling and disposal as a public utility. Once the politicians got involved in the trash business, however, politics very nearly destroyed it. According to Paul Kleindorfer of the University of Pennsylvania, political opposition to passing garbage-disposal costs along to consumers effectively ended investment in landfills. In 1972, there were 331 landfills operating in New Jersey; by 1991, the number had fallen to 50, because the state-regulated fees payable to landfill operators simply didn't cover the rising costs of operation. More than half of the state's municipal solid waste is now exported to neighboring Pennsylvania, in part because only about twenty landfills remain open in New Jersey.

Pennsylvania's situation provides a sharp contrast. The state does not regulate the deals that communities make with landfill and incinerator operators; the market takes care of matters instead. For example, despite the state's hands-off policy, tipping fees (the charges for disposing of garbage in landfills) are below the national average in Pennsylvania, effectively limited by competition between disposal facilities. The market seems to be providing the right **incentives;** in one recent year, there were thirty-one pending applications to open landfills in Pennsylvania but only two in New Jersey, despite the fact that New Jersey residents are paying the highest disposal rates in the country to ship garbage as far away as Ohio and Georgia.

Ultimately, two issues must be solved when it comes to trash. First, what do we do with it once we have it? Second, how do we reduce the amount of it that we have? As hinted at by the Pennsylvania story and illustrated further by developments elsewhere in the country, the market mechanism can answer both questions. The fact of the matter is that in many areas of the country, population densities are high and land is expensive. Hence a large amount of trash is produced, and it is expensive to dispose of locally. In contrast, there are some areas of the country where there are relatively few people around to produce garbage, where land for disposal facilities is cheap, and where wide-open spaces minimize any potential air-pollution hazards associated with incinerators. The sensible thing to do, it would seem, is to have the states that produce most of the trash ship it to states where it can be most efficiently disposed of—for a price, of course. This is already being done to an extent, but residents of potential recipient states are (not surprisingly) concerned, lest they end up being the garbage capitals of the nation. Yet Wisconsin, which imports more than a million tons of garbage each year, is demonstrating that it is possible to get rid of the trash without trashing the neighborhood. Landfill operators in Wisconsin are now required to send water-table monitoring reports to neighbors and to maintain the landfills for forty years after closure. Operators have also guaranteed the value of neighboring homes to gain the permission of nearby residents and in some cases have purchased homes to quiet neighbors' objections. These features all add to the cost of operating landfills, but as long as prospective customers are willing to pay the price and neighboring residents are satisfied with their protections—and so far these conditions appear to have been met—it would seem tough to argue with the outcome.

Some people might still argue that it does not seem right for one community to be able to dump its trash elsewhere. Yet the flip side is this: Is it right to prevent communities from accepting trash if that is what they want? Consider Gilliam County, Oregon (population 1,950), which wanted Seattle's garbage so badly that it fought Oregon state legislators' attempts to tax out-of-state trash coming into Oregon. Seattle's decision to use the Gilliam County landfill generated $1 million per year for the little community—some 25 percent of its annual budget and enough to finance the operations of the county's largest school.

Faced with the prospect of paying to dispose of its garbage, Seattle had to confront the problem of reducing the amount of trash its residents were generating. Its solution was to charge householders according to the amount they put out. Seattle began charging $16.55 per month for each can picked up weekly. Yard waste that has been separated for composting costs $5.35 per month, and paper, glass, and metal separated for recycling are hauled away at no charge. In the first year that per-can charges were imposed, the total tonnage that had to be buried fell by 22 percent. Voluntary recycling rose from 24 percent of waste to 36 percent—a rate almost triple the national average at the time. The "Seattle stomp" (used to fit more trash into a can) became a regular source of exercise, and the city had trouble exporting enough garbage to fulfill its contract with Gilliam County.

The Seattle experience is paralleled by a similar program in Charlottesville, Virginia. A few years ago, this university town of forty thousand began charging 80 cents per 32-gallon bag or can of residential garbage collected at the curb. The results of the city's new policy suggest that people respond to garbage prices just as they do to all other prices: When an activity becomes more expensive, people engage in less of it. In fact, after controlling for other factors, the introduction of this unit-pricing plan induced people to reduce the volume of garbage presented for collection by 37 percent.

Where did all of the garbage go? Well, some of it didn't go anywhere because many residents began practicing their own version of the Seattle stomp, compacting garbage into fewer bags. Even so, the total weight of Charlottesville's residential garbage dropped by 14 percent in response to unit pricing. Not all of this represented a reduction in garbage production because some residents resorted to "midnight dumping"—tossing their trash into commercial Dumpsters or their neighbors' cans late at night. This sort of behavior is much like the rise in gasoline thefts that occurred in the 1970s when gas prices jumped to the equivalent of over $3 per gallon. But just as locking gas caps ended most gas thefts, there may be a simple way to prevent most midnight dumping. Economists who have studied the Charlottesville program in detail suggest that property taxes or monthly fees could be used to cover the cost of one bag per household each week, with a price per bag applied only to additional bags. According to these estimates, a one-bag allowance would stop all midnight dumping by most one-person households and stop almost half the dumping by a hypothetical three-person household. Moreover, such a scheme would retain most of the environmental benefits of the garbage-pricing program.

The message beginning to emerge across the country, then, is that garbage is no different from the things we consume in the course of producing it. As long as the trashman is paid, he will come, and as long as we must pay for his services, his burden will be bearable.

DISCUSSION QUESTIONS

1. How do deposits on bottles and cans affect the incentives of individuals to recycle these products?

2. Why do many communities mandate recycling? Is it possible to induce people to recycle more without requiring that all residents recycle?

3. How do hefty per-can garbage pickup fees influence the decisions people make about what goods they will consume?

4. A community planning on charging a fee for trash pickup might structure the fee in any of several ways. It might, for example, charge a fixed amount per can, an amount per pound of garbage, or a flat fee per month without regard to amount of garbage. How would each of these affect the amount and type of garbage produced? Which system would lead to an increase in the use of trash compactors? Which would lead to the most garbage?

Chapter 27

BYE-BYE, BISON

The destruction of animal species by humans is nothing new. For example, the arrival of human beings in North America about twelve thousand years ago is tied to the extinction of most of the megafauna (very large animals) that then existed. The famous La Brea Tar Pits of Southern California yielded the remains of twenty-four mammals and twenty-two birds that no longer exist. Among these are the saber-toothed tiger, the giant llama, the 20-foot ground sloth, and a bison that stood 7 feet at the hump and had 6-foot-wide horns.

Although many experts believe that human hunting was responsible for the demise of these species and that hunting and habitat destruction by humans have led to the extinction of many other species, the link is not always as clear as it might seem at first glance. For example, it is estimated that only about 0.02 percent (1 in 5,000) of all species that have ever existed are currently extant. Most of the others (including the dinosaurs) disappeared long before humans ever made an appearance. The simple fact is that all species compete for the limited resources available, and most species have been outcompeted, with or without the help of *Homo sapiens.* Just as important is that basic economic principles can help explain why various species are more or less prone to meet their demise at the hands of humans and what humans might do if they want to delay the extinction of any particular species.[1]

Let's begin with the passenger pigeon, which provides the most famous example of the role of human beings in the extinction of a species. At one time, these birds were the most numerous species of birds in North America and perhaps in the world. They nested and migrated in huge flocks and probably numbered in the billions. When flocks passed

---

1. We say "delay" rather than "prevent" extinction because there is no evidence to date that any species—*Homo sapiens* included—has any claim on immortality.

overhead, the sky would be dark with pigeons for days at a time. The famous naturalist John James Audubon measured one roost at 40 miles long and 3 miles wide, with birds stacked from treetop down to nearly ground level. Although the Native Americans had long hunted these birds, the demise of the passenger pigeon is usually tied to the arrival of the Europeans, who increased the **demand** for pigeons as a source of food and sport. The birds were shot and netted in vast numbers; by the end of the nineteenth century, an animal species that had been looked on as almost indestructible because of its enormous numbers had almost completely disappeared. The last known passenger pigeon died in the Cincinnati Zoo in 1914.

The American bison only narrowly escaped the same fate. The vast herds that roamed the plains were easy targets for hunters; with the advent of the railroad and the need to feed crews of workers as the transcontinental railroads were built, hunters such as Buffalo Bill Cody killed bison by the thousands. As the demand for bison hides increased, the animals became the target of more hunting. Like the passenger pigeon, the bison had appeared to be indestructible because of its huge numbers, but the species was soon on the road to extinction. Despite the outcries of the Native Americans who found their major food source being decimated, it was not until late in the nineteenth century that any efforts were made to protect the bison.[2]

These two episodes, particularly that of the bison, are generally viewed as classic examples of humans' inhumanity to our fellow species, as well as to our fellow humans, for many Native American tribes were ultimately devastated by the near demise of the bison. A closer look reveals more than simply wasteful slaughter; it discloses exactly why events progressed as they did and how we can learn from them to improve modern efforts to protect species threatened by human neighbors.

Native Americans had hunted the bison for many years before the arrival of Europeans and are generally portrayed as both carefully husbanding their prey and generously sharing the meat among tribal members. Yet the braves who rode their horses into the thundering herds marked their arrows so that it would be clear who had killed each bison. The marked arrows gave the shooter rights to the best parts of the animal. Tribal members who specialized in butchering the kill also received a share as payment for processing the meat. Indeed, the Native American hunting parties were organized remarkably like the parties of the

2. For the bison's cousin, the eastern buffalo—which stood 7 feet tall at the shoulder, was 12 feet long, and weighed more than a ton—the efforts came too late. The last known members of the species, a cow and her calf, were killed in 1825 in the Allegheny Mountains.

Europeans who followed: Once an animal was killed, its ownership was clearly defined, fully enforced, and readily transferable. Moreover, the rewards were distributed in accordance with the contribution that each person had made to the overall success of the hunt.

Matters were different when it came to the ownership rights to living bison. Native Americans, like the white hunters and settlers who came later, had no economically practical way to fence in the herds. The bison could (and did) migrate freely from one tribe's territory into the territory of other tribes. If the members of one tribe economized on their kill, their conservation efforts would chiefly provide more meat for another tribe, who might well be their mortal enemies. This fact induced Native Americans to exploit the bison, so that the herds disappeared from some traditional territories on the Great Plains by 1840—before Buffalo Bill was even born.

Two factors made the efforts of the railroad hunters more destructive, hastening the disappearance of the bison herds. First, the white population (and thus the demand for the meat and hides) became much larger than the Native American population. Second, white hunters used firearms—a technological revolution that increased the killing capacity of a given hunter by a factor of 20 or more, compared to the bow and arrow. Nevertheless, the fundamental problem was the same for whites and Native Americans alike: The **property rights** to live bison could not be cheaply established and enforced. To own a bison, one had to kill it, and so too many bison were killed.

The property rights to a **scarce good** or **resource** must be clearly defined, fully enforced, and readily transferable if that resource is to be used efficiently—that is, in the manner that yields the greatest net benefits. This is true whether the resource in question is the American bison, the water in a stream, or a pepperoni pizza. If these conditions are satisfied, the resource will be used in the manner that best benefits both its owner and society.[3] If they are not satisfied—as they were not for bison on the hoof or passenger pigeons on the wing—the resource will generally not be used in the most efficient manner. In the case of animal species that are competing with human beings, this sometimes means extinction.

In modern times, the government has attempted to limit hunting and fishing seasons and the number of animals that may be taken by imposing state and federal regulations. In effect, a rationing system (other than

---

3. This does not mean that all species will be permanently protected from extinction, for reasons that are suggested in Chapter 3, "Flying the Friendly Skies?" It does mean that extinction will be permitted to occur only if the benefits of letting it occur exceed the costs.

prices) is being used in an attempt to induce hunters and fishermen to act as though the rights to animals were clearly defined, fully enforced, and readily transferable. The results have been at least partly successful. It is likely, for example, that there are more deer in North America today than there were at the time of the colonists—a fact that is not entirely good news for people whose gardens are sometimes the target of hungry herds.

The threatened status of many species of whales illustrates that the problem is far from resolved. The pattern of harvesting whales has been the subject of international discussion ever since World War II, for migratory whales are like nineteenth-century bison: To own them, one must kill them. It was readily apparent that without some form of restraint, many species of whales were in danger of extinction. The result was the founding in 1948 of the International Whaling Commission (IWC), which attempted to regulate international whaling. But the IWC was doomed from the start, for its members had the right to veto any regulation they considered too restrictive, and the commission had no enforcement powers in the event that a member nation chose to disregard the rules. Moreover, some whaling nations (such as Chile and Peru) refused to join the IWC, so commission quotas had little effect on them. Some IWC members have used nonmember flagships to circumvent agreed quotas, while others have claimed that they were killing the whales solely for exempt "research" purposes.

The story of the decimation of a species is well told in the events surrounding blue whales, which are believed to migrate thousands of miles each year. A blue whale, which can weigh almost 100 tons, is difficult to kill even with the most modern equipment; nevertheless, intensive hunting gradually reduced the stock from somewhere between 300,000 and 1 million to, at present, somewhere between 3,000 and 4,000. In the 1930–1931 winter season, almost 30,000 blue whales were taken, a number far in excess of the species' ability to replenish through reproduction. Continued intense harvesting brought the catch down to fewer than 10,000 by 1945–1946, and in the late 1950s, the yearly harvest was down to around 1,500 per year. By 1964–1965, whalers managed to find and kill only 20 blue whales. Despite a 1965 ban by the IWC, the hunting of blues continued by nonmembers such as Brazil, Chile, and Peru.

Humpback whales were also hunted to near-extinction. From an original population estimated at 300,000, stocks plunged to 5,000 or fewer, although as many as 60,000 to 80,000 humpbacks are alive today. It is generally agreed that the IWC ban on hunting humpbacks has played a key role in the species' ongoing recovery.

Whales are not the only seagoing creatures to suffer from an absence of clearly defined, cheaply enforceable, and transferable property rights.

Codfish off the New England and eastern Canadian coasts were once so abundant, it was said, that a person could walk across the sea on their backs. The fish grew into 6-foot-long, 200-pound giants, and generations of families from coastal communities knew they could count on the fish for a prosperous livelihood. The problem was that the fish had to be hauled from the sea before rights to it could be established. The result was overfishing, which led to declining yields and shrinking fish. Between 1970 and 2000, the catch dropped more than 75 percent, and the typical fish caught these days weighs but 20 pounds. As a result, the Canadians have closed down their cod fishery, and the American fleet is a ghost of its former self.

The cod is not alone in its demise. The world's ocean fisheries are in decline. Since 1950, nearly 30 percent of all fisheries have collapsed, and some scientists project that in forty years, *all* of the world's fisheries could disappear. The problem, it is widely agreed, is a failure of humans to manage fisheries in a way that is consistent with both maximum economic benefit and long-term survival of ocean fish stocks. But it is now becoming increasingly apparent that a simple property-rights system has the power to stop and even reverse these declines.

A system of catch shares called individual transferable quotas (ITQs) is stunningly successful in protecting fisheries. Where such rights have been assigned, there is no evidence of collapse. In fact, the assignment of catch share rights often halts and even reverses potential collapse. And in fisheries where they are used, ITQs have permitted the return of economically viable fishing activities.

Command-and-control systems of fisheries management have historically held sway around the world. These systems limit, for example, fishing gear and season length, in an effort to keep total harvests within **quotas.** But even the best of them suffer from a profound misalignment of **incentives:** the self-interest of the individual harvester is generally inconsistent with actions that would both maximize the value of the fishery and ensure its sustainability. Because individuals lack secure rights to part of the harvest, they are motivated to "race to fish" to outcompete others. The results are poor stewardship and lobbying for ever-larger harvest quotas, causing excessive harvests, reduced stocks, and eventual collapse.

In recent years, the failure of command-and-control fishery management has become increasingly clear, but the question has been, is there a viable alternative? Economists have suggested that catch shares assigned to individual harvesters (such as ITQs) offer such an alternative, because property-rights systems, of which ITQs are an example, are generally the most effective way to conserve resources.

Catch-share systems combine two features. First, based on biological and other scientific criteria, an allowable catch size is determined. Then members of the fishing community (individuals or cooperatives, for example) are assigned shares of the total allowable catch. These shares can then be used or be sold or leased to others; no one is allowed to harvest in excess of the amount specified in the harvester's quota. The ITQs give fishermen de facto property rights in the catch, much as they have rights in their boats and gear. Collectively, these rights owners then have an incentive to protect and maintain the value of the fishery, just as they do to maintain their other property.

Case studies of the use of ITQs suggest that catch shares can dramatically improve both the biological and the economic health of fisheries. Alaska, British Columbia, Iceland, and New Zealand all represent locations where ITQs are regarded as having succeeded. But recent research covering more than eleven thousand fisheries around the world reveals that ITQs are effective worldwide. In fact, the outcomes for fisheries with and without catch-share systems have been studied systematically, accounting for factors (such as ecosystem characteristics and fish species) that might have played a role in the health and viability of the fish stocks. This amounts to conducting a statistically controlled experiment—and the results are striking.

A conventional measure of collapse for a fishery is a decline in catch to a level that is less than 10 percent of the maximum recorded catch for that fishery. By this criterion, an average of more than fifty fisheries has reached collapse each year since 1950, in a worldwide pattern that seems to be pointing toward the demise of all fisheries. But in fisheries where a catch-share system is implemented, the process of collapse halts—completely. Moreover, in many of the ITQ fisheries, recovery of fish stocks begins soon after implementation, even as fishermen continue to profitably catch fish.

It is now estimated that had ITQs been implemented in all fisheries beginning in 1970, the incidence of collapse would have been cut by two-thirds. Moreover, instead of watching fisheries collapse today, we would be seeing them getting healthier, even as they were supporting fishermen and nourishing consumers. Most important, it appears that the power of ITQs to prevent and even reverse fishery collapse applies to species and ecosystems throughout the world.

Until now, skeptics of the property-rights approach to solving environmental problems have argued that fisheries are profoundly different from other resources, somehow immune to the benefits of instituting catch shares. That argument is no longer viable. Catch shares are being implemented in growing numbers around the world. It is now clear that an expansion of ITQs and other catch-share systems can lead to the recovery of fish stocks and of the profits from harvesting them—one more illustration that the clear assignment of enforceable, transferable property rights remains the most effective way we know to protect other species from the depredations of *Homo sapiens*.

DISCUSSION QUESTIONS

1. Has there ever been a problem with the extinction of dogs, cats, or cattle? Why not?

2. Some people argue that the best way to save rare species is to set up private game reserves to which wealthy hunters can travel. How could this help save endangered species?

3. Is government *ownership* of animals needed to protect species from extinction?

4. In the United States, most fishing streams are public property, with access available to all. In Britain, most fishing streams are privately owned, with access restricted to those who are willing to pay for the right to fish. Anglers agree that over the past thirty years, the quality of fishing in the United States has declined, while the quality of fishing in Britain has risen. Can you suggest why?

Chapter 28

SMOG MERCHANTS

Pollution is undesirable, almost by definition. Most of us use the term so commonly it suggests we all know, without question, what it means. Yet there is an important sense in which "pollution is what pollution does." Consider, for example, ozone (O_3), an unstable collection of oxygen atoms. At upper levels of the atmosphere, it is a naturally occurring substance that plays an essential role in protecting life from the harmful effects of ultraviolet radiation. Without the ozone layer, skin cancer would likely become a leading cause of death, and spending a day at the beach would be as harmful as snuggling up to an open barrel of radioactive waste. At lower levels of the atmosphere, however, ozone occurs as a by-product of a chemical reaction between unburned hydrocarbons (as from petroleum products), nitrogen oxides, and sunlight.[1] In this form, it is a major component of smog, and breathing it can cause coughing, asthma attacks, chest pain, and possibly long-term lung-function impairment.

Consider also polychlorinated biphenyls (PCBs), molecules that exist only in synthetic form. Because they are chemically quite stable, PCBs are useful in a variety of industrial applications, including insulation in large electrical transformers. Without PCBs, electricity generation would be more expensive, as would the thousands of other goods that depend on electricity for their production and distribution. Yet PCBs are also highly toxic; acute exposure (as from ingestion) can result in rapid death. Chronic (long-term) exposure is suspected to cause some forms of cancer. Illegal dumping of PCBs into streams and lakes has caused massive fish kills and is generally regarded as a threat to drinking-water supplies. And because

---

1. Ozone is also produced as a by-product of lightning strikes and other electrical discharges. Wherever and however it occurs, it has a distinctive metallic taste.

PCBs are chemically stable (that is, they decompose very slowly), once they are released into the environment, they remain a potential threat for generations.

As these examples suggest, the notion of pollution is highly sensitive to context. Even crude oil, so essential as a source of energy, can become pollution when it washes up on Alaska's pristine shores. Despite this fact, we shall assume in what follows that (1) we all know what pollution is when we see, smell, taste, or even read about it, and (2) holding other things constant, less of it is preferable to more.

There are numerous ways to reduce or avoid pollution. Laws can be passed banning production processes that emit pollutants into the air and water or specifying minimum air- and water-quality levels or the maximum amount of pollution allowable. Firms would then be responsible for developing the technology and for paying the price to satisfy such standards. Or the law could specify the particular type of production technology to be used and the type of pollution-abatement equipment required in order to produce output legally. Finally, subsidies could be paid to firms that reduce pollution emission, or taxes could be imposed on firms that engage in pollution emission.

No matter which methods are used to reduce pollution, **costs** will be incurred and problems will arise. For example, setting physical limits on the amount of pollution permitted discourages firms from developing the technology that will reduce pollution beyond those limits. The alternative of subsidizing firms that reduce pollution levels may seem a strange use of taxpayers' dollars. The latest solution to the air-pollution problem—selling or trading the rights to pollute—may seem even stranger. Nevertheless, this approach is now being used around the nation, especially in Los Angeles, the smog capital of the country.

Under the plan that operates in the Los Angeles area, pollution allowances have been established for about 400 of the area's largest polluters. Both nitrous oxide (NO_x) and sulfur dioxide (SO_2), the two main ingredients of Southern California's brown haze, are covered. Prior to the plan, which went into effect in 1994, the government told companies such as power plants and oil refineries what techniques they had to use to reduce pollutants. Under the new rules, companies are simply told how much they must reduce emissions each year, and they are then allowed to use whatever means they see fit to meet the standards. Over the initial ten years of the plan, firms had their baseline emissions limits cut by 5 to 8 percent a year. Emissions of NO_x from these sources are down by 75 percent, and SO_2 emissions have been cut by 60 percent.

The key element in the program is that the companies are allowed to buy and sell pollution rights. A firm that is successful in reducing pollutants below the levels to which it is entitled receives emission reduction credits for doing so. The firm can sell those credits to other firms, enabling the latter to exceed their baseline emissions by the amount of credits they purchase.

Presumably, firms that can cut pollutants in the lowest-cost manner will do so, selling some of their credits to firms that find it more costly to meet the standards. Because the total level of emissions is determined ahead of time by the area's air-quality management district, the trading scheme will meet the requisite air-quality standards. Yet because most of the emission reductions will be made by firms that are the most efficient at doing so, the standards will be met at the lowest cost to society.

A similar market-based plan covering SO_2 has been adopted by the Environmental Protection Agency (EPA) on a nationwide level. Each emission allowance issued under this plan permits a power utility to emit one ton of SO_2 into the air. Based on their past records, utilities have been given rights to emit SO_2 into the air at a declining rate into the future. Companies can use their allowances to comply with the clean-air regulations, or they can beat the standards and sell their unused allowances to other utilities. There are also EPA-initiated trading programs for the emissions produced by heavy-duty on-highway engines (such as found in large trucks) and for NO_x emissions from power plants in the eastern United States.

The private markets in tradable allowances seem to be quite efficient at doing what they are designed to do—move allowances to their highest-valued locations, permit equalization of control costs across sources, and generate information about the costs of reducing emissions. Because firms can freely choose between either abating or releasing a given amount of emissions, they will pay no more for an allowance than it will save them in abatement costs. Equivalently, a company will pay no more for abatement than it would pay for an allowance to emit the pollutant. Thus the existence of a common price for allowances assures us that the cost per ton of cutting emissions must be at that same level. If the price of a permit to emit a ton of SO_2 is $1,000, for example, then the costs of abating SO_2 emissions must be running about $1,000 per ton.

According to the U.S. Council of Economic Advisers, the tradable-permit plans have not only helped contribute to substantial cuts from major sources but have also reduced the costs of achieving this environmental improvement. It also appears that the **transaction costs** of trading allowances are quite low—about 2 percent of the prevailing price—and that the prices at which trade takes place at any point in time are all quite close together. Hence this market is not only doing what it is supposed to be doing, but it is accomplishing it at low costs.

Perhaps not surprisingly, the notion of selling the right to pollute has been controversial, particularly among environmental organizations. The activist group Greenpeace, for example, claims that selling pollution allowances "is like giving a pack of cigarettes to a person dying of lung cancer." Nonetheless, other environmental groups have chosen to buy some of the allowances and retire them unused. One such group was the Cleveland-based National Healthy Air License Exchange, whose president said, "It is our intent . . . to have a real effect on this market and on the quality of air."

Some observers have been disappointed that the government has taken so long to approve emission-trading schemes. There appear to be two key reasons why progress has been so slow. First, many environmentalists have been vigorously opposed to the very concept of tradable emissions, arguing that it amounts to putting a price on what has traditionally been considered a "priceless" **resource**—the environment. Because most of the cost savings that stem from tradable-emissions rights accrue to the polluters and their customers, government agencies have proceeded carefully, to avoid charges that they are somehow selling out to polluters.

Ironically, the second reason for the delay in developing markets for tradable pollution rights has been the reluctance on the part of industry to push harder for them. Similar programs in the past involved emissions credits that could be saved up (banked) by a firm for later use or bartered on a limited basis among firms. Under these earlier programs, environmental regulators would periodically wipe out emissions credits that firms thought they owned, on the ground that doing so provided a convenient means of preventing future environmental damage.

Not surprisingly, some companies believe that any credits purchased under a tradable-rights plan might be subject to the same sort of confiscation. Under such circumstances, these firms have been understandably reluctant to support a program that might not prove to be of real value.[2] Indeed, even under the tradable-emissions plan adopted for Los Angeles, the regulators have explicitly stated that the emissions credits are *not* property rights and that they can be revoked at any time. Sadly, unless obstacles such as these can be removed, achieving environmental improvement at the lowest **social cost** is likely to remain a goal rather than an accomplishment.

---

2. One can imagine the enthusiasm people would feel toward, say, the market for automobiles if the government announced that because cars were a source of pollution, the **property rights** to them might be revoked at any time, for any reason.

DISCUSSION QUESTIONS

1. Does marketing the right to pollute mean that we are allowing too much destruction of our environment?

2. Who implicitly has property rights to the air when the EPA sells SO_2 permits? Does your answer depend on who gets the revenue raised by the sale?

3. Some environmental groups have opposed tradable pollution rights on the grounds that this puts a price on the environment when in fact the environment is a priceless resource. Does this reasoning imply that we should be willing to give up *anything* (and therefore everything) to protect the environment? Does environmental quality have an infinite value? If not, how should we place a value on it?

4. Environmental regulations that prohibit emissions beyond some point implicitly allow firms and individuals to pollute up to that point at no charge. Don't such regulations amount to giving away environmental quality at no charge? Would it be better to charge a price via emissions taxes, for example, for the initial amount of pollutants? Would doing so reduce the amount of pollution?

Chapter 29

GREENHOUSE ECONOMICS

The sky may not be falling, but it is getting warmer—maybe. The consequences will not be catastrophic, but they will be costly—maybe. We can reverse the process but should not spend very much to do so right now—maybe. Such is the state of the debate over the greenhouse effect— the apparent tendency of carbon dioxide (CO_2) and other gases to accumulate in the atmosphere, acting like a blanket that traps radiated heat, thereby increasing the earth's temperature. Before turning to the economics of the problem, let's take a brief look at the physical processes involved.

Certain gases in the atmosphere, chiefly water vapor and CO_2, trap heat radiating from the earth's surface. If they did not, the earth's average temperature would be roughly 0°F instead of just over 59°F, and everything would be frozen solid. Human activity helps create some so-called greenhouse gases, including CO_2 (mainly from combustion of fossil fuels) and methane (from landfills and livestock). We have the potential, unmatched in any other species, to profoundly alter our ecosystem.

There seems little doubt that humankind has been producing these gases at a record rate and that they are steadily accumulating in the atmosphere. Airborne concentrations of CO_2, for example, are increasing at the rate of about 0.5 percent per year; over the past fifty years, the amount of CO_2 in the atmosphere has risen a total of about 25 percent. Laboratory analysis of glacial ice dating back at least 160,000 years indicates that global temperatures and CO_2 levels in the atmosphere do, in fact, tend to move together, suggesting that the impact of today's rising CO_2 levels may be higher global temperatures in the future. Indeed, the National Academy of Sciences (NAS) has suggested that by the middle of the twenty-first century, greenhouse gases could be double the levels they were in 1860 and that global temperatures could rise by 2°F to 9°F.[1] The possible consequences of such a temperature increase include a rise in the average sea level, inundating coastal areas, including much of Florida; the spread of algal blooms capable of deoxygenating major bodies of water, such as Chesapeake Bay; and the conversion of much of the midwestern wheat and corn belt into a hot, arid dust bowl.

When an individual drives a car or heats a house, greenhouse gases are produced. In economic terms, this creates a classic **negative externality.** Most of the **costs** (in this case, those arising from global warming) are borne by individuals *other than* the one making the decision about how many miles to drive. Because the driver enjoys all the benefits of the activity but suffers only a part of the cost, that individual engages in more than the economically efficient amount of the activity. In this sense, the problem of greenhouse gases parallels the problem that occurs when someone smokes a cigarette in an enclosed space or litters the countryside with fast-food wrappers. If we are to get individuals to reduce production of greenhouse gases to the efficient rate, we must somehow induce them to act *as though* they bear all the costs of their actions. The two most widely accepted means of doing this are government regulation and taxation, both of which have been proposed to deal with greenhouse gases.

The 1988 Toronto Conference on the Changing Atmosphere, attended by representatives from forty-eight nations, favored the regulation route. The conference recommended a mandatory cut in CO_2 emissions by 2005 to 80 percent of their 1988 level—a move that would have required a major reduction in worldwide economic output. The 1997 Kyoto conference on climate change, attended by representatives from 160 nations, made more specific but also more modest proposals. Overall, attendees agreed that by 2012, thirty-eight developed nations should cut greenhouse emissions by 5 percent relative to 1990 levels. Developing nations, including China and India (the two most populous nations in the world), would be exempt from emissions cuts. On the taxation front, one prominent U.S. politician has proposed a tax of $100 per ton on the carbon emitted by fuels. It is estimated that such a tax would raise the price of coal by $70 per ton and elevate the price of oil by $8 per barrel. These proposals, and others like them, clearly have the potential to reduce

---

1. This may not sound like much, but it does not take much to alter the world as we know it. The global average temperature at the height of the last ice age eighteen thousand years ago—when Canada and most of Europe were covered with ice—was 51°F, a mere 8°F or so cooler than today.

the buildup of greenhouse gases but only at substantial costs. It thus makes some sense to ask, what are we likely to get for our money?

Perhaps surprisingly, the answer to this question is not obvious. Consider the raw facts of the matter. On average over the past century, greenhouse gases have been rising, and so has the average global temperature. Yet most of the temperature rise occurred before 1940, whereas most of the increase in greenhouse gases occurred after 1940. In fact, global average temperatures fell about 0.5°F between 1940 and 1970; this cooling actually led a number of prominent scientists during the 1970s to forecast a coming ice age!

Between 1975 and 2000, the upward march of global temperatures resumed, accompanied by rising concentrations of greenhouse gases. At the same time, however, sunspot and other solar activity rose considerably, and the sun became brighter than in a thousand years. Then temperatures started falling, accompanied by diminished solar activity. Many scientists believe that the sun has thus contributed to the earth's temperature fluctuations. Debate remains, however, over how big this contribution has been.

Let us suppose for the moment that barring a significant reduction in greenhouse gas emissions, global warming is under way and that more is on the way. What can we expect? It appears that the answer is a "good news, bad news" story.

The bad news is this: The likely rise in sea level by 1 to 3 feet will inundate significant portions of our existing coastline; the expected decline in precipitation in key regions will necessitate more widespread use of irrigation; the higher average temperatures will compel more widespread use of air conditioning, along with the associated higher consumption of energy to power it; and the blazing heat in southern latitudes may make these areas too uncomfortable for all but the most heat-loving souls. The good news is that the technology for coping with changes such as these is well known and the costs of coping are surprisingly small (on a scale measured in hundreds of billions of dollars, of course). Moreover, many of the impacts that loom large at the individual level will represent much smaller costs at a societal level. For example, although higher average temperatures could prove disastrous for farmers in southern climes, the extra warmth could be an enormous windfall farther north, where year-round farming might become feasible. Similarly, the loss of shoreline due to rising sea levels would partly just be a migration of coastline inland—current beachfront property owners would suffer, but their inland neighbors would gain.[2]

---

2. There would be a net loss of land area and thus a net economic loss. Nevertheless, the net loss of land would be chiefly in the form of less valuable inland property.

None of these changes are free, of course, and there remain significant uncertainties about how global warming might affect species other than *Homo sapiens.* It is estimated, for example, that temperate forests can "migrate" only at a rate of about 60 miles per century, not fast enough to match the speed at which warming is expected to occur. Similarly, the anticipated rise in the sea level could wipe out between 30 and 70 percent of today's coastal wetlands. Whether new wetlands would develop along our new coastline and what might happen to species that occupy existing wetlands are questions that have not yet been resolved.

Yet the very uncertainties that surround the possible warming of the planet suggest that policy prescriptions of the sort that have been proposed—such as the cut in worldwide CO_2 emissions agreed to at Kyoto—may be too much, too soon. Caution seems particularly wise, because the exclusion of China, India, and other developing nations from any emissions cuts could result in huge costs for developed nations but little or no reduction in worldwide greenhouse gases. Some sense of the damage that can be wrought by ignoring such counsel and rushing into a politically popular response to a complex environmental issue is well illustrated by another atmospheric problem: smog.

Although gasoline is a major source of the hydrocarbons in urban air, its contribution to smog plummeted because cars now run far cleaner than their predecessors. In the 1970s, cars spewed about 9 grams of hydrocarbons per mile; emissions controls brought this down to about 1.5 grams per mile by 1995. The cost of this reduction is estimated to be approximately $1,000 for each ton of hydrocarbon emissions prevented—a number that many experts believe to be well below the benefits of the cleaner air that resulted. Despite the improvements in air quality, smog is still a problem in many major cities. Additional federal regulations aimed primarily at the nine smoggiest urban areas, including New York, Chicago, and Los Angeles, went into effect in 1995. Meeting these standards meant that gasoline had to be reformulated at a cost of about 6 cents per gallon. This brought the cost of removing each additional ton of hydrocarbons to about $10,000—ten times the per-ton cost of removing the first 95 percent from urban air.

Over the past fifteen years, new Environmental Protection Agency (EPA) rules for reformulated gasoline (RFG) have added even more to the cost of gasoline and have had other (presumably unintended) adverse consequences. For example, initially, the RFG standards could be met only with the addition to gasoline of ethanol or methyl tertiary butyl ether (MTBE). Because ethanol was considerably more expensive than MTBE, refiners used MTBE. But after a few years, it appeared that leakage of MTBE from storage tanks was contaminating groundwater and that the substance was highly carcinogenic. Numerous states banned its use on the grounds that whatever it did to improve air quality, its adverse effects elsewhere were likely far more damaging. (The EPA has since allowed refiners more flexibility in meeting the RFG standards.)

Overall, EPA rules on RFG have led to a "patchwork quilt" of regulations across the country: Some dirty-air locations must use one type of gas, while others, with cleaner air, can use different gas. The presence of multiple EPA standards across the country has left supplies of gasoline vulnerable to disruption, because fuel often cannot be transshipped from one area to another to meet temporary **shortages.** This fact has contributed substantially to large spikes in the price of gasoline in major midwestern cities, such as Milwaukee and Chicago, every time there has been even a minor supply disruption.

Overall, the costs of EPA-mandated gasoline reformulation are huge, even though the EPA has never shown that RFG is necessary to meet its air-quality standards. The potential benefits of RFG appear to be small compared to the costs, yet we are stuck with this EPA mandate because few politicians want to be accused of being in favor of smog.

There is no doubt that atmospheric concentrations of greenhouse gases are rising and that human actions are the cause. It is probable that as a result, the global average temperature is rising. If temperatures rise significantly, the costs will be large, but the consequences are likely to be manageable. Given the nature of the problem, private action, taken on the individual level, will not yield the optimal outcome for society. Thus the potential gains from government action, in the form of environmental regulations or taxation, are substantial. But the key word here is *potential* because government action, no matter how well intentioned, does not automatically yield benefits that exceed the costs. As we seek solutions to the potential problems associated with greenhouse gases, we must be sure that the consequences of action are not worse than those of first examining the problem further. If we forget this message, greenhouse economics may turn into bad economics—and worse policy.

DISCUSSION QUESTIONS

1. Why will voluntary actions, undertaken at the individual level, be unlikely to bring about significant reductions in greenhouse gases such as CO_2?

2. Does the fact that the CO_2 produced in one nation results in adverse effects on other nations have any bearing on the likelihood that CO_2

emissions will be reduced to the optimal level? Would the problem be easier to solve if all the costs and benefits were concentrated within a single country? Within a single elevator or office?

3. The policy approach to greenhouse gases will almost certainly involve limits on emissions rather than taxes on emissions. Can you suggest why limits rather than taxes are likely to be used?

4. It costs about $80,000 per acre to create wetlands. How reasonable is this number as an estimate of what wetlands are worth?

PART SEVEN

Globalization and Economic Prosperity

Introduction

Many of the key public issues of our day transcend national borders or affect the entirety of our $15 trillion economy. The rapid developments in information processing, communications, and transportation over the past thirty years are gradually knitting the economies of the world closer together. Political developments, most notably the demise of the Iron Curtain and the dissolution of the Soviet Union, have contributed to this growing **globalization** of world economies, as have reductions in long-standing barriers to international trade. Moreover, over the past decade or so, awareness has been growing that the economic vitality of individual markets is importantly affected by decisions made in Washington, D.C.

The passage of the North American Free Trade Agreement (NAFTA) and the creation of the **World Trade Organization (WTO)** have substantially reduced the barriers to trade between the United States and most of the rest of the world. If we take advantage of these lower **trade barriers,** we have the opportunity to make ourselves far better off by specializing in activities in which we have a **comparative advantage** and then trading the fruits of our efforts with other nations. Yet voluntary exchange also often redistributes wealth, in addition to creating it, so there will always be some individuals who oppose free trade. There are many smoke screens behind which the self-interested opposition to globalization is hidden, as we see in Chapter 30, "Globalization and the Wealth of America." Nevertheless, although **protectionism**—the creation of trade barriers such as **tariffs** and **quotas**—often sounds sensible, it is in fact a surefire way to reduce rather than enhance our wealth. If we ignore the value of free trade, we do so only at our peril.

To illustrate the tremendous damage that can result when protectionism gains the upper hand, Chapter 31, "The $750,000 Steelworker," examines what happens when tariffs and quotas are imposed in an effort to "save" U.S. jobs from foreign **competition.** The facts are that in the long run, it is almost impossible to protect U.S. workers from globalization, and efforts to do so not only reduce Americans' overall living standards but also end up costing the jobs of other Americans. The moral is that competition is just as beneficial on the international scene as it is on the domestic front.

For decades, Americans have worried about competition from cheap labor in China. As you will see in Chapter 32, "The Lion, the Dragon, and the Future," China has been adopting capitalist **institutions** over the past thirty years and has reaped the rewards, most notably in the form of a rapidly rising standard of living for its people. But accompanying this has been the emergence of China as a major player in world markets. Indeed, China is now America's number two trading partner (after Canada) and may even have risen to number one by the time you read this. The growing volume of trade between the United States and China has created enormous wealth for people in both nations, albeit not without costly adjustments for some individuals. India, too, is becoming an important player in world markets, although its relatively late entry into global competition makes it less significant than China—for the moment. When discussing trade with any nation, however, the crucial fact to keep in mind is that international trade is fundamentally no different from interstate trade or interpersonal trade: As long as it is voluntary, the result is a higher standard of living for all participants.

Chapter 30

GLOBALIZATION AND THE WEALTH OF AMERICA

The past two decades have been a time of great change for international trade and **globalization.** The North American Free Trade Agreement (NAFTA), for example, substantially reduced the **trade barriers** among citizens of Canada, the United States, and Mexico. On a global scale, the Uruguay round of the General Agreement on Tariffs and Trade (GATT) was ratified by 117 nations, including the United States. Under the terms of this agreement, GATT was replaced by the **World Trade Organization (WTO),** whose membership now numbers about 150, and **tariffs** were cut worldwide. Agricultural **subsidies** were reduced, patent protections were extended, and the WTO established a set of arbitration boards to settle international disputes over trade issues.

Many economists believe that both NAFTA and the agreements reached during the Uruguay round were victories not only for free trade and globalization but also for the citizens of the participating nations. Nevertheless, many noneconomists, particularly politicians, opposed these agreements, so it is important that we understand what is beneficial about NAFTA, the Uruguay round, and free trade in general.

Voluntary trade creates new wealth. In voluntary trade, both parties in an exchange gain. They give up something of lesser value in return for something of greater value. In this sense, exchanges are always unequal. But it is this unequal nature of exchange that is the source of the increased **productivity** and higher wealth that occurs whenever trade takes place. When we engage in exchange, what we give up is worth less than what we get—for if this were not true, we would not have traded. And what is true for us is also true for our trading partner, meaning that both partners end up better off.

Free trade encourages individuals to use their talents and abilities in the most productive manner possible and to exchange the fruits of their efforts. The **gains from trade** lie in one of the most fundamental ideas in economics: A nation gains from doing what it can do best *relative to other nations*, that is, by specializing in endeavors in which it has a **comparative advantage.** Trade encourages individuals and nations to discover ways to specialize so that they can become more productive and enjoy higher incomes. Increased productivity and the subsequent increase in economic growth are exactly what the signatories of the Uruguay round and NAFTA sought—and are obtaining—by reducing trade barriers.

Globalization differs from free trade chiefly in the degree of integration across nations. For example, although there is free trade in wine, the wines produced in Australia, California, and France are each created wholly within the geopolitical borders indicated by their labels. Moreover, each remains a distinct economic entity, in that significant relative price changes between, say, French and California wines are observed. In contrast, the market for automobiles has become truly "global": If you purchase a "Japanese" automobile in the United States, assembly of the vehicle may have taken place in Japan, the United States, or even Mexico, and the components of the car may have come from a half-dozen or more different nations. And if you call for customer support for your car, the person answering the phone may be at a call center located in any of a variety of English-speaking nations. Globalization thus means that trade between nations becomes as seamless as trade between states, provinces, or cities within a given nation.

Despite the enormous gains from exchange, globalization is routinely opposed by some people. Many excuses are offered for this opposition, but they all basically come down to one issue: When our borders are fully open to trade with other nations, some individuals and businesses in our nation face more competition. As you saw in Chapter 19, most firms and workers hate competition, and who can blame them? After all, if a firm can keep the competition out, **profits** are sure to rise. And if workers can prevent competition from other sources, they can enjoy higher wages and greater selection among jobs. So the real source of most opposition to globalization is that the opponents to trade dislike the competition that comes with it. There is nothing immoral or unethical about this—but there is nothing altruistic or noble about it, either. It is self-interest, pure and simple.

One aspect of globalization that looms large in the minds of its opponents is the unremitting competitive vigilance that it requires. When world markets are completely integrated, one's competitors may emerge at any time from any place—often from corners of the world that one may least expect. And because competitors may only need to create a Web site to get started and can have their products delivered the next day by air freight, that competition can emerge devastatingly quickly. Thus when operating in a global economy, firms and their employees must contend with a level of uncertainty that is simply not present when trade patterns are less integrated. Note that this highly competitive atmosphere ultimately benefits all of us, but that doesn't make it any less unnerving for those who must endure its pressures, day after day. Competition is tough, and global competition is toughest of all.

Because of this, opposition to globalization is nothing new. One of the most famous examples of such opposition led to passage of the Smoot-Hawley Tariff of 1930. This major federal statute was a classic example of **protectionism**—an effort to protect a subset of American producers at the expense of consumers and other producers. It included tariff schedules for more than twenty thousand products, raising taxes on affected imports by an average of 52 percent.

The Smoot-Hawley Tariff encouraged beggar-thy-neighbor policies by the rest of the world. Such policies represent an attempt to improve (a portion of) one's domestic economy at the expense of foreign countries' economies. In this case, tariffs were imposed to discourage **imports** so that domestic import-competing industries would benefit. The beggar-thy-neighbor policy at the heart of Smoot-Hawley was soon adopted by the United Kingdom, France, the Netherlands, and Switzerland. The result was a halt to globalization and a massive reduction in international trade that almost certainly exacerbated the worldwide depression of the 1930s.

Opponents of globalization sometimes claim that beggar-thy-neighbor policies benefit the United States by protecting import-competing industries. In general, this claim is not correct. It is true that some Americans benefit from such policies, but two large groups of Americans lose. First, there are the purchasers of imports and import-competing goods. They suffer from higher prices and reduced selection of goods and suppliers caused by tariffs and import **quotas.** Second, the decline in imports caused by protectionism also causes a decline in **exports,** thereby harming firms and employees in these industries. This follows directly from one of the most fundamental propositions in international trade: *In the long run, imports are paid for by exports.* This proposition simply states that when one country buys goods and services from the rest of the world (imports), the rest of the world eventually wants goods from that country (exports) in exchange. Given this fundamental proposition, a corollary becomes obvious: *Any restriction on imports leads to a reduction in exports.* Thus any business for import-competing industries gained as a result of tariffs or quotas means at least as much business lost for exporting industries.

Opponents of globalization raise a variety of objections in their efforts to restrict international trade. For example, it is sometimes said that foreign companies engage in dumping, that is, selling their goods in America below cost. The first question to ask is, below *whose* cost? Clearly, if the foreign firm is selling in America, it must be offering the good for sale at a price that is at or below the cost of American firms, or else it could not induce Americans to buy it. But the ability of individuals or firms to get goods at lower cost is one of the *benefits* of free trade, not one of its negatives.

What about claims that import sales are taking place at prices below the foreign company's costs? This amounts to arguing that the owners of the foreign company are voluntarily giving some of their wealth to us, namely, the difference between their costs and the lower price they charge us. It is possible, though unlikely, that they might wish to do this as a way of getting us to try a product that we would not otherwise purchase. But if so, why would we want to refuse this gift? As a nation, we are richer if we accept it. Moreover, it is a gift that will be offered for only a short while, for there is no point in selling below one's cost unless one hopes soon to raise price profitably above cost!

Another argument sometimes raised against globalization is that the goods are produced abroad using unfair labor practices (such as the use of child labor) or using production processes that do not meet American environmental standards. Such charges are sometimes correct. But we must remember two things. First, although we may find the use of child labor (or perhaps sixty-hour work weeks with no overtime pay) objectionable, such practices were once common in the United States. They used to be prevalent in America for the same reason they are now practiced abroad: The people involved were (or are) too poor to do otherwise. Some families in developing nations cannot survive unless all members of the family contribute. As unfortunate as this is, if we insist on imposing our attitudes—shaped in part by our great wealth—on peoples whose wealth is far lower than ours, we run the risk of making them worse off even as we think we are helping them.

Similar considerations apply to environmental standards[1] It is well established that individuals' and nations' willingness to pay for environmental quality is very much shaped by their wealth: Environmental quality is a **luxury good;** that is, people who are rich (such as Americans)

---

1. There is one important exception to this argument. In the case of foreign air or water pollution generated near enough to our borders (for example, with Mexico or Canada) to cause harm to Americans, good public policy presumably dictates that we seek to treat such pollution as though it were being generated inside our borders.

want to consume much more of it per capita than people who are poor. Insisting that other nations meet environmental standards that we find acceptable is much like insisting that they wear the clothes we wear, use the modes of transportation we prefer, and consume the foods we like. The few people who manage to comply will indeed be living in the style to which we are accustomed, but most people will simply be impoverished by the attempt.

Our point is not that foreign labor or environmental standards are, or should be, irrelevant to Americans. Our point is that achieving high standards of either is costly, and trade restrictions are unlikely to be the most efficient or most effective way to achieve them. Just as important, labor standards and environmental standards are all too often raised as smoke screens to hide the real motive: keeping the competition out.

If it is true that globalization is beneficial and that restrictions on trade are generally harmful, we must surely raise the question, how does legislation like the Smoot-Hawley Tariff (or any other such restriction) ever get passed? As Mark Twain noted many years ago, the reason the free traders win the arguments and the protectionists win the votes is this: Foreign competition often clearly affects a narrow and specific import-competing industry such as textiles, shoes, or automobiles, and thus trade restrictions benefit a narrow, well-defined group of economic agents. For example, restrictions on imports of Japanese automobiles in the 1980s chiefly benefited the Big Three automakers in this country: General Motors, Ford, and Chrysler. Similarly, long-standing quotas on the imports of sugar benefit a handful of large American sugar producers. And when tariffs of up to 30 percent were slapped on many steel imports in 2002, an even smaller number of American steelmakers and their employees benefited. Because of the concentrated benefits that accrue when Congress votes in favor of trade restrictions, sufficient funds can be raised in those industries to convince members of Congress to impose those restrictions.

The eventual reduction in exports that must follow is normally spread in small doses throughout all export industries. Thus no specific group of workers, managers, or shareholders in export industries will feel that it should contribute money to convince Congress to reduce barriers to globalization. Furthermore, although consumers of imports and import-competing goods lose due to trade restrictions, they too are typically a diffuse group of individuals, none of whom will be individually affected a great deal because of any single import restriction. It is the simultaneous existence of concentrated benefits and diffuse costs that led to Mark Twain's conclusion that the protectionists would often win the votes. (Concentrated benefits and dispersed costs are at the heart of Chapter 2,

"Ethanol Madness," and Chapter 23, "Raising Less Corn and More Hell," in explaining some U.S. domestic policies.)

Of course, the protectionists don't win all the votes—after all, almost one-sixth of the U.S. economy is based on international trade. Despite the opposition to globalization that comes from many quarters, its benefits to the economy as a whole are so great that it is unthinkable that we might do away with international trade altogether. Thus when we think about developments such as NAFTA and the WTO, it is clear that both economic theory and empirical evidence indicate that Americans will be better off after—and because of—globalization.

DISCUSSION QUESTIONS

1. During the late 1980s and early 1990s, American automobile manufacturers greatly increased the quality of the cars they produced relative to the quality of the cars produced in other nations. What effect do you think this had on American imports of Japanese cars, on Japanese imports of American cars, and on American exports of goods and services other than automobiles?

2. Over the past twenty years, some Japanese automakers have opened plants in the United States so that they could produce (and sell) "Japanese" cars here. What effect do you think this had on American imports of Japanese cars, on Japanese imports of American cars, and on American exports of goods and services other than automobiles?

3. For a number of years, Japanese carmakers voluntarily limited the number of cars they exported to the United States. What effect do you think this had on Japanese imports of American cars and on American exports of goods and services other than automobiles?

4. Until recently, American cars exported to Japan had driver controls on the left side (as in the United States), even though the Japanese drive on the left side of the road and Japanese cars sold in Japan have driver controls on the right side. Suppose the Japanese tried to sell their cars in the United States with the driver controls on the right side. What impact would this likely have on their sales in this country? Do you think the unwillingness of American carmakers to put the driver controls on the correct side for exports to Japan had any effect on their sales of cars in that country?

Chapter 31

THE $750,000 STEELWORKER

In even-numbered years, particularly years evenly divisible by 4, politicians are apt to give speeches about the need to protect U.S. jobs from the evils of **globalization.** We are thus encouraged to buy American. If further encouragement is needed, we are told that if we do not voluntarily reduce the amount of imported goods we purchase, the government will impose (or make more onerous) either **tariffs** (taxes) on imported goods or **quotas** (quantity restrictions) that physically limit **imports.** The objective is to save U.S. jobs.

Unlike black rhinos or blue whales, U.S. jobs are in no danger of becoming extinct. There are an infinite number of potential jobs in the American economy, and there always will be. Some of these jobs are not very pleasant, and many others do not pay very well, but there will always be employment of some sort as long as there is **scarcity.** Thus when a steelworker making $72,000 per year says that imports of foreign steel should be reduced to save his job, what he really means is this: He wants to be protected from **competition** so he can continue his present employment at the same or higher salary rather than move to a different employment that has less desirable working conditions or pays a lower salary. There is nothing wrong with the steelworker's goal (better working conditions and higher pay), but it has nothing to do with saving jobs.

In any discussion of the consequences of restrictions on international trade, it is essential to remember two facts. First, *we pay for imports with exports.* It is true that in the short run, we can sell off assets or borrow from abroad if we happen to import more goods and services than we export. But we have only a finite amount of assets to sell, and foreigners do not want to wait forever before we pay our bills. Ultimately, our accounts can be settled only if we provide (export) goods and services to the trading partners from whom we purchase (import) goods and services.

Trade, after all, involves *quid pro quo* (literally, something for something). The second point to remember is that *voluntary trade is mutually beneficial to the trading partners.* If we restrict international trade, we reduce those benefits, both for our trading partners and for ourselves. One way these reduced benefits are manifested is in the form of curtailed employment opportunities for workers. In a nutshell, even though tariffs and quotas enhance job opportunities in import-competing industries, they also cost us jobs in export industries; the net effect seems to be *reduced* employment overall.

What is true for the United States is also true for other countries: They will buy our goods only if they can market theirs, because they too have to export goods to pay for their imports. Thus any U.S. restrictions on imports—via tariffs, quotas, or other means—ultimately cause a reduction in our exports, because other countries will be unable to pay for our goods. Hence import restrictions must inevitably decrease the size of our export sector. So imposing trade restrictions to save jobs in import-competing industries has the effect of costing jobs in export industries.

Import restrictions also impose costs on U.S. consumers. By reducing competition from abroad, quotas, tariffs, and other trade restraints push up the prices of foreign goods and enable U.S. producers to hike their own prices. Perhaps the best-documented example of this is the automobile industry.

Due in part to the enhanced quality of imported cars, sales of domestically produced automobiles fell from 9 million units in 1978 to an average of 6 million units per year between 1980 and 1982. **Profits** for U.S. automobile manufacturers plummeted as well, turning into substantial losses for some of them. U.S. automakers and autoworkers' unions demanded protection from import competition. They were joined in their cries by politicians from automobile-producing states. The result was a voluntary agreement by Japanese car companies (the most important competitors of U.S. firms) that restricted U.S. sales of Japanese cars to 1.68 million units per year. This agreement—which amounted to a quota even though it never officially bore that name—began in April 1981 and continued into the 1990s in various forms.

Robert W. Crandall, an economist with the Brookings Institution, has estimated how much this voluntary trade restriction has cost U.S. consumers in terms of higher car prices. According to his estimates, the reduced supply of Japanese cars pushed their prices up by $2,000 apiece, measured in 2009 dollars. The higher price of Japanese imports in turn enabled domestic producers to hike their prices an average of $800 per car. The total tab in the first full year of the program was over $8 billion. Crandall also estimated the number of jobs in automobile-related industries that were saved by the voluntary import restrictions at about 26,000. Dividing $8 billion by 26,000 jobs yields a cost to consumers of about $300,000 *per year* for every job saved in the automobile industry. U.S. consumers could have saved over $5 billion on their car purchases each year if instead of implicitly agreeing to import restrictions, they had simply given $100,000 to every autoworker whose job was preserved by the voluntary import restraints.

The same types of calculations have been made for other industries. Tariffs in the apparel industry were increased between 1977 and 1981, saving the jobs of about 116,000 U.S. apparel workers at a cost of $50,000 per job each year. At about the same time, the producers of citizens band radios also managed to get tariffs raised. Approximately six hundred workers in the industry kept their jobs as a result, at an annual cost to consumers of over $90,000 per job.

The cost of **protectionism** has been even higher in other industries. Jobs preserved in the glassware industry due to trade restrictions cost $200,000 apiece each year. In the maritime industry, the yearly cost of trade protection is $290,000 per job. In the steel industry, the cost of preserving a job has been estimated at an astounding $750,000 per year. If free trade were permitted, each worker losing a job could be given a cash payment of half that amount each year, and consumers would still save a lot of money.

Even so, this is not the full story. None of these studies estimating the cost to consumers of saving jobs in import-competing industries have attempted to estimate the ultimate impact of import restrictions on the flow of exports, the number of jobs lost in the export sector, and thus the total number of jobs gained or lost.

When imports to the United States are restricted, our trading partners will necessarily buy less of what we produce. The resulting decline in export sales means fewer jobs in exporting industries. And the total reduction in trade leads to fewer jobs for workers such as stevedores (who unload ships) and truck drivers (who carry goods to and from ports). On both counts—the overall cut in trade and the accompanying decline in exports—protectionism leads to job losses that might not be immediately obvious.

Several years ago, Congress tried to pass a domestic-content bill for automobiles. In effect, the legislation would have required that cars sold in the United States have a minimum percentage of their components manufactured and assembled in this country. Proponents of the legislation argued that it would have protected 300,000 jobs in the U.S. automobile manufacturing and auto parts supply industries. Yet the legislation's supporters failed to recognize the negative impact of the bill on trade in general and its ultimate impact on U.S. export industries. A U.S. Department of Labor study did recognize these impacts, estimating that the domestic-content legislation would actually cost more jobs in trade-related and export industries than it protected in import-competing businesses. Congress ultimately decided not to impose a domestic-content requirement for cars sold in the United States.

More recently, when President Bush decided in 2002 to impose tariffs of up to 30 percent on steel imports, the adverse effects on the economy were substantial and soon apparent. To take but one example, prior to the tariffs, the Port of New Orleans relied on steel imports for more than 40 percent of its revenues, in part because once steel coming into the port is offloaded, the ships are cleaned and refilled with U.S. grain for export. By reducing imports, the tariffs slashed economic activity at the port and also reduced U.S. grain exports. Businesses and farms all up and down the Mississippi River were adversely affected. More broadly, the higher costs of imported steel produced a decline in employment in U.S. industries that use steel as an input. Indeed, one study estimated that due to the tariffs, some 200,000 people lost their jobs in 2002 in these industries alone—a number that exceeded the total number of people actually employed by the steel manufacturing firms protected by the tariff.

In principle, trade restrictions are imposed to provide economic help to specific industries and to increase employment in those industries. Ironically, the long-term effects may be just the opposite. Researchers at the **World Trade Organization (WTO)** examined employment in three industries that have been heavily protected throughout the world: textiles, clothing, and iron and steel. Despite stringent trade protection for these industries, employment *declined* during the period of protection, in some cases dramatically. In textiles, employment fell 22 percent in the United States and 46 percent in the European Union. The clothing industry had employment losses ranging from 18 percent in the United States to 56 percent in Sweden. Declines in employment in the iron and steel industry ranged anywhere from 10 percent in Canada to 54 percent in the United States. In short, restrictions on free trade are no guarantee against job losses, even in the industries supposedly being protected.

The evidence seems clear: The cost of protecting jobs in the short run is huge. And in the long run, it appears that jobs cannot be protected, especially if one considers all aspects of protectionism. Free trade is a tough platform on which to run for office. But it is the one that yields the most general benefits if implemented. Of course, this does not mean that politicians will embrace it, and so we end up "saving" jobs at a cost of up to $750,000 each.

DISCUSSION QUESTIONS

1. Who gains and who loses from import restrictions?

2. What motivates politicians to impose trade restrictions?

3. If it would be cheaper to give each steelworker $375,000 per year in cash than impose restrictions on imports of steel, why do we have the import restrictions rather than the cash payments?

4. Most U.S. imports and exports travel through our seaports at some point. How do you predict that members of Congress from coastal states would vote on proposals to restrict international trade? What other information would you want to know when making such a prediction?

Chapter 32

THE LION, THE DRAGON, AND THE FUTURE

For decades after the Communists' rise to power in 1949, China was best known for poverty and repression, and its aggression came mostly on the military front. But in recent years, *economic* aggression has become the byword. Although both poverty and repression are still the norm, both are changing for the better. China, it seems, is trying to learn from capitalism, even if not converting to it.

China's economic offensive began thirty years ago in its southeastern province of Guangdong. The Chinese leadership decided to use this province as a test case, to see if capitalist **direct foreign investment** could stimulate **economic growth** in a way that could be politically controlled. The experience was deemed a success—economic growth soared amid political stability. What the government learned from the experience helped it smooth the 1997 transition of Hong Kong from British to Chinese control. Most important in terms of China's long-term economic aspirations, many foreign investors came to view the Guangdong experiment as solid evidence that they could invest in China without fear that the Communist government would confiscate their capital. The result: foreign investment in China soared.

There are two powerful forces that are attracting economic investment to China: **demand** and **supply.** On the demand side, 1.3 billion people live there, some 20 percent of the world's population. Although **per capita income** is still low by world standards, it has been increasing by more than 6 percent per year, after adjusting for inflation. At that rate, the standard of living for the Chinese people—and hence their **purchasing power** in world markets—is doubling every decade or so. China is already the world's largest cell-phone market, and within a few years, it is estimated, China will account for 25 percent of the world's purchases of personal computers. Indeed, China now spends over $100 billion per year on information technology and services. By 2030, the Chinese economy will likely have eclipsed the United States' and become the world's largest.

With its huge population, China also offers attractions on the supply side. Highly skilled workers have been plentiful in the Chinese labor market with hundreds of thousands of engineering graduates each year. In many cities, the fact that the Chinese workforce is generally well educated and often English-speaking has helped make the country attractive to foreign employers. Collaborative scientific ventures between Chinese researchers and U.S. firms are becoming increasingly common. A research team at Beijing University played a role in deciphering the genetic makeup of rice, for example. American computer hardware and software firms Intel, IBM, Oracle, and Microsoft have shifted some key components of their research to China in recent years. Indeed, American firms of all types are setting up operations in China. Chinese firms, meanwhile, are proving to be formidable competitors both at home and abroad.

The situation has become critical in Japan, where wages are much higher than in China but whose technological lead over China is gradually eroding. "Are we to become a vassal of the Chinese dynasty again?" asked one Japanese official, clearly concerned that his nation's manufacturing firms were having trouble competing with Chinese firms. Eventually, Japanese firms will adjust to the growing economic presence of China, but the transition may be unpleasant.

Americans are more concerned about the likely impact on the U.S. economy of China's capitalist ambitions. Will the dragon consume American firms and jobs as it grows? The short answer is no. The long answer has two elements. To this point, a key element of China's competitiveness has been the low wages there. Even though American and European firms operating in China choose to pay their workers more than state-owned enterprises pay, this has still yielded considerable savings. As recently as five years ago, unskilled and semiskilled labor in China cost only 25 percent as much as in Europe. Moreover, in the past, foreign firms have been able to hire engineers for salaries that are only 10 to 20 percent of the cost of hiring engineers in the West.

Labor markets in China are changing rapidly, however. Between 2000 and 2008, average wages rose 50 percent, with bigger increases among higher-skilled workers. Many firms were unable to hire as many workers as they would have liked, and most firms had to upgrade their fringe benefits and other on-the-job amenities just to retain existing workers. Wages are still well below American and European levels, but the gap has closed, thereby cutting the competitive advantage of many Chinese firms. The recent worldwide recession has altered labor market conditions as significantly in China as anywhere. But it is unlikely to impede China's march to economic superpower status.

Higher wages in China will also translate into higher demand for goods produced by American and European firms. China, like all nations, must in the long run import goods equal in value to those it exports (unless China intends to give its exports away, which so far no one is claiming). This means that just as China has become a potent supplier of many goods and services, it is at the same time becoming a potent demander of still other goods and services.

Thus far, the Chinese demand for goods has not been as visible in American markets because American firms tend to produce goods and services designed for higher-income consumers, and China has relatively few of those. In the meantime, the demand-side influence of the Chinese economy is already showing up, albeit in odd places. To take one example, right now China's most important import from the United States is trash. Ranging from used newspapers to scrap steel, Chinese companies buy billions of dollars' worth of the stuff every year to use as raw materials in the goods they produce. In addition to yielding profits (and employment) in these U.S. export industries, this exportation of U.S. trash reduces the burden on U.S. landfills and, by pushing up the prices of recyclable scrap, encourages more recycling in the United States.

Eventually, of course, we'd like to be sending China more than our rubbish, and that time is coming. As China's economy grows, so will the number of affluent Chinese, and with 1.3 billion potential candidates, that ultimately means *plenty* of consumers for America's high-end goods. Thus the long-run effects of China's growth will mean a different American economy—we'll be producing and consuming different mixes of goods and services—but America will also be a richer nation. Voluntary exchange creates wealth, and the Chinese dragon is big enough to create a lot of wealth.

To China's southwest, another giant is stirring. Around 1990, the lion of India began to throw off the self-imposed shackles of nearly a half-century of markets largely closed to international **competition.** The central government, for example, began opening state-owned companies to competition from private-sector rivals. FedEx and United Parcel Service (UPS) have made huge inroads on the Indian postal service, and numerous foreign firms are now competing with the state-owned telephone service, which had long been a complete **monopoly.**

Entry into the Indian market brought familiarity with its workforce, many of whose members are fluent in English. The technical capabilities of graduates of top Indian universities, combined with their English skills and low wages, made them perfect staffers for a proliferation of call centers that have opened throughout India. Tens of thousands of technical and customer-relations jobs that used to go to Middle America are now held by the growing middle class in India. As we discussed in Chapter 14, "A Farewell to Jobs," it was in many respects this very movement that brought **outsourcing** to the forefront of the American consciousness.

But India, too, is struggling with growth. The talent pool at the top is thin: Only a dozen or so of India's seventeen thousand universities and colleges can compete with America's best, and the wages of graduates of these top schools are soaring. Moreover, India suffers from overwhelming infrastructure problems: Much of its road system is either overcrowded or in disrepair, and its port facilities are in desperate need of modernization. For the time being, such transportation problems are likely to keep India from becoming a major manufacturing powerhouse. India has also been hampered by its huge and seemingly permanent government bureaucracy. For example, despite the fact that the postal service there has lost more than half of its business to newcomers such as FedEx and UPS, none of the 550,000 postal service employees can be fired.

At least India is a democracy, and its legal system, inherited from the British, who ruled there for so long, is in close conformity with the legal systems of most developed nations. Matters are rather different in China. As noted in Chapter 4, "The Mystery of Wealth," political and legal **institutions** are crucial foundations for sustained economic growth. Despite the advances China has made over the past thirty years, its wealth-creating future may be clouded unless it can successfully deal with two crucial institutional issues.

First, there is the matter of resolving the tension inherent when a Communist dictatorship tries to use capitalism as the engine of economic growth. Capitalism thrives best in an environment of freedom and itself creates an awareness of and appreciation for the benefits of that freedom. Yet freedom is antithetical to the ideological and political tenets of the Communist government of China. Will the government be tempted to confiscate the fruits of capitalist success to support itself? Or will growing pressure for more political freedom force the government to repress the capitalist system to protect itself? Either route would likely bring economic growth in China to a swift halt.

The second potential long-run problem faced by China lies in that nation's cultural attitude toward **intellectual property.** In a land in which imitation is viewed as the sincerest form of flattery, it is routine to use the ideas of others in one's own pursuits. As a result, patent and copyright laws in China are far weaker than in Western nations. Moreover, actions elsewhere considered to be commercial theft (such as software piracy) are largely tolerated in China. If foreign firms find that they cannot protect their economic **assets** in the Chinese market, foreign investment will suffer accordingly, and so will the growing dragon that depends on it so heavily.

DISCUSSION QUESTIONS

1. Currently, AIDS is spreading rapidly in China and India. If the governments of these nations fail to stop the spread of AIDS, what are the likely consequences for future economic growth in China and India?

2. In 1989, a massive protest against political repression in China was halted by the government's massacre of more than 150 individuals at Tiananmen Square in Beijing. What impact do you think that episode had on foreign investment and growth in China during the years immediately thereafter?

3. Most of the advances in institutions in China have come in the cities rather than in the countryside. Indeed, local officials in farming villages actively redistribute wealth among villagers to keep the distribution of income among local farmers roughly equal. Thus a farmer's success or failure with his crops has little impact on his family's standard of living. Given these facts, where do you think the economic growth in China has occurred over the past thirty years, in the cities or on the farms? Explain.

4. Explain how the following factors will influence India's ability to succeed in a highly competitive, rapidly changing global marketplace: (a) an educational system that is largely state-operated and that emphasizes job security for teachers and professors; (b) a transportation infrastructure that is largely antiquated and in disrepair; and (c) a political system that is adept at protecting favored constituents from competition and handing out favors that have concentrated benefits and widely dispersed costs.

G L O S S A R Y

Absolute advantage: The ability to produce more of a good, without regard for the costs of forgone output of other goods.

Acreage-restriction program: A federal government limit on the number of acres that a farmer can plant with a particular crop.

Adjustable-rate mortgages (ARMs): Debt obligations for which houses serve as the collateral and on which the lender may move the interest rate up or down by specified amounts at specified times.

Adverse selection: A process in which "undesirable" (high-cost or high-risk) participants tend to dominate one side of the market, causing adverse effects for the other side; often results from *asymmetric information.*

Assets: All tangible and intangible items to which an individual or institution holds a legal claim of ownership.

Asymmetric information: Circumstance in which participants on one side of a market have more information than participants on the other side of the market; often results in *adverse selection.*

Bank run: The simultaneous attempt by many of a bank's depositors to convert checkable and savings deposits into currency because of a perceived fear for the bank's solvency.

Biofuels: Fuels made from once-living organisms or their by-products.

Capital stock: The collection of productive assets that can be combined with other inputs, such as labor, to produce goods and services.

Cartel: A group of independent businesses, often on an international scale, that agree to restrict trade, to their mutual benefit.

Civil law system: A legal system in which statutes passed by legislatures and executive decrees, rather than judicial decisions based on precedent, form the basis for most legal rules.

Common law system: A legal system in which judicial decisions based on precedent, rather than executive decrees or statutes passed by legislatures, form the basis for most legal rules.

Comparative advantage: The ability to produce a good at a lower opportunity cost than others. The principle of comparative advantage implies that individuals, firms, and nations will specialize in producing goods for which they have the lowest opportunity cost compared to other entities.

Compensating differential: Additional pay given to workers employed in particularly hazardous or unpleasant jobs.

Competition: Rivalry among buyers or sellers of outputs or among buyers or sellers of inputs.

Constant-dollar price: Price corrected for changes in the purchasing power of the dollar, taking inflation and deflation into account.

Constant-quality price: The price of a good adjusted upward or downward to reflect the higher- or lower-than-average quality of that good.

Consumer price index: A measure of the dollar cost of a typical bundle of consumer goods relative to the cost of that bundle in a base year.

Cost: The highest-valued (best) forgone alternative; the most valuable option that is sacrificed when a choice is made.

Demand: The willingness and ability to purchase goods.

Demand curve: A graphic representation of demand: a negatively sloped line showing the inverse relationship between the price and the quantity demanded.

Direct foreign investment: Resources provided to individuals and firms in a nation by individuals or firms located in other countries, often taking the form of foreign subsidiary or branch operations of a parent company.

Disposable income: The maximum amount of spending consumers can undertake after they have paid direct taxes, such as income taxes.

Dynamic analysis: An assessment of the economic impact of a policy that takes into account the induced responses to that policy.

Earned-income tax credit: A tax policy that offers payments from the government to people who earn relatively low wages.

Economic good: Any good or service that is scarce.

Economic growth: Sustained increases over time in real per capita income.

Economic profits: Profits in excess of competitive profits, which are the minimum necessary to keep resources employed in an industry.

Elastic demand: Characteristic of a demand curve in which a given percentage change in price will result in a larger inverse percentage change in quantity demanded. Total revenues and price are inversely related in the elastic portion of the demand curve.

Elasticity: A measure of the responsiveness of one variable to a change in another variable; it is the ratio of two percentage changes.

Elasticity of demand: Responsiveness of the quantity of a commodity demanded to a change in its price per unit.

Elasticity of supply: Responsiveness of the quantity of a commodity supplied to a change in its price per unit.

Entitlement program: A government program that guarantees a certain level of benefits to persons who meet the requirements set by law.

Equilibrium price: Price that clears the market when there is no excess quantity demanded or supplied; the price at which the demand curve intersects the supply curve. *Also called* Market-clearing price.

Exports: Sales of goods or services to a foreign country.

Externalities: Benefits or costs of an economic activity that spill over to a third party. Pollution is a negative spillover or externality.

Fixed exchange rates: A system of legally fixed prices (rates) at which two or more national currencies trade (exchange) for one another.

Foreclosure: The legal process by which a borrower in default under a mortgage is deprived of his or her interest in the mortgaged property.

Free good: Any good or service available in larger quantities than desired at a zero price.

Full cost: The combined measure of all of the things that must be given up to undertake an activity; includes both the money price (other goods that must be sacrificed) and the value of the time that must be sacrificed.

Gains from trade: The extent to which individuals, firms, or nations benefit by engaging in exchange.

Globalization: The integration of national economies into an international economy as a result of lower trade barriers and reduced transportation and communication costs.

Human capital: The accumulated training, education, and knowledge of workers.

Illiquid: Not readily convertible to cash.

Imports: Purchases of goods or services from a foreign country.

Import tariff: A tax applied specifically to imports of goods or services from another nation.

Incentives: Perceived consequences of actions or decisions; they may be positive or negative, monetary or nonmonetary.

Income elasticity of demand: A measure of the responsiveness of demand to changes in income, calculated as the percentage change in demand for a good divided by the percentage change in consumer income.

Income mobility: The tendency of individuals to move around in the income distribution over time.

Inelastic: Relatively unresponsive.

Inelastic demand: Characteristic of a demand curve in which a given change in price will result in a less than proportionate inverse change in the quantity demanded. Total revenue and price are directly related in the inelastic region of the demand curve.

Inflation: A rise in the dollar cost of achieving a given level of satisfaction, often measured in terms of the dollar cost of a particular standard bundle of goods.

In-kind transfers: Grants of goods and services rather than cash to recipients who meet certain criteria. Examples include Medicare, Medicaid, subsidized housing, food stamps, and school lunches.

Insolvent: In a financial condition in which the value of one's assets is less than the value of one's liabilities.

Institutions: The basic rules, customs, and practices of society.

Intellectual property: Creative ideas and expressions of the human mind that have commercial value and receive the legal protection of a property right, as through the issuance of a patent, copyright, or trademark.

Labor force participation rate: The sum of all people who are working or are available for and looking for work, divided by the population; both numerator and denominator are generally restricted to persons age sixteen and above.

Law of demand: Law stating that quantity demanded and price are inversely related—more is bought at a lower price and less at a higher price (other things being equal).

Law of supply: Law stating that a direct relationship exists between price and quantity supplied (other things being equal).

Liabilities: Amounts owed; monetary claims against an individual or an institution.

Luxury good: A good for which the income elasticity of demand is greater than 1, meaning that people spend an increasing proportion of their income on the good as they get richer.

Marginal analysis: Analysis of what happens when small changes take place relative to the status quo.

Marginal benefits: Additional benefits associated with one more unit of a good or action; the change in total benefits due to the addition of one more unit of production.

Marginal costs: Changes in total costs due to a change in one unit of production.

Market-clearing price: *See* Equilibrium price.

Market share: The proportion of total sales in an industry accounted for by a specific firm or group of firms in that industry.

Market supply: Total quantities of a good offered for sale by suppliers at various prices.

Median age: Age that exactly separates the younger half of the population from the older half.

Minimum wage: The lowest hourly wage that firms may legally pay their workers.

Models, or theories: Simplified representations of the real world used to make predictions or to better understand the real world.

Monitoring costs: Costs that must be incurred to observe the behavior of a politician or other agent to whom responsibilities have been delegated.

Monopolistic competition: The situation that exists when producers and sellers offer for sale similar products with slight variations in features or quality; although the products are priced above their average minimum cost, competition among firms reduces long-run economic profits to zero.

Monopoly: A single supplier; a firm that faces a downward-sloping demand curve for its output and therefore can choose the price at which it will sell the good; an example of a *price searcher.*

Monopoly power: The ability of a company to charge a price for its product that is in excess of the marginal cost of producing the product.

Monopsonist: A firm operating as a monopsony.

Monopsony: A single buyer; a firm that faces an upward-sloping supply curve for its input and therefore can choose the price at which it will buy the good; an example of a *price searcher.*

Moral hazard: The tendency of an entity insulated from risk to behave differently than it would behave if it were fully exposed to the risk.

Natural-resource endowments: The collection of naturally occurring minerals (such as oil and iron ore) and living things (such as forests and fish stocks) that can be used to produce goods and services.

Negative externality: A cost associated with an economic activity that is paid by third parties. Pollution is a negative externality because, for example, someone other than the driver of an automobile bears part of the cost of the car's exhaust emissions.

Negative tax: A payment from the government made to supplement the incomes of people who earn low wages.

Nominal prices: The costs of goods, expressed in terms of a nation's currency, such as the dollar.

Nonprice competition: Offering additional services or higher product quality to attract business instead of cutting prices to do so.

Oligopoly: A firm that is one of very few sellers (or buyers) in a market; in such a case, each firm reacts to changes in the prices and quantities of its rivals.

Opportunity cost: The highest-valued alternative that must be sacrificed to attain something or to satisfy a want.

Outsourcing: The practice of having workers located in foreign lands perform tasks (typically services) that have traditionally been performed by domestic workers.

Per capita income: Average income per person.

Perfectly elastic: Characterized by an infinite value for the ratio of the percentage change in quantity over the percentage change in price; visually, a perfectly inelastic curve appears horizontal.

Perfectly inelastic: Characterized by a zero value for the ratio of the percentage change in quantity over the percentage change in price; visually, a perfectly inelastic curve appears vertical.

Physical capital: Nonhuman productive resources.

Political economy: The study of the causes and consequences of political decision-making.

Price discrimination: Selling at prices that do not reflect differences in marginal costs; different prices with the same marginal costs, for example, or the same prices with different marginal costs.

Price elasticity of demand: The percentage change in quantity demanded divided by the percentage change in price. *See also* Elasticity of demand.

Price elasticity of supply: The percentage change in quantity supplied divided by the percentage change in price. *See also* Elasticity of supply.

Price searcher: A firm that must search for the profit-maximizing price because it faces a downward-sloping demand curve (if it is a seller) or an upward-sloping supply curve (if it is a buyer); often used as a synonym for *monopoly* or *monopsony*.

Price-support program: A government program that mandates minimum prices for crops.

Price taker: Any economic agent that takes the market price as given; often used as a synonym for a firm operating in a market characterized by *pure competition*.

Private costs: Costs incurred by the relevant decision maker.

Product differentiation: Distinguishing products by brand name, color, and other minor attributes.

Productivity: Output produced per unit of input.

Profit: Income generated by selling something for a higher price than was paid for it. In production, the income generated is the difference between total revenues received from consumers who purchase the goods and the total cost of producing those goods.

Property and contract rights: Legal rules governing the use and exchange of property and enforceable agreements between people or businesses.

Property rights: Set of rules specifying how a good may be used and exchanged.

Protectionism: The imposition of rules designed to protect certain individuals or firms from competition, usually competition from imported goods.

Proven reserves: Estimated quantities of oil and gas that geological and engineering data demonstrate with reasonable certainty to be recoverable in future years from known reservoirs under existing economic and operating conditions.

Purchasing power: Ability or means to acquire goods and services.

Pure competition: A market structure in which participants individually have no influence over market prices; all act as *price takers*.

Quota: A limit on the amount of a good or an activity; often used in international trade to limit the amount of some foreign good that may be imported into a country.

Rate of return: The net benefit, in percentage terms, of engaging in an activity. For example, if the investment of $1.00 yields a gross return of $1.20, the net benefit is $0.20 and the rate of return is $0.20/$1.00 = 20 percent.

Rational ignorance: A state in which knowledge is incomplete because obtaining perfect information is too costly.

Real per capita income: Gross domestic product (GDP) corrected for inflation and divided by population.

Real price: A price that is adjusted for inflation and is expressed in terms of some base year.

Relative prices: The costs of goods, expressed in terms of other goods or in terms of a basic bundle of goods.

Rent control: A system in which the government tells building owners how much they can charge for rent.

Resource: Any input used in the production of desired goods and services.

Revealed preferences: The likes and dislikes of consumers, as demonstrated by the choices they make in the marketplace.

Rule of law: The principle that relations between individuals, businesses, and the government are governed by clearly enumerated rules that apply to everyone in society.

Scarce: Not free; something must be sacrificed to obtain.

Scarce good: Any good that commands a positive price.

Scarcity: State of nature in which resources are limited even though wants are unlimited. Scarcity means that nature does not freely provide as much of everything as people want.

Shortage: Situation in which an excess quantity is demanded or an insufficient quantity is supplied; the difference between the quantity demanded and the quantity supplied at a specific price below the market-clearing price.

Social cost: The full cost that society bears when a resource-using action occurs. For example, the social cost of driving a car is equal to all private costs plus any additional cost that other members of society bear (such as air pollution and traffic congestion).

Solvent: In a financial condition in which the value of one's assets is greater than the value of one's liabilities.

Static analysis: Any assessment of the economic impact of a policy that does not fully take into account the induced responses to that policy.

Stock: The quantity of something at a particular point in time. An inventory of goods is a stock. A bank account at a point in time is a stock. Stocks are defined independent of time, although they are assessed at a point in time.

Subsidies: Government payments for the production of specific goods, generally designed to raise the profits of the firms receiving the subsidies and often intended to increase the output of the subsidized goods.

Supply: The willingness and ability to sell goods.

Supply curve: A graphic representation of supply, which slopes upward (has a positive slope), reflecting the positive relationship between price and quantity supplied.

Supply schedule: A set of prices and the quantity supplied at each price; a schedule showing the rate of planned production at each relative price for a specified time period.

Support price: The minimum price that farmers are guaranteed to receive for their crop, as set by the federal government. If the market price falls below the support price, the government purchases enough of the crop to bring the market price up to the support price.

Surplus: Excess quantity supplied or an insufficient quantity demanded; the difference between the quantity supplied and the quantity demanded at a price above the market-clearing price. As applied to the government budget, an excess of tax receipts over expenditures.

Target price: The minimum price that farmers are guaranteed to receive for their crop, as set by the federal government. If the market price falls below the target price, farmers receive a payment equal to the difference between the two (multiplied by their production of the crop).

Tariff: A tax levied on imports.

Tax credit: An offset against current or future income taxes.

Tax rate: Proportion of the value of the taxed item that is collected in taxes.

Tax revenue: Total dollar value of taxes collected.

Technological change: A change in the set of feasible production possibilities, typically the result of the productive implementation of new knowledge.

Trade barriers: Any rules having the effect of reducing the amount of international exchange. *Tariffs* and *quotas* are trade barriers.

Trade-off: Term relating to opportunity cost. In order to get a desired economic good, it is necessary to trade off (give up) some other desired economic good in a situation of scarcity. A trade-off involves making a sacrifice in order to obtain something.

Transaction costs: Costs of conducting exchanges of goods.

Type I error: An error of commission, such as might arise when an unsafe drug is mistakenly permitted to be sold.

Type II error: An error of omission, such as might arise if a beneficial drug is mistakenly prevented from reaching the market.

User fees: Charges imposed for the use of a good or service; often applied to the charges applied by governments for the use of government-owned resources, ranging from roads to parks.

Voucher: A document that authorizes a person to receive a specified dollar amount of services at no charge.

White-collar jobs: Employment in which workers rely chiefly on their intellect and knowledge rather than their physical skills.

World Trade Organization (WTO): An association of more than 145 nations that helps reduce trade barriers among its members and settles international trade disputes among them.

Zone pricing: Setting different retail prices in different geographic areas, depending on the characteristics of customers in those areas; a practice of major oil companies.

SELECTED REFERENCES

Chapter 1   DEATH BY BUREAUCRAT

Kazman, Sam. "Deadly Overcaution: FDA's Drug Approval Process." *Journal of Regulation and Social Cost* 1, no. 1 (1990): 35–54.

Peltzman, Sam. "An Evaluation of Consumer Protection Legislation: The 1962 Drug Amendments." *Journal of Political Economy* 81, no. 1 (1973): 1049–1091.

Walker, Steven. "S.O.S. to the FDA." *Wall Street Journal Online*, August 26, 2003. (http://online.wsj.com/article/SB1061854102951501000-search.html)

Chapter 2   ETHANOL MADNESS

Barrionuevo, Alexei. "Boom in Ethanol Reshapes Economy of Heartland." *New York Times*, June 25, 2006, p. 1.

Environmental Protection Agency. *Regulatory Announcement: Removal of Reformulated Gasoline Oxygen Content Requirement and Revision of Commingling Prohibition to Address Non-Oxygenated Reformulated Gasoline*. Document no. EPA420-F-06–020. Washington, D.C.: Environmental Protection Agency, February 2006.

Tokgoz, Simla. "Policy and Competitiveness of U.S. and Brazilian Ethanol." *Iowa Ag Review Online*, Spring 2006. (www.card.iastate.edu/iowa_ag_review/spring_06/article3.aspx)

www.eia.doe.gov. Official Web site of the Energy Information Administration.

Chapter 3   FLYING THE FRIENDLY SKIES?

Mitchell, Mark L., and Michael T. Maloney. "Crisis in the Cockpit? The Role of Market Forces in Promoting Air Travel Safety." *Journal of Law and Economics* 32, no. 2 (1989): 139–184.

www.airsafe.com. Statistics on airline safety.

www1.faa.gov. Official Web site of the Federal Aviation Administration.

Chapter 4   THE MYSTERY OF WEALTH

Easterly, William, and Ross Levine. "Tropics, Germs, and Crops: How Endowments Influence Economic Development." *Journal of Monetary Economics* 50, no. 1 (2003): 3–39.

Mahoney, Paul G. "The Common Law and Economic Growth: Hayek Might Be Right." *Journal of Legal Studies* 30, no. 3 (2001): 503–525.

Chapter 5   SEX, BOOZE, AND DRUGS

Becker, Gary, Kevin M. Murphy, and Michael Grossman. "The Market for Illegal Goods: The Case of Drugs." *Journal of Political Economy* 114, no. 1 (2006): 38–60.

Benjamin, Daniel K., and Roger LeRoy Miller. *Undoing Drugs: Beyond Legalization.* New York: Basic Books, 1993.

Hardy, Quentin. "Inside Dope." *Forbes*, November 10, 2003, pp. 146–154.

Miron, Jeffrey A., and Jeffrey Zwiebel. "Alcohol Consumption during Prohibition." *American Economic Review* 81, no. 2 (1991): 242–247.

Chapter 6   KIDNEYS FOR SALE

Adler, Jerry. "Are Kidneys a Commodity?" *Newsweek*, May 26, 2008.

"The Gap between Supply and Demand." *Economist*, October 9, 2008.

Harrington, David E., and Edward A. Sayre. "Paying for Bodies, but Not for Organs." *Regulation*, Winter 2006–2007, pp. 14–19.

Meckler, Laura. "A Shortage of Available Kidneys Inspires a Radical Idea: Organ Sales." *Wall Street Journal*, November 16, 2007.

Chapter 7   WHEN HIGH PRICES ARE LOW PRICES

Alchian, Armen A., and Reuben Kessel. "The Effects of Inflation." *Journal of Political Economy* 70, no. 6 (1962): 521–537.

Goklany, Indur M., and Jerry Taylor. "A Big Surprise on Gas." *Los Angeles Times*, August 11, 2008.

Kokoski, Mary F. "Quality Adjustment of Price Indexes." *Monthly Labor Review* 116, no. 12 (1993): 34–46.

www.bls.gov/bls/inflation.htm. Statistics on inflation.

Chapter 8   ARE WE RUNNING OUT OF WATER?

Anderson, Terry, and Pamela S. Snyder. *Water Markets: Priming the Invisible Pump*. Washington, D.C.: Cato Institute, 1997.

Casselman, Ben. "Desperate Sprinklers." *Wall Street Journal*, July 20, 2007.

Libecap, Gary. *Owens Valley Revisited: A Reassessment of the West's First Great Water Transfer*. Stanford, Calif.: Stanford University Press, 2007.

Santos, Fernanda. "Inch by Inch, Great Lakes Shrink, and Cargo Carriers Face Losses." *New York Times*, October 22, 2007.

Yardley, Jim. "Beneath Booming Cities, China's Future Is Drying Up." *New York Times*, September 28, 2007.

Chapter 9   THE (DIS)INCENTIVES OF HIGHER TAXES

Feenberg, Daniel R., and James M. Poterba. "The Alternative Minimum Tax and Effective Marginal Tax Rates." *National Tax Journal* 57, no. 2 (2004): 407–427.

Harber, Arnold. *Taxation and Welfare*. New York: Little, Brown, 1974.

Mitchell, Daniel J. "What Can the United States Learn from the Nordic Model?" *Cato Institute Policy Analysis*, November 5, 2007.

Chapter 10   BANKRUPT LANDLORDS, FROM SEA TO SHINING SEA

Downs, Anthony. *Residential Rent Controls: An Evaluation*. Washington, D.C.: Urban Land Institute, 1988.

Glaeser, Edward L., and Erzo F. P. Luttmer. "The Misallocation of Housing under Rent Control." *American Economic Review* 93, no. 4 (2003): 1027–1046.

Chapter 11   (WHY) ARE WOMEN PAID LESS?

Becker, Elizabeth, and Cotton M. Lindsay. "The Limits of the Wage Impact of Discrimination." *Managerial and Decision Economics* 26 (2005): 513–525.

Becker, Gary. *The Economics of Discrimination*. Chicago: University of Chicago Press, 1957.

Heckman, James J. "Detecting Discrimination." *Journal of Economic Perspectives* 12, no. 1 (1998): 101–116.

Chapter 12   THE EFFECTS OF THE MINIMUM WAGE

Baker, Michael, Dwayne Benjamin, and Shuchita Stanger. "The Highs and Lows of the Minimum Wage Effects: A Time-Series Cross-Section Study of the Canadian Law." *Journal of Labor Economics* 17, no. 2 (1999): 318–350.
Card, David, and Alan Krueger. "Minimum Wages and Employment: A Case Study of the Fast-Food Industry in New Jersey and Pennsylvania." *American Economic Review* 84, no. 3 (1994): 772–793.
Neumark, David, and William Wascher. "Minimum Wages and Employment: A Case Study of the Fast-Food Industry in New Jersey and Pennsylvania: Comment." *American Economic Review* 90, no. 5 (2000): 1362–1396.
Rottenberg, Simon (ed.). *The Economics of Legal Minimum Wages.* Washington, D.C.: American Enterprise Institute, 1981.

Chapter 13   IMMIGRATION, SUPERSTARS, AND POVERTY

Borjas, George. *Heaven's Door: Immigration Policy and the American Economy.* Princeton, N.J.: Princeton University Press, 2001.
Rosen, Sherwin. "The Economics of Superstars." *American Economic Review* 71, no. 5 (1981): 845–858.
U.S. Bureau of the Census. "The Effects of Government Taxes and Transfers on Income and Poverty, 2004." April 27, 2006. (www.census.gov/hhes/www/poverty/effect2004/effect2004.html)

Chapter 14   A FAREWELL TO JOBS

Browning, Lynnley. "Outsourcing Abroad Applies to Tax Returns, Too." *New York Times*, February 15, 2004, p. 12.
Federal Reserve Bank of Dallas. *The Fruits of Free Trade.* Annual Report. Dallas, Tex.: Federal Reserve Bank, 2002.
Madigan, Kathleen. "Outsourcing Jobs: Is It Bad?" *Business Week,* August 25, 2003, pp. 36–38.

Chapter 15   BIG OIL, BIG OIL PRICES?

Edmonds.com Editors. "Torch My Ride: Arson for Hire." CNN.com .autos, June 11, 2006. www.edmunds.com/apps/vdpcontainers/do/vdp/articleId=115584/pageNumber=1.

Maugeri, Leonardo. "Oil, Oil Everywhere." *Forbes*, July 24, 2005, p. 42.
"A Survey of Oil." *Economist*, April 30, 2005, pp. 3–9, 25–26.
www.eia.doe.gov/oil_gas/petroleum/data_publications/wrgp/mogas_ history.html. A useful source for weekly gasoline prices around the country.

Chapter 16 CONTRACTS, COMBINATIONS, AND CONSPIRACIES

Kanfer, Steven. *The Last Empire: DeBeers, Diamonds, and the World.* New York: Farrar, Straus & Giroux, 1993.
www.eia.doe.gov. Official Web site of the Energy Information Administration.
Zimbalist, Andrew. *Unpaid Professionals: Commercialism and Conflict in Big-Time College Sports.* Princeton, N.J.: Princeton University Press, 2001.

Chapter 17 COFFEE, TEA, OR TUITION-FREE?

Chevalier, Judith, and Austan Goolsbee. "Measuring Prices and Price Competition Online: Amazon.com versus BarnesandNoble.com." *Quantitative Marketing and Economics* 1, no. 2 (2003): 203–222.
Odlyzko, Andrew. "Privacy, Economics, and Price Discrimination on the Internet." St. Paul: University of Minnesota, Digital Technology Center, 2003.
"They're Watching You." *Economist*, October 18, 2003, p. 77.

Chapter 18 COLLEGE COSTS (. . . AND COSTS AND COSTS)

Ehrenberg, Ronald G. *Tuition Rising: Why Colleges Cost So Much.* Cambridge, Mass.: Harvard University Press, 2002.
U.S. News & World Report Staff. *U.S. News Ultimate College Guide, 2006.* New York: Source Books, 2006.
Vedder, Richard. "Why Does College Cost So Much?" *Wall Street Journal*, August 23, 2005, p. 9.

Chapter 19 KEEPING THE COMPETITION OUT

Lipton, Eric. "Finding the Intersection of Supply and Demand." *New York Times,* November 23, 2003, p. 31.
www.schallerconsult.com/taxi/topics.htm. Facts on the New York City taxicab and taxi medallion markets.

Chapter 20 MORTGAGE MELTDOWN

Liebowitz, Stan J. "Anatomy of a Train Wreck." The Independent Institute, October 3, 2008.

Lucchetti, Aaron, and Serena Ng. "Credit and Blame: How Rating Firms' Calls Fueled Subprime Mess—Benign View of Loans Helped Create Bonds, Led to More Lending." *Wall Street Journal*, August 15, 2007.

Simon, Ruth. "FirstFed Grapples with Payment-Option Mortgages." *Wall Street Journal*, August 6, 2008.

www.ofheo.gov/HPI.aspx. Web site of the Office of Federal Housing Enterprise Oversight.

www2.standardandpoors.com. Standard & Poor's/Case-Shiller home price indexes.

Chapter 21 THE POLITICAL ECONOMY OF COLLAPSING BRIDGES

Doyle, Martin W., et al. "Aging Infrastructure and Ecosystem Reconstruction." *Science* 319, no. 5861 (2008): 286–287.

Powers, Kyna. *Aging Infrastructure: Dam Safety.* Washington, D.C.: The Library of Congress, Congressional Research Service, 2005.

Timiraos, Nick. "Aging Infrastructure: How Bad Is It?" *Wall Street Journal*, August 4, 2007.

Chapter 22 IS YOUR BANK MANAGER HEADED TO VEGAS WITH YOUR MONEY?

Allen, Franklin, and Douglas Gale. "Competition and Financial Stability." *Journal of Money, Credit & Banking* 36, no. 13 (2004): S453–S480.

Bordo, M., H. Rockoff, and A. Redish. "The U.S. Banking System from a Northern Exposure: Stability versus Efficiency." *Journal of Economic History* 54, no. 2 (1994): 325–341.

Diamond, D., and P. Dybvig. "Bank Runs, Deposit Insurance, and Liquidity." *Journal of Political Economy* 91, no. 3 (1983): 401–419.

Friedman, Milton, and Anna J. Schwartz. *A Monetary History of the United States, 1867–1960.* Princeton, N.J.: Princeton University Press, 1963.

Chapter 23 RAISING LESS CORN AND MORE HELL

Becker, Elizabeth. "U.S. Corn Subsidies Said to Damage Mexico: Study Finds Farmers Lose Livelihoods." *New York Times*, August 27, 2003, p. C4.

Edwards, Chris, and Dan DeHaven. *Save the Farms—End the Subsidies.* Washington, D.C.: Cato Institute, 2002.

Fackler, Martin. "Japanese Farmers Losing Clout." *Wall Street Journal,* February 20, 2004, p. A10.

Chapter 24 CRIME AND PUNISHMENT

Levitt, Stephen. "The Effect of Prison Population Size on Crime Rates: Evidence from Prison Overcrowding Litigation." *Quarterly Journal of Economics* 111, no. 2 (1996): 319–351.

Levitt, Stephen. "Using Electoral Cycles in Police Hiring to Estimate the Effect of Police on Crime." *American Economic Review* 87, no. 3 (1997): 270–290.

Levitt, Stephen. "Juvenile Crime and Punishment." *Journal of Political Economy* 106, no. 6 (1998): 1156–1185.

Chapter 25 THE GRAYING OF AMERICA

Council of Economic Advisers. "Restoring Solvency to Social Security," *Economic Report of the President.* Washington, D.C.: Government Printing Office, 2004, ch. 6.

Miron, Jeffrey A., and David N. Weil. "The Genesis and Evolution of Social Security." In Michael D. Bordo, Claudia Goldin, and Eugene N. White (eds.), *The Defining Moment: The Great Depression and the American Economy in the Twentieth Century.* Chicago: University of Chicago Press, 1998, pp. 297–322.

Chapter 26 THE TRASHMAN COMETH

Benjamin, Daniel K. *Eight Great Myths of Recycling.* Policy Series no. PS-28. Bozeman, Mont.: Property and Environment Research Center, 2003.

Fullerton, Don, and Thomas C. Kinnaman. "Household Responses to Pricing Garbage by the Bag." *American Economic Review* 88, no. 2 (1996): 971–984.

Hocking, Martin B. "Paper versus Polystyrene: A Complex Choice." *Science,* February 1991, pp. 504–505.

Hocking, Martin B. "Disposable Cups Have Eco-Merit." *Nature,* May 1994, p. 107.

Rathje, William, and Cullen Murphy. *Rubbish: The Archeology of Garbage.* New York: HarperCollins, 1992.

Chapter 27 BYE-BYE, BISON

Adler, Jonathan. "Bad for Your Land, Bad for the Critters." *Wall Street Journal*, December 31, 2003, p. A8.

Anderson, Terry L., and Peter J. Hill. *The Not So Wild, Wild West: Property Rights on the Frontier.* Stanford, Calif.: Stanford University Press, 2004.

Coase, Ronald. "The Problem of Social Cost." *Journal of Law and Economics* 3, no. 2 (1960): 1–40.

Grafton, R. Quentin, Dale Squires, and Kevin J. Fox. "Private Property and Economic Efficiency: A Study of a Common-Pool Resource." *Journal of Law and Economics* 43, no. 2 (2000): 679–713.

Lueck, Dean, and Jeffrey A. Michael. "Preemptive Habitat Destruction under the Endangered Species Act." *Journal of Law and Economics* 46, no. 1 (2003): 27–60.

Chapter 28 SMOG MERCHANTS

Foster, Vivien, and Robert W. Hahn. "Designing More Efficient Markets: Lessons from Los Angeles Smog Control." *Journal of Law and Economics* 38, no. 1 (1995): 19–48.

Joskow, Paul L., Richard Schmalensee, and Elizabeth M. Bailey. "The Market for Sulfur Dioxide Emissions." *American Economic Review* 88, no. 5 (1998): 669–685.

www.epa.gov/airmarkets/trading. EPA Web site for tradable emissions.

Chapter 29 GREENHOUSE ECONOMICS

Bradsher, Keith. "China's Boom Adds to Global Warming Problem." *New York Times,* October 22, 2003, p. A1.

Castles, Ian, and David Henderson. "The IPCC Emission Scenarios: An Economic-Statistical Critique." *Energy and Environment* 14, nos. 2, 3 (2003): 159–185.

Lomborg, Bjorn. *The Skeptical Environmentalist.* New York: Cambridge University Press, 2001.

Sohngen, Brent, and Robert Mendelsohn. "Valuing the Impact of Large-Scale Ecological Change in a Market: The Effect of Climate Change on U.S. Timber." *American Economic Review* 89, no. 4 (1999): 686–710.

Chapter 30 GLOBALIZATION AND THE WEALTH OF AMERICA

Eichengreen, Barry. "The Political Economy of the Smoot-Hawley Tariff." *Research in Economic History* 12, no. 1 (1989): 1–43.

Federal Reserve Bank of Dallas. *The Fruits of Free Trade*. Annual Report. Dallas, Tex.: Federal Reserve Bank, 2002.

Irwin, Douglas A. "From Smoot-Hawley to Reciprocal Trade Agreements: Changing the Course of U.S. Trade Policy in the 1930s." In Michael D. Bordo, Claudia Goldin, and Eugene N. White (eds.), *The Defining Moment: The Great Depression and the American Economy in the Twentieth Century*. Chicago: University of Chicago Press, 1998, pp. 325–352.

Chapter 31 THE $750,000 STEELWORKER

Berry, Steven, James Levinsohn, and Ariel Pakes. "Voluntary Export Restraints on Automobiles: Evaluating a Trade Policy." *American Economic Review* 89, no. 3 (1999): 400–430.

Crandall, Robert W. "The Effects of U.S. Trade Protection for Autos and Steel." *Brookings Papers on Economic Activity* 1987, no. 1 (1987): 271–288.

Chapter 32 THE LION, THE DRAGON, AND THE FUTURE

Eckholm, Erik, and Joseph Kahn. "China's Power Worries Neighbors." *New York Times*, December 1, 2002, p. 7.

Goodman, Peter S. "China Takes Pivotal Role in High-Tech Production." *International Herald Tribune*, December 5, 2002, p. 2.

Restall, Hugo. "New Property Rights for Chinese Farmers?" *Wall Street Journal Europe*, October 3–5, 2003, p. A7.

INDEX